LIFE AMONG THE
QALLUNAAT

FIRST VOICES, FIRST TEXTS

SERIES EDITOR: WARREN CARIOU

First Voices, First Texts aims to reconnect contemporary readers with some of the most important Aboriginal literature of the past, much of which has been unavailable for decades. This series reveals the richness of these works by providing newly re-edited texts that are presented with particular sensitivity toward Indigenous ethics, traditions, and contemporary realities. The editors strive to indigenize the editing process by involving communities, by respecting traditional protocols, and by providing critical introductions that give readers new insights into the cultural contexts of these unjustly neglected classics.

1. *Devil in Deerskins: My Life with Grey Owl* by Anahareo
2. *Indians Don't Cry / Gaawiin Mawisiiwag Anishinaabeg* by George Kenny
3. *Life Among the Qallunaat* by Mini Aodla Freeman
4. *From the Tundra to the Trenches* by Eddy Weetaltuk

LIFE AMONG THE
QALLUNAAT

MINI AODLA FREEMAN

Edited and with an afterword by Keavy Martin and Julie Rak

UNIVERSITY OF MANITOBA PRESS

University of Manitoba Press
Winnipeg, Manitoba, Canada
Treaty 1 Territory
uofmpress.ca

Cataloguing data available from Library and Archives Canada
First Voices, First Texts, ISSN 2291-9627 ; 3
ISBN 978-0-88755-775-0 (PAPER)
ISBN 978-0-88755-492-6 (PDF)
ISBN 978-0-88755-490-2 (EPUB)

Cover image: Elisapee Ishulutaq, "Downtown Vancouver,"
stencil, 66 cm x 51 cm
Cover design: Mike Carroll
Interior design: Jess Koroscil

Printed in Canada

The University of Manitoba Press acknowledges the financial
support for its publication program provided by the Government of
Canada through the Canada Book Fund, the Canada Council
for the Arts, the Manitoba Department of Sport, Culture,
and Heritage, the Manitoba Arts Council, and
the Manitoba Book Publishing Tax Credit.

Funded by the Government of Canada | Canadä

To

Milton, Graham, Elaine and Malcolm
and for Caroline, Jennifer, Jasmine, Grant, Emily,
Evan, Megan, and Alexandra

Teach, learn, care and love while you can
for nothing ever stays the same.

Love, Moms

CONTENTS

Photographs follow page 126

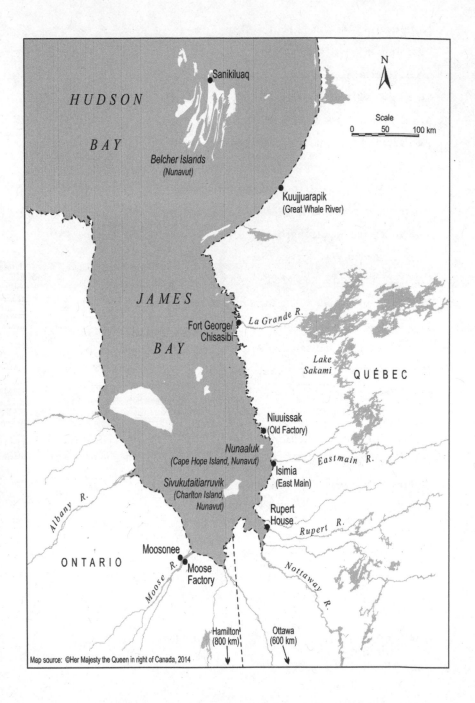

"ONE DAY, SOMEBODY IS GOING TO FORGET"

A CONVERSATION WITH MINI AODLA FREEMAN

The original publication of *Life Among the Qallunaat* began with a foreword by Alex Stevenson, the "Administrator of the Arctic" who had worked at the Department of Northern Affairs and Natural Resources during the time when Mini Aodla Freeman was employed there as a translator (1957–1960). To provide context for this new edition, Aodla Freeman detailed her experiences of writing and publishing the original text in an interview with Keavy Martin and Norma Dunning. This excerpt is taken from a longer discussion recorded on March 20, 2014, at Aodla Freeman's home in Edmonton.

KEAVY MARTIN: Can you tell us how you came to write *Life Among the Qallunaat*?[1]

---

1. The etymology of the term "qallunaat" is subject to debate, but it is used variously to refer to "Southerners," "white people," or even "English speakers." For Aodla Freeman's more detailed discussion of the connotations of this term, see p. 86–87.

MINI AODLA FREEMAN: We were living in Burlington, Ontario, while my husband was teaching at the university in Hamilton [McMaster University]. My last baby had gone—started going to school—and I had nothing to do, it seems. And I had wanted to...I didn't *want* to, but I said to Milton, "Maybe I should write a book." And he said, "You know, you have a lot of experience in James Bay that you've told me over and over about." So that's when I decided to write a book about James Bay and the people there. And it didn't take me long; I think I wrote that big book for six or eight months. And I didn't know my family for six to eight months [laughing]. They were so glad when I finished that!

I phoned Mr. Hurtig, who lived here in Edmonton, and he never hesitated: he just said, "Send it!" So I sent it, and before you knew, he was publishing it. I belonged to the Hamilton Writers Guild at that time because I was interested in writing, and they asked me if I'd done anything with my book. And I said, "It's going to be published."

"Oh my God! I've had a book I keep sending to ten, twelve publishers!"

So, Mr Hurtig, when he saw it, he said he's going to have to get it edited a lot—cut a lot—because it's too long. So that's what they did.

And then while I was writing it, I discovered that I really like writing. You know, I really enjoy writing. It's not because I wanted to force myself; I couldn't force myself. I just really enjoyed it. I'm book crazy, you know: I belong to the library across the street and I go there every month, I think [laughing]. Yes, and it's something that I have questioned myself over and over, because in my culture, we are not 'writing people'; we memorize everything: everything what people say, everything of where we went, everything what we plan to do. You know, it was all done by memory. And all our culture, our rules, our laws, our games are all from memory, passed on from one generation to another. And I said to myself, "One day, somebody is going to forget." So that's when I decided to write the book.

KM: And who came up with the title? Was that your idea?

MAF: I had a different title, and Mr. Hurtig phoned me and he said, "We're going to change your title to 'Life Among the Qallunaat' in order to.... How he did it put it? Something about "fighting back [against the book] *Life Among the Eskimos.*" I said, "Go ahead." You know that book, *Life Among the Eskimos*? Written by... what's his name? He was a scientist from Germany [Bernhard Adolph Hantzsch]. And that's how I ended up with that title, "Life Among the Qallunaat."

KM: So what did you want to call it?

MAF: Something about "James Bay Inuit."

KM: Yes, because when you're reading it, only some parts are actually about qallunaat and being in the South. A lot of it is about James Bay, Nunaaluk [Cape Hope Island], and your family, and being at home.

MAF: A lot of it was cut off.

KM: Well, one of things that we are hoping to do is to find the parts that were taken out of your manuscript and to put them back in.

MAF: Okay.

KM: Because it's not *that* long. And we thought that the parts that were cut out are important; we learned a lot from reading them.

MAF: Okay, but I will see it when you get it all together before you send it to publish. Will I?

KM: Yes, of course. Absolutely. And then, if there's anything that you want us to change or take out, we'll be asking you to tell us that.

MAF: Okay.

NORMA DUNNING: After you published, Mini, you went on a bit of a speaking tour. You went up north, didn't you?

MAF: There was three of us; there was Daphne Odjig, and Alice French from the Western Arctic. Her book [*My Name is Masak*] had come out earlier, and we went on tour in the northern parts of provinces—just the northern part. We stopped in, I think, Winnipeg—that's the only place we stopped—but the rest were all small communities. Met a lot of Indians and Inuit in northern parts of Manitoba and Alberta.

ND: When did you know that your book got put into the basement of Indian and Northern Affairs?

MAF: I think the people in Northern Affairs had feared that I might tell something, you know? That's how guilty they are [laughing]. We had been invited—all the writers, magazine writers, artists from Cape Dorset—we were all invited to Ottawa, and I was one of them. And people kept saying to me, "I haven't seen your book. Where is it?" And I couldn't answer with all those people there, you know. So I just said, "Well, it should be out somewhere."

And then somebody told me the whole 3,000 of them were in the basement of Northern Affairs. Just kept it there until somebody read it and started distributing it up north. And the man who reads all the books for awards from Toronto [Peter Buitenhuis]—he somehow got it; I think Hurtig sent him one, and he read it. And he was asking where he could find copies and saying that he recommended it to get an award [the Governor General's Award for Nonfiction]. And it never happened because they couldn't find the book.

KM: Do you remember how long it was that they were in the basement?

MAF: I think it was at least six to eight months. I think they were afraid that I might talk badly about residential schools. And remember: at that time, Northern Affairs kept denying, denying about residential schools. When an Indian person came up and talked about it really badly, they would shut them up. And then, I think they thought I wrote something bad about residential schools, which I *should* have, but I didn't [laughing]. I think that was the worry, and when they discovered there wasn't something about residential schools, they decided to put it out. And they paid our airfares after that to travel north.

ND: Has your brother ever said anything about the book? Did he ever say, "Mini, we didn't fight that much!" [Laughing]

MAF: As you know, Inuit don't read or write much. And he never said anything about it. But they didn't know until about—let's see—it must have been till the '80s, '90s, when they started to say, "I saw your book. I saw your book." That's how long it took.

KM: And how did people respond when they read it? Did you get any responses?

MAF: I have a bunch of clippings from newspapers somewhere in the box. Mr. Hurtig would send me one for me to see. Out of all those, I only had one woman saying really bad things about it. She said something about eating raw food—I just ignored her. That's the only bad thing I got; the rest enjoyed it, loved it....

KM: So how do you feel about the book coming out again after all these years?

MAF: People kept saying to me, "It's about time, it's about time. You should have done that right after the book was sold out—you should have done that long time ago." But I kept ignoring it, and I was busy with the other things, you know, being an Elder there and here and there. I feel good about it now—I'm ready to take it again. Yes. At least nice people are handling it.

[Laughter]

KM: You're nice to put up with us!

MAF: You have time for tea?

Whenever I meet a person for the first time I am always asked "How do you like the weather?". The weather is something I am very aware of just as much as I am with the way of living in the South, and a lot of things Qallunaat take so much for granted.

Surely people in the South must have more interesting question besides "How do you like the weather?". There are countless things I am very facinated with in the South. Going back to 1957 when I first arrived to Ottawa and stepping out of the train at the Union Station my mind had many questions; noticing the train tracks first thing I asked myself was: Am I suppose to walk on them or shall I just walk on cement? Which gate way shall I use? Then to my own observations I noticed they had special door opening for arriving people. Getting into a car was, I think the moment I was ever to be quiet in full five minutes. The man who drove to Laurentian Terrace where I was to reside as a Government working girl, asked me how did I enjoy the weather during my trip? I do not think his question sank into my mind as I was too busy watching cars and cars and more cars everywhere I looked; some were going, some were parked. How does the man who is driving know when to stop and go, does he count? or does the other car let him know when to go? I noticed the car ahead of us had blinking red light at rear. The red light never entered in my mind that it mean't so much.

My first two months in the South were trying days. And I mean trying days! First, because of my very shyness. Meeting five to ten different people every day was agony for me. I could never look at them and I would barely

-2-

The first page of Mini Aodla Freeman's original typescript.

LIFE AMONG THE
QALLUNAAT

Whenever I meet a person for the first time, I am always asked, "How do you like the weather?" The weather is something I am very aware of, just as I am aware of many things which the qallunaat take so much for granted. Surely people in the South must have more interesting questions than "How do you like the weather?"

There are countless things that I am very fascinated with in the South. When I first arrived in Ottawa in 1957 and stepped out of the train at Union Station, my mind had many questions. Noticing the train tracks, the first thing I asked myself was: am I supposed to walk on them or shall I just walk on the cement? Which gateway shall I use? Is there a special door for arriving people?

Getting into a car was, I think, the first moment I was ever to be quiet for a full five minutes. There were cars and more cars everywhere I looked—some were moving, some were parked. How does the man who is driving know when to stop and go? Does he count to a certain number? Or does the other car let him know when to go? I noticed that the car ahead of us had a blinking red light at the rear. It never entered into my mind that the red light meant so much. Meanwhile, the man who drove me to Laurentian Terrace—where I was to reside as a government working girl—asked me, how did I enjoy the weather during my trip?

My first two months in the South were trying days. And I mean trying days! First, because of my shyness. Meeting five to ten people every day was agony for me. I could never look at them and I would barely say hello. To be honest, I don't really know why I was shy. It was not that I was ashamed of myself or that I was aware of my different colouring; having been brought up among Indian people, I was forever told to ignore differences of race and always to treat all equally.

Laurentian Terrace had high ceilings; the room appeared to me to be very large. I felt like a little ant. Why all the sofas and chairs, pictures on the walls and so many doors? The matron of the Terrace kindly asked me to sit down. Which chair? I sat on the nearest one that I was standing by. Little did I know I was to sit there for an hour, reading the rules I was to conform to, rules and more rules that made me feel I could not move unless I was told. Rules are things we Inuit children were never brought up with—we eat when we are hungry, sleep when we are tired, come and go with the weather. If it was a nice day, we left for the day and hunted as much food as we could, and if it was a bad day, we stayed home—the women to sew, the men to work with their tools, the children to learn from their parents.

As I was walking down the hall with the matron, she showed me the bathroom. Is this one mine? By myself, I found out I was to share it with 300 girls. "This is the telephone you will be called on." Who is going to call me? How will anyone know I am here? Finally, after endless steps, she said, "This is your room. The rules are to change your bed once a week. Here is your key, lock your room when you leave. Here is the key for your locker, don't lose the combination." What a difference from living in a tent! We come and go with no locks and no combinations to remember.

I met the girl who was to share my room. She was very surprised by my hairdo—apparently, it was out of date and too long. But she was more surprised that my clothes were as up to date as hers. When I began to open my trunk, she went out, but before long others started to come in, one-two-three-four-five-six different girls. I concluded that she had invited them to see what kind of clothes I had, and that they expected to see sealskin clothing, maybe along with a folding igloo. When I got to the bottom, one of them asked, "Where are your clothes?" I wanted to laugh and say, as to any well-known friend, what do you mean? I have been putting them in this locker. We sat and talked afterwards, and they asked, "How do you like the weather?" I am afraid that I was as disappointed with their questions as they were with my clothes. One of them insisted, "Where are your own clothes?" and I replied, there, pointing to the locker. But she kept on insisting, "Where are your, you know, clothes where you come from? Skins." She practically vomited out the word, and her face had a sick look. Well, it was too much for me. One of the girls seemed to have the knack of saving everyone from the feeling of intrusion and said, "How awful we are, watching her unpack." The others took the hint, said goodnight and left.

Eating rules were the hardest for me to get used to. They always went with the time, never with one's own hunger. I must say, the leader of the South is the clock! Everything is about time: time to get up, time to eat, time to get to work, time to go home, time for everything. Two days after my arrival, I stayed in for two solid days. I felt I would not be able to see the outside for a long time. Nobody told me that I could go out for walks and explore my surroundings, so I stayed in, as all the rules I had been asked to follow so far seemed to say that I should never move unless I was told to.

The first day at work I will never forget. The matron had told me that some woman was going to take me where I will work. What does she look like? is all I could think about. I stood for some time where I was told to wait for her. Suddenly a woman was examining me, and I looked at her. She said, "I can't remember your name, but are you the Eskimo?" What a jolt! This was the first time I had met a person who did not have to give me rules to follow. I just nodded my head, accepted her as she was, and followed her out.

ELEVATOR

The woman who took me with her "walked" and I followed behind her. The cement hurt my feet. There was so much to see and yet she did not seem to be aware of anything. I watched her walk and wondered: She is so old and nothing seems to bother her, there is so much to see and yet she is not interested—probably she has only one thing on her mind: her destination.

When we arrived where I was to work, my first ride in an elevator was fascinating. The woman just punched a button and up we went, and I wondered if I had to do the same thing later. ME? Run machinery like that? What would I have to say to make it go, or what will I think? Shall I just push the button like she did? I was not afraid of the elevator but was very leery about getting in it. I always made sure I went in with somebody: no matter if it went up or down, somehow I always knew I would reach my destination.

FIRST DAY AT WORK

I had come to Ottawa in May of 1957 to work as a translator for the federal government, for what was then the Department of Northern Affairs and Natural Resources. My first day at work was very tiring. The man in charge of the division where I was to be a translator introduced me around, which I hated, and I felt mad at him for doing so. Being very shy, introductions were the last thing I wanted—to face person after person. I wanted to cry and just stay in one place. The desk I was given to sit at was most comforting that day. I never moved from it, no matter how much I wanted to. Finally, I met the lady who showed me the rules of the office, and at the end of the day she walked back with me to Laurentian Terrace.

LOST

I had no problem going to work, but one frightful day, I had to walk home alone. I never paid much attention to the names of the streets but would go by the shapes of stores or commercial signs. This was how I had learned to find my way in my culture—our way of travel demanded it. Passing the Chateau Laurier every day, I saw a big sign, "Red Feather Week," over its door and knew that I was heading in the right direction. But one frightful day the sign was gone and all the buildings looked the same to me. So I walked and walked. I was getting very hungry. Then I remembered a friend had told me before I left North that I should never go to a stranger but always look for a policeman, who has a navy blue uniform and a hat with a peak. I began to look around to see if I could see such a man. My friend was right—they were not hard to find. Sure enough, there was one standing on the corner of the street, just as my friend had described him. I went up to him rather shyly and asked if he could tell me where Sussex Street was. Up that way, he said, ten blocks! I wanted to ask him so much what had happened to the "Red Feather Week" sign, but I told myself that I would never go by it or any signs again, other than street names.

I never felt so safe as when I finally got home. I looked at the clock as I entered—I had been walking for two hours. Supper hour had passed. I entered my room, where my roommate was lying on her bed, just like she had been there all day—so relaxed.

"Mini, what happened to you? Did you have to work late?" I tried to explain. "Mini, you could have been kidnapped or raped!" My head was shaking and nodding, trying to keep up with her questions. When she finally slowed down, I had to admit I had been lost. Her eyes got round like the moon and she started all over again about how I could have been kidnapped or raped. She then reminded me that supper hour was over and if I wanted anything to eat, I would have to go out to a restaurant or bring the food back to our room. Well, I was hungry, but I did not feel like eating. I just could not face the streets again. That night was not the last that I went to bed hungry as it was not the last time I got lost.

I always made sure to cross the street on a red light as I thought that when the cars went, they would see me much better. But every time I crossed, cars would honk and I would wonder why. And no matter that there were ten or fifteen people standing on the corner with me, not one took time to tell me that I should not cross on the red light, until I began to walk with a girl who lived at the Terrace too.

"I saw you yesterday," she said. "Where do you work? What time do you get off? How long is your lunch hour? Do you have coffee breaks? Who do you work for? What is your name? Where do you come from? Ooooooh! HOW DO YOU LIKE THE WEATHER?" I found her to be curious in an interesting way until she asked me that famous question. Anyway, we decided we would meet after work and walk home together. As we were walking home together, the questions were reversed. I found out that she too was just getting used to city life because she had been brought up on a farm. Figuring out red and green lights was pure shock for her too. I can still hear her: "Oh Mini! You could have been killed! Don't you have lights where you come from?" How I longed to step out of a tent and turn in any direction, without having to look for some kind of crawling beast, ready to crush me if I didn't stay out of his way. From that day on, my friend became for me the only qallunaaq in the whole of Ottawa.

"Stranger"—how odd is the meaning of that word and yet that is what I was in my own country. It is a word I never heard used in my own language. Even white people have a beautiful Inuit name, qallunaat—"people who pamper their eyebrows." After two months, I decided that the qallunaat were the saddest, most worried, most in-a-hurry, never-smiling people. I have to say that my parents wasted a lot of their time telling me, "If you have nothing to say, smile." I could neither speak nor smile in the South.

ALIKATU

I began to meet a lot of people. My first visit to a qallunaat family and first long ride by car were exhausting. While in the car, I did not know what to look at. There were other cars—big ones, little ones, and all colours—buildings, stores and, how odd, people in the front of windows were smiling. I had a good look at these people later—they were model dummies. In my mind, I concluded that it was one way to get people to buy, which my grandmother would have called alikatu—showing off or competing with others. And there were people standing about, others walking as if they had big loads on their backs, but there was nothing on their backs, just a little handbag in their hands.

The man who was driving was telling me that he had just learned to drive. I looked at him, surprised. I thought he had known how to drive since childhood, just as I knew how to hitch a dog team at the age of five. It is only now that I know why he did not drive since the age of five. That is one of the many laws of the qallunaat world that I, too, eventually had to conform to: hitching up a car.

The home of the first qallunaat family I visited was even more surprising. I was offered a chair. I had only been sitting an hour in the car, but that was not what surprised me—it was the children. They were not allowed to be normal the way children in my culture are allowed: free to move, free to ask questions, free to think aloud, and most of all, free to make comments so that they will get wiser. As they grow older, questioning becomes a boring habit—they have gained wisdom and eventually become more intelligent. The more intelligent they become, the quieter they are. That is the reason why children are allowed to be children. I very often have been asked by qallunaat who have gone north and lived in the settlements why Inuit children are so spoiled. They do not have an idea of what Inuit home life is like, and they do not believe in systems of Inuit child-rearing. (Most of the questioners have expected me to give them an answer and a full explanation in two minutes flat. It would take me another whole book to really explain about Inuit child-rearing.)

When I entered this qallunaat home, I could not help but notice the treatment of the children by the parents. One child asked, "What is that girl sitting in a little red dress?" She was answered with whispers and told to leave. Instead of being proud that the child could actually question about the girl sitting in a red dress, instead of examining the way the child used her wording upon asking questions, she was right away shut down. To my people, such discipline can prevent a child from growing mentally, killing the child's sense of interest. "Is it very cold where she comes from? Did she live in an igloo before she came here?" Shhhh! the mother was cautioning. "Go outside! Don't do that! No! Move away!" How I wanted to pick up the child and say, "It is not very cold where I come from because we wear warm clothes." But words like "DON'T," "NO," "MOVE" were to me like talking to a dog who was eating from some other dog's dish, or who was going in another direction instead of following orders during sled travel, or who was in the doorway. The whole episode stuck in my mind, as it was very different from what my culture demanded in terms of how to handle children: whenever I asked questions that my parents did not want to answer, I was always told to hand them a needle and thread—that my mouth would be sewn up. But it did not kill my sense of questioning because I was not told to shut up instantly. The word "NO" I never heard; instead, I would be distracted and shown something else. My culture tells me that the word "No" leads to disobedient children who become very hard to handle later on. And the only place that I could not MOVE was in a canoe out in the water. My visit that day was an event, though I could not express my thoughts and feelings. Being very shy, all I said was Yes, No and Thank you.

LONELINESS HAD MANY REASONS

My weekends and evenings were very lonely. At times, I would just lie on my bed, wishing I was with my family, and out of nowhere, tears would come down my cheeks. I missed visiting people who I know, open air, howling dogs, even the chores I had to do—washing, cleaning, cutting wood, filling the water pails. I missed the sound of the sea just a few feet from our home, carrying branches off a tree, gathering twigs from the shore, welcoming a dog team just back from a hunting trip, and most of all, joking, laughing and smiling through these everyday events. I missed my food, especially frozen seal liver with seal fat. I would wonder if I would see and feel all these things again. I missed going out on canoe trips to pick berries and the smell of tea brewed on an open fire.

I missed my brother, with whom I shared all these chores. I would burst out crying when I got a letter from him saying, "I do all the work alone now. Today I put up snares; I am still allowed to use one dog, but I miss your help pushing the sled with me." He made me cry because I was having such an easy life and because I knew what he was going through.

I could just picture him. He had to get up as soon as he opened his eyes because of our culture's tradition that we not lie around. That can lead to hard times in bringing up children, and for a girl it means that she will have hard times while giving birth. We were never allowed to eat before we went outside. Grandmother would remind us, "Go out, look at the world, look around you, greet and adore the things that are disposed to us." Having to do this every day in our childhood became a joke to me and my brother. We would burst out laughing. What were we looking for? Grandmother always knew that we were laughing at something that we were not supposed to, and she would warn us that we would bear unhealthy children. Naturally, we would get scared and try not to laugh at anything again.

I KNEW HIM AND YET NOT

I joined the church's young people's association. My first meeting with the group was very happy. The minister who seemed to be the leader of the group looked familiar, and I guess he felt the same about me. Upon repeating my name and asking if I had ever been to Bishop Horden School in Moose Factory, he realized who I was and I too began to remember. As we talked, I discovered that he had been my teacher in the 1941–2 and 1942–3 school years. I had been too young to say that I knew him well, but I felt elated to discover someone I sort of knew. I knew him and yet not, and he too knew me and yet not, as I had grown a bit both mentally and physically.

He introduced me, and—still as shy as ever—I got through meeting the group. I sat through the whole meeting and observed everything that was said and done. It was interesting to see that they had a person for every task: one spoke, one collected money, one made up name tags to be pinned on us, one organized dancing, and one served food. Different people were invited to speak about other countries. When my turn came, I could not believe that I would stand up in front of all those people (about twenty of them) to speak. At that moment, I wished the spot where I was standing would fall down and make me disappear. I felt so shy! I remember having the gestures of my father: I put my hands in my skirt pockets, my legs swayed back and forth, and with my head down as low as I could get it, I spoke about Christmas where I came from. I said that we did not give gifts at Christmas, but on New Year's Day. They began to ask questions when I only wished it were over. Whenever anybody asked me about home, I just wanted to cry, missing it very much.

They began to ask me to speak more often than I wanted to, and this was when my whole way of thinking about qallunaat collapsed. I used to think they knew everything, were capable of anything, could make anything, just picked what they wanted like magic, could change anything from bad to good. And most of all, I thought they knew all about the Inuit. All of the qallunaat who had come to my land had that attitude. But here, all they knew was that it was cold in the North, that Inuit rub noses—and even that was the wrong impression, as we caress with our noses like they caress with their lips. Sooner or later came the question I had learned to expect: "HOW DO YOU LIKE THE WEATHER?"

THE SCREEN HAD TO DO WITH IT

Going to a theatre to see a movie for the first time made me gasp. I could not decide if the show was real or not. One scene where there was fighting just made me scared. I dreamed about it for weeks: it was the first fight I ever witnessed in my whole life. And everything I saw made me wonder if qallunaat really live like that. The film was titled *Oklahoma*.

MY CLOTHES WERE VALUABLE

Washing my clothes taught me that nothing was free in the South. I remember going down to the basement with my qallunaaq friend. I expected to see a washing board; instead, I saw a square, white box. I watched my qallunaaq but asked no questions, and she took it for granted that I knew how to operate the machine. Not a word was said between us, and I copied her all the way. I put in my clothes, added soap, inserted a quarter and away it went. From all that noise out of the machine, I expected never to see my clothes again. While we waited, my friend said that she wished they had a dryer. What is a dryer? All this time, I thought they had a wash line outside. I even pictured myself standing out in a breeze and my washing being gently shaken and a nice smell of air getting into them. That was the way my grandmother had taught me to love washing. Later, when we went to get our clothes, she showed me the wash line—in another room in the basement! The breeze and the smell of nice air died out of my mind right there. The thought of me walking around smelling like musty, grey cement hung in my mind.

I was told to be careful not to leave my clothes there too long or they would be stolen. Who would want to steal my clothes? At home, I was taught never to steal, and surely qallunaat would not do that either. But in the evening, when I went for my clothes, by gum, two pairs of my panties, two pairs of nylons and a slip were missing. Nothing is impossible, no matter how much I believed that qallunaat never do anything bad. Missionaries themselves stressed to me that stealing was a sin—that gave me the impression that qallunaat do not steal either. To this day, my friend does not know that I had never run an automatic washing machine before that day. And I often wonder why her underwear was not valued highly enough to be stolen.

SO CLOSE TOGETHER AND YET SO FAR APART

My first ride on a bus during rush hour made me think the bus would never move with all its passengers. When I travelled with my family, the sled would not move if it was too full and heavy—the dogs could not move it without help. But the bus, run by a motor, was something else. It was full! I was with a man, and we were on our way to visit his family. I sat while he stood, but I felt rather awkward, as I was taught to let my elders sit, man or woman. Much later, I learned that it was his custom to be a gentleman to a female, young or old.

No one spoke. Now and then, I would hear a little bell and I learned that the bell meant that somebody was getting off. (I decided I would never ride the bus alone, because I would be too shy to ring the bell.) I thought while I sat there that people can be so close together and yet so far apart. No one seemed to know each other. I could not understand how people could ignore each other when they were sharing a bus, let alone one seat. While the bus lulled me into daydreams, making my mind drunk with the smell of gasoline, I thought of big gatherings at home. When a whale or seal or any other big animal was divided among the families, children would be laughing and throwing stones into the water, and dogs yapping, and everybody enjoying the food. I could hear the swishing water at the shore and the merriment down the banks, which I used to enjoy so much.

EXHIBITION

The month of August came, and it seemed that everywhere I turned or looked, there was talk about the Exhibition. I asked my friend, "What will be done there?" Right away she said, "Didn't you ever see one?" I hadn't. Every word that I didn't understand I looked up in the dictionary, so I understood the word "exhibition," but still, my curiosity was not satisfied. I began to get very excited about it as my friend never seemed to miss a day to mention it. She would tell me about the rides and cotton candy and shows. When the day of the Exhibition came, my friend and I went in the evening. As I had suspected, it was not free. I never saw so many people and my friend just seemed to know where to go. I felt like I was going in circles. Every time I was in the crowds, I felt so tired. Everybody seemed to hurry all the time.

My friend said, "Let's take a ride first on the Ferris wheel." I wondered, what the heck is that? I found out, and the two minutes I was on it seemed to be hours. I just closed my eyes and held on to the seat as hard as I could. I wished I had never got on it. When it stopped while we were right on top, I want to tell my friend off for not telling me what it was like, but when I got off I wanted to go on it again. So, my friend said, "Let's go on the Caterpillar this time." For the rest of the evening I was in caterpillar motion. Then my friend wanted to go on the Mouse. Well, I had a good look at it, and that was one ride I would not go on as I can still hear the screams that were coming from it.

Then we went where they have mirrors that made you look all shapes and sizes. It seemed that I had not heard myself laugh in such a long time. I began to think about my brother and how we used to laugh so much whenever we played ajaraq—a game played using seal flipper bones. Grandmother used to tell us we were cheating if we checked too close to see which bone is right-side-up, as we were supposed to be able to know which one is right-side-up just by looking normally. She always seemed to know we were not playing the right way, no matter how busy she was with her sewing. I guess our laughter told her we were not concentrating very hard. Looking at myself in funny shapes in the mirrors and laughing made me think how much my brother and I used to laugh. Tears were rolling down my face when my friend and I came out of there.

Then we had cotton candy. When I put it in my mouth, right away it reminded me of the bubbles that grow at the shore of salt water. Then we went to the Bingo: there I had fun. I suppose because I was not really taking it seriously, I won a panda bear toy for thirty-four cents. When we finally got home, I could not forget the Exhibition. I enjoyed it just as I used to enjoy gathering down on the banks of Cape Hope Island.

EXCITING FOR A QALLUNAAT GIRL

One day, I stopped off at the mail office (another routine I had to get used to), and I picked up a rare-looking envelope. Its contents told me to vote. What is vote? What will be my reason to vote? I did not understand it; I had never heard of it. My qallunaaq, who was four years younger than I, said to me that I was lucky, that she had to wait another four years before she could vote. She was very excited about it but I could not see any reason why. What is vote? What do I do? Who is the person I have to vote? My qallunaaq told me where I had to go, that there were two men whose names would be written on a piece of paper, and that I should try to put an X on the right line or it would not count. What would not count? If I put it below or above the line? This was CRAZY! Who were these two men? What were they? What is going to happen to them? I went to vote but still did not understand. Putting an X on a piece of paper was something I did not find exciting.

IT'S A TERRIBLE DREAM

I began to take walks by myself, and my favourite spot was behind Parliament Hill, near the water. There, all the memories of home would come to mind. Many times, I would sit on a stone and tears would begin coming.

I pictured a tent near the shore and heard waves smacking against canoes that were left there tied to a rock. I yearned to get pails and pails of water for drinking or for next day's wash. But the water I was looking at did not look normal at all. The water seemed like it was part of a terrible dream. I would wonder why qallunaat stressed to Inuit people that they keep their houses clean, when the water right in their backyard looked so filthy. When I got back from my walks, my qallunaaq would ask me where I had been and why. What did I see there? Somehow, I could never explain. I had no words to tell her that somehow it made me feel at home to hear water smacking against the shore.

TO PLEASE A FRIEND

There were things that I was willing to try, but others I did not care for. Bicycling was one of the things I did not care for. There were things imposed on me that I could refuse, but to please a friend, one day, I agreed to go bicycling. We started off from Rideau Street and planned to cycle up to Sussex Drive. I got on: in that instant, I had to summon all the senses that had not been used since I left home, my eyes, my ears, my sense of direction, my balance and most of all my nerves. All these things I had been taught to use in order to survive. A car screeched behind me. I looked, and all I could see was the driver shouting with a very mad look on his face. And there was my friend yelling, "Mini! Stop! Stop!" I stopped with a swish with my feet on the cement. My nerves went all tense and the beat of my heart just seemed to be all over my body. My friend was right behind me, reminding me to stay on the right side. She had put more pressure on my nerves than ever when she asked me to go cycling with her, but I went in order to please her. By the time I got back, the fee on my rental was overdue, and when we finally got home, my friend was able to relax casually on her bed, while I was still shaking. And all I whispered to myself was Mini, peace, peace, peace, peace.

THEY ARE OUT OF THE BOX

Television was something I could not get over. If I had the freedom to watch it day and night, I could have. Commercials fascinated me the most, not because of what they advertised, but because of the way they came on—everything seemed to flash quick and disappear just as quick, as if they didn't really want people to see what it was. It made me wonder how it happened. Where does the picture come from? How do people that are on television get inside? How do they know what to say? Where are they? They cannot be in that little box! I found out quite by accident one black day.

A man came to me and said that I had to be televised. I was given fifteen minutes to get ready and be there by taxi. I did not know what was going to happen to me. Will I be boxed in? My imagination began to take over. My second-worst enemy, other than shyness, began to work within me: I will not be able to breathe! Whenever I go where there is no light or daylight, I feel like I am being smothered. My mind begins to work fast, wanting to get out.

I was told to tell the taxi driver where to go. Me? Tell him where to go? He should know where it is—he is from around here. But I relayed the instructions politely to the driver, and to my relief, he did not seem to mind being told by a person who was younger than himself. In fact, he was very polite and kept saying "Yes, ma'am." I looked out the window of the car; now and then, I would look at the driver. He looked like he knew where he was taking me. I felt secure. Not long after, I saw a sign over a building with red lights looking so pretty against the blue sky. The sign said "CBC". When I entered the building, everyone I saw had a beautiful smile and seemed very friendly. A man came over and shook my hand and introduced himself. His name was Percy Saltzman. He asked me questions. "What do you miss most from home? What can you not get used to here?" I was amazed by him. He was the first qallunaaq I had met who asked very human questions. How come the people I see every day do not ask me those questions? For a long time, he stood out in my memory. I told myself that somewhere in this fascinating world of the qallunaat lived people with incredible minds.

The next day, people kept coming to tell me that they had seen me on television. I felt shy and awkward that I was seen by so many people and that my very private thoughts were known by so many. But I stopped worrying about how television works after that. I know now that people on television are not boxed in.

I DID NOT HEAR HIM ARRIVE

I had been a year in the South before I saw another Inuk. The man, just returned from Greenland, was on his way home to Cornwallis Island, Northwest Territories. I wanted to hug him. I wanted to welcome him the way I would have in my own home, to make tea and converse about his trip. But I could not. My surroundings did not at all allow me to be me. The steel desks seemed to say, you are part of us, do not act like a human being. There was a great big lump in my throat and my tears were hard to keep back.

I was so happy to see him, not only because he was Inuk, but because he knew Inuk ways. For the first time, I really felt that I was so alone—his awakening of the Inuk ways in me made me realize that. But his questions and answers and my questions and answers kept me from crying. He told me about his family and I told him about my parents. He told me that he had a daughter almost the same age as me. That I would meet her one day. He made me wish that I had an Inuk girl to chum with, to make comments about things I see in an Inuit way. No matter how hard I tried to communicate with my qallunaaq, my comments never seemed to hit her right. Half the time, my qallunaaq's question was "What do you mean?" My visitor also made me realize that I was losing the sense of humour that my parents had considered so important in order to survive on unfamiliar ground. My "Inukism" was slowly disappearing, or getting buried deeper and deeper. I felt dumbfounded, so I tried to bring out my normal reaction to his arrival and said, "I did not hear you arrive, where did you park your dogs?" That hit him right on the Inuk funny spot and he laughed. My welcoming instincts slowly began to come back.

GRANDMOTHER'S QULLIK WAS VERY BRIGHT

I have known about electricity since I was five years old, but its power was not known to me until I saw electric lights. In school, I was taught that electricity came from thunder and lightning. To me, it meant danger, and I was brought up to be very cautious of lightning and thunder at home. When there was a thunderstorm, my brother and I were always reminded to put our hands on our ears as the sound could injure the nerves inside us, even kill us. We were never allowed to be near anything shiny, such as iron or metal cans, while it stormed. We were told that such objects attracted thunder and lightning.

I learned that electricity is dangerous but also very wonderful, and useful, and I compared it to the qullik—the seal oil lamp, which was also wonderful, useful and a comfort to us. Every evening, women would sit down on the floor or ground, catching the last speck of daylight, to clean and fix the wick of the qullik. Watching my grandmother, it never occurred to me that there was another such light, brighter than what I thought was so bright. To my thinking, that is what the qallunaat woman has as a source of comfort. If she could have seen Inuit women, what they have to go through. Here in the South, she has light merely by flicking a most innocent-looking gadget on the wall. The Inuit woman has first of all to make sure there is seal oil ready to be poured into a pot, the oil having been rendered by a slow process to liquify the fats of the seal. The wick has to be cut neat and even so it will not give smoke or cause any odour. The burned part of the wick has to be trimmed off so it will give an even flame. The oil has to be poured into another pan from the original processing pan in order to get out the saturated parts of cooked fat. That was the comfort of an Inuk woman.

Sometimes these lamps were lit early in the morning, before the sun came up, so the women could finish sewing the garments to be worn by the men that same morning. The qullik was her only light during the early darkness of winter. Who can say who enjoys more comfort? It is me who is comfortable today because I can reach up and switch on a gadget that nobody seems to pay attention to except when it's needed, and because I do not have to reach down and put in all that work in order to get one flame. Though I realize how lucky and in comfort I am, I will never cease to believe that my ancestors were smart and resourceful. But I do have a reason to be afraid of thunderstorms, because I can see now what it can do in the hands of the qallunaat.

I have been told by qallunaat individuals that thunderstorms cannot hurt me. I have never been out during thunderstorms when I was with my parents, but here in the south, I have had to be out a few times on my way home from work. It was unbearable for me the first time. Having been told from two sides about the storm, it was very uncomfortable walking on the streets, especially around shining objects. I felt caught in a trap. No matter how much I tried to tell myself that it will not hurt me, I could not help feeling that I was about to be killed. I was watching other people; they were walking just as if the storm was not there—they did not seem to react to the sound of thunder. I assured myself: it does not bother them; I, too, will not be hurt. Eventually, I had to get used to walking out on a stormy day. But I still will not stay close to shining objects. If it storms while I am at home, I cover everything that shines.

IT AND HER

While I was riding in a car with a friend, we stopped at a gas station, which was beyond my description. I had been so busy being amazed by so many cars that I had never really thought about what makes them go until that moment. The smell of gas told me that the car I was in was being fed. As usual, with so many things going through my mind, I wanted to ask so many questions. Where does the gas come from? What makes the dollar signs add up? I was trying to hear what the driver would say. Everything was happening too fast. The driver said, "Fill her up," at least to my ears, that's how it sounded. A teacher I had once came flashing into my mind, pointing at me with her finger and trying to make me see the difference between "her" and a non living thing, or "it." Today, I get terribly nervous when I realize my car is running out of gas. I can still hear my friend saying, "Fill her up," and all the way to the gas station I tell myself, "fill it up," and when I get there I say, "Three dollars' worth." Then I look at the dollar signs add up on the pump, am nauseated at the smell of gas, and I tell myself that the car has a mind of its own.

ALMOST LOST AN ARM FOR A STAMP

Sooner or later, I had to write letters to my family and friends. I had known for a long time that a letter had to have a stamp in order to be mailed, but I had never quite understood what it was for. I knew neither where the stamps came from nor where to buy them. We did not have post offices where I come from. The mail used to go free from person to person. And in my earlier writing days, someone always gave me a stamp. One day, I found out where these little stickers were available. It was one of those days when my qallunaaq and I met after work; she said that she had to get stamps from the post office. I just followed her until we arrived at an enormous building.

The first thing I noticed were the funny-looking doors. I was afraid to enter through them, but my qallunaaq did not seem bothered. I was right behind her and did not notice that when she pushed it, it began to revolve. I was so busy trying to figure out what made it go around that I forgot myself. The next thing I knew, my arm was caught. A person behind me was screaming, "She's caught!" over and over. I was panicking so much that nothing was coming out of me but little aching sounds. By this time, a crowd had gathered, and someone managed to pull the revolving door backwards. My arm was so sore that I was in tears. This made me feel all the more awkward as I was taught never to shed a tear in public. I tried to ignore my ache so that no one would look at me anymore. I learned two things at that moment: that someone getting hurt is very exciting to people, and that this was the place where stamps came from.

I felt a bit afraid to handle the stamps I bought, and many questions began to pour into my mind. Why does a letter have to have a stamp? Is there something that has to be done to it? Not quite knowing anything about it, I handled them very carefully, with high respect, as if I might break some law if I did not take care of them. The image of the Queen on the stamp also made me feel afraid, as if she would know how I was handling it. I did not really learn why stamps were necessary at that time, though I have now, after many years. I have decided that everything has its own place in the South.

GRANDMOTHER'S HELPERS

When I was very little, I heard about policemen. I used to be told that they arrest anybody and put people in jail and tie them up. I was never told that they do that to people who broke a law. I did not even know what "law" was at the time. Every summer, the Royal Canadian Mounted Police boat would arrive at Old Factory River (our summer camping place). When they were spotted coming, I used to be careful to select a good hiding place in a bush so that I would not be arrested. I must have had a real guilty conscience to be so well prepared. Today, I know that it was one of my grandmother's wonderful tricks to make me listen to her. Come to think of it, the police never even hurt me when they came to our tents. When they said something to me, I knew it was something nice, though I did not understand their language, I could tell by their voices. But little did I know that they came just to check my E9-438 number. And little did I know that they too are just as arrestable as I am if they do not follow the law. But they were indeed Grandmother's helpers to make me follow her rules.

GRANDMOTHER'S ELEGANCE CAME IN HANDY

On my way to work, I passed many shops. I would ask myself, who goes to these shops? I wonder if I can go in too? They did not look quite like the Hudson's Bay stores I had known in the North. I wondered if one had to be special to enter them? Having met many girls at the Terrace, I knew of one who enjoyed sewing as I did. She told me about shops where I could buy material to make dresses. If she can enter such shops, so can I.

Walking into a shop in the South made me want to tiptoe. So elegant! A lady came to me. "Can I help?" I had never known the freedom to select the fabric and colour I wanted. I was used to Hudson's Bay Company clerks making the choices; it did not matter the colour or size, they simply handed it to you and told you the price—that was that. Somehow I felt a little helpless making my own choice. The lady made me feel worse standing around, not saying a word after offering her help. I decided that the longer I stayed, the longer I would suffer. I chose what hit my eyes first: a wool fabric in turquoise. I went home and decided to make a jumper.

Not long after I finished the jumper, I needed something to wear underneath it. I felt nervous just thinking about the lady and about choosing. This time, I was wiser and made up my mind beforehand. Off I went, this time to a big department store. Entering the store, I again had the impression of a crowd of people, each person carrying a heavy load. Some hurrying, some browsing and none enjoying this elegant store. No matter what my purpose was when I went shopping, I always forgot it when I got into the crowds. All I wanted to do was sit and watch all these people.

That's what I was doing when a lady woke me out of it—again, with such elegance: "Can I help?" I suddenly realized that I was not anywhere near the item I wanted, so I asked her where I could find a sweater. She directed me to the second floor and pointed the way. I went where she pointed. What I saw there amazed me—a crawling thing with a sign above it, "ESCALATOR." Qanuk taima?—What now? To me, it was unbelievable. I just stood there and did not move and just watched. I felt very far removed from the sweater I wanted, though it did not seem so important anymore. The crawling thing was now mine to master. I informed myself that people were on it, to reassure myself. I watched the others for a while, especially their feet. I walked over, and just as I stepped onto the moving part, it did not feel as scary as it looked from the bottom. I kept my eyes on the feet of the person in front of me and copied. What a short ride. I thought while I was downstairs that it must have no ending, that it went up and up. I love to watch people, and I told myself that that would be a good place to watch them one by one, without them disappearing into the crowds. It is amazing how one can feel like one of the crowd just because one is doing something that others are doing. That's how I felt at that moment, riding on the crawling thing—pardon me—escalator.

But once I was at the other end, I felt very much alone. I did not see any sign of sweaters. My greatest worry now was how to get back downstairs. I told myself to forget the sweater and started to walk around to find a way down. Not far from the escalator I read a sign: "ELEVATOR." Well! I know what that is; I use it everyday at my working place. I felt like shouting at the top of my lungs, "Taika!"—there it is! I was so relieved and went straight home to think about my adventure. Elevator and escalator. I told myself that they are related, but one goes straight up and down, and one crawls.

ARTIFICIAL RIVER

My qallunaaq decided one day that we should go for a boat ride. That made some sense to me, but I also had questions, such as: What reasons do I have for taking a boat ride? Where do we get a boat? In the North, when people take such trips, it's either for hunting, berry picking or to make a seasonal move from one camp to another. This, of course, is done for joy as well as for work and to get resources.

But taking a boat ride in Ottawa was something else. I just followed my qallunaaq without question. As usual, she just seemed to know where everything was. I had my own picture in my mind about where to go for a boat ride—that was either straight to the beach or to the river. But as I followed my qallunaaq, my picture just did not form. First of all, we had to go to a man who was standing on a street, and he gave us a sheet of paper. When I read it, my picture completely changed, and when we got to the place for the boat ride, my picture was turned completely upside-down. I had pictured my qallunaaq and me rowing or running a motor alone in a boat along the shore, with beautiful scenery going by. But there we were in the midst of people, in a line-up waiting for our turn. And I thought people bought tickets only to the theatre and the exhibition grounds.

Embarking on that boat was something else. I could not understand where the loud voice was coming from and I couldn't see the sites it was describing. All I could see was the mass of heads of other people who were in the boat with us. My qallunaaq was so excited about the whole thing. The river we were in just did not seem normal to me. It did not have the shape or form of the rivers I had boated on. All it reminded me of was one straight long bathtub filled with water. When we disembarked, my qallunaaq was bubbling with excitement. I felt like asking her, "Suukainnaqita? What did we do?"

I WOULD LIKE TO SEE TO WHOM I AM TALKING

When I was first shown the telephone at Laurentian Terrace, I had wondered who would call me. I had never really thought much about this machine and it took me ages to ever think about using it. At the office where I worked, I was often alone during lunch hours. Occasionally, the phone, which was sitting next to my desk, would ring—always when I was alone, it seemed. I suppose I didn't pay much attention to it when people were around. When it rang while I was alone, I ignored it. I would not know exactly what to say if I picked it up. That was one machine I was not very anxious to master. In fact, I felt awkward about talking to someone I could not see.

It was one of those days when I was alone and the telephone started to ring. I completely ignored it, but this time, it would not stop. It got to the point that it sounded like it was saying, "Mini! Answer me!" over and over. And it got to the point that I could not ignore it—at least, I thought of everything to do so. I even thought of leaving the office, but on leaving, I would have to pass it. I felt a bit ridiculous about my plan. Finally, I decided to answer and told myself that whoever was wanted was not there; I would simply say so and hang up fast. I do not know how I sounded from the other end, but the voice said, "Speak up, Mini, I cannot hear you." The voice I recognized! "I thought you would never answer," it said. "Mini, it is only me. Wait, I will hang up and come over. I am just across the hall."

Here, it had been the lady who had been taking me various places for civil service tests. It was one of her tests. She had tricked me to answer the telephone. She then explained to me how to answer, take messages and so on. Why can't the caller just call back? was my question, but I never questioned her on that.

My qallunaaq worked in another building. I asked her if I could phone her the next day. I discovered that it was not so scary after all to be normal as you are on the telephone, and it was rather fun to feel that I had mastered another machine. But each time, when I did learn something new, I felt a little change in me. Somehow I seemed braver and braver, but still very shy.

SOMETHING FAMILIAR?

The first farm I visited was the only place I recognized in the South. At least it was something I had read about while I was in school with the missionaries. It was the first time I did not have to follow my qallunaaq to find the cows, horses, pigs and chickens. I even knew where to go to gather eggs. Somehow my qallunaaq did not seem at all excited; she took it for granted, it was her home. My hunger to have a real home so close made me decide that I would call it my home. Of course, I did not tell my qallunaaq what I was thinking. We made many visits to this farm and before long, I was calling her mother "Mom."

"Mom" became very ill two years later. She ended up in a hospital. I went to visit her a couple of times, but she did not look at all like the "Mom" who used to serve me hot buns fresh out of the oven. As the tragedy of death had come my way many times, I had no doubt that I would never see her again. She died of yellow jaundice a couple of weeks later. I went to her funeral service and, as I watched her coffin being lowered into the ground, her last words to me became louder and louder in my ears: "Mini, look after yourself."

MEETING A GRAND LADY

I do not know the lady personally. I only call her a grand lady because I see her pictures in the papers so often with little children. I think any woman who takes time to see children, especially not her own, is a grand lady. One day, I was sent a notice to meet this woman. Upon arriving at her home, which later I learned is called the Governor General's residence, I wanted to tiptoe as I often felt on entering elegant shops. I do not know what I had thought before arriving. I suppose I had visions that she would meet me at the door as does any other visited person. It was fascinating to find out that such grand ladies have ladies-in-waiting. I met the lady-in-waiting who took me down a long hallway. My feet never made a sound. It felt like walking on fresh-fallen snow, this hall covered with deep pile red carpet. Almost at the end of the hall, we entered a room furnished with many chairs. I felt I was just arriving again to Laurentian Terrace, only I did not have to feel lost in choosing a chair. In the room was the grand lady, Mrs. the late Governor General Georges Vanier.

As usual, I felt shy and speechless, but the grand lady made it possible for me to be completely at ease. That was also the first time I was shown a greenhouse. Flowers in the middle of winter? I could not believe it. Here in this greenhouse were all kinds of flowers. That was the day that I fell in love with flowers for the first time. I had always taken them for granted, as wildflowers grow all over where I come from, though these ones were much bigger than I was used to seeing. The grand lady gave me one which she called a chrysanthemum. It was the first time that I learned that different flowers have different names. It was also the first time that I learned there was such a thing as a visiting book where you can sign your name.

DOG MEAT IN THE SOUTH?

It was one of those days when my qallunaaq and I met after work. She suggested that we eat at a restaurant. I had no idea just exactly what you do there. I understood that it was an eating place, but I thought you served yourself. As usual, I followed my qallunaaq without question. I kept my mouth shut, while all the time I was asking myself, why are we sitting down? A lady came over and handed us a folded sheet of paper. "Menu," it read. I watched my qallunaaq. Do we sit here and figure out what to cook for ourselves? I felt very lost—it was not at all like the place where we ate at the Terrace. Finally, I became aware of the other people in this restaurant. They were not doing anything but eating. The lady was passing food around. Ah! I have to tell the lady what I want and she will go and cook it.

I had discovered that there was nothing free in the South, so I had to think about the cost of what I was about to ask the lady to cook for me. For the first time, I had a good look at the sheet of paper. There it showed the prices. Anything that sounded good was beyond the amount in my purse. Finally, my qallunaaq said that she would have a hot dog. I burst out laughing and could not stop. What is a hot dog? Do not tell me people in the South eat dog meat! I felt a bit sick. Which one is that? She pointed: wiener on a bun, twenty-five cents. I asked the lady to cook one for me as well; in fact, I asked for everything my qallunaaq asked for—Coke, jello and a hot dog. When the dog was brought to our table, I stared at it. I was very hungry at that moment and began to picture nice fresh seal meat, but the aroma of the dog killed it. I did not like it. I washed the taste down with Coke. That became a habit of mine; I drank so much that my face broke into a million pimples, even down to the soles of my feet.

THEY TOO HAVE
THEIR OWN WAY OF WRITING

Not very long after my visit and after many, many bottles of Coke, my right foot got infected to the point where I could not walk. My foot became so badly infected that a red streak began to show going up my leg.

Besides following so many rules where we lived, my qallunaaq and I had our own little rules. She would wake me up, and if she did not, I would wake her up. That morning, I had to wake her and tell her about my pain. For the first time since I met her, I did not have to follow her. She told me what she was going to do. She told me not to get up, that she would go and tell our matron and phone the place where I worked. I wanted to express to her that I was happy for her help and concern. I could not bring myself to tell her that, mostly because I was a bit surprised that she had turned into a caring mother.

The matron came and examined my foot, and then she made arrangements for me to see a doctor. Waiting in a doctor's office taught me this was something else new besides other new things I had seen. My experience taught me again that everything has its own place in the South. This time, I learned about drugstores. I had thought that once I saw the doctor, he would do something for me right there. But I learned that the only way one can get medicine is by taking a little piece of paper and going to a drugstore. I also learned that there is more than one drugstore. I waited for the doctor to give directions to a specific store, but all he said was that any drugstore would fill the prescription. I looked at the piece of paper. I did not understand one word said on it. In fact, it looked like scribbling to me. Surely the doctor cannot be teasing me by giving me something with such messy writing. Surely no doctor would play around with my pain, especially after seeing my foot. But when I handed the paper to the man behind the counter, he took it with an appearance of comprehension. This was just unbelievable! I waited, and sure enough, I got the medicine, but when I looked at the bottle, it was readable in plain English. In fact, it said: "Soak foot twice a day in hot water for half an hour." I told myself that druggists and doctors have their own language and must have translators, like I am at work. After that, I never drank any Coke—I sort of like it, but it did not like me.

I HATE WATER

Water and beach I can understand. My qallunaaq and I decided to go swimming one day. I did not know how to swim, but I liked the sound of the beach—it sounded familiar. Upon arriving at the beach, all I could say was amisuaaluit! Many, many! Just like a mass of geese feeding on a swamp. Some were in the water, some lying around, some walking. The whole area sounded like millions of bees. But they were not "together." There were some couples, others in fours, and others alone. It amazed me that so many people could ignore each other when they were only a few inches apart.

I do not know what I was doing at that beach, especially since I hated water. I have hated water since I was six years old. It was during springtime, in May, that my family and I were returning from goose hunting. At this time of the year at Cape Hope Island, the ice on the sea is very thin. We were approaching our camp when suddenly I fell off the sled and went straight into the water, right up to my neck. I was barely holding on to the sled when our dogs stopped themselves and looked back as if they knew something was wrong. My grandmother and brother moved to pull me out. I looked down at the hole I had just come out of. It was so dark and looked so deep that I have never really erased it from my mind. It came back to me at this beach where I was watching my qallunaaq swim without fear. I had no desire at all to try what she was doing. All I did was go in as far as my waist and came out and never went in again. Instead, I sat on the sand and watched people. Many, many people just fascinated me so.

MY MOST SILLY MOMENT

I felt like wanting to crawl into a little hole many times, but there was never a moment quite like the way I felt on the street while I was getting into a bus. My qallunaaq was rushing around and excited as usual on the day she decided to take me to a square dance. We both got all dressed up in full flare skirts and crinolines. I was following behind her when our bus arrived. Just as I was getting into the bus, as I put one of my feet down, my heel got caught on my crinoline and down it came. I do not quite remember how I managed to do this, but I will never forget the red, red feeling on my face. My qallunaaq was just as red when she discovered my predicament. I sat down and somehow tried to pull the crinoline back up where it belonged. Every time I think about that moment I feel like saying: OH NO!

MY FIRST SQUARE DANCE IN THE SOUTH

My Inuk mind has had many disappointments since I came to the South. When my qallunaaq suggested that we go square dancing, it sounded like lots of fun. It sounded like everybody being themselves. But anything that sounded familiar never seemed to turn out the way I had in my mind.

We entered the dance hall and I felt excited. (Even fun was not free—it cost fifty cents to enter.) I had done square dancing at home, but never experienced it in the South. "May I have this dance?" a gentleman asked. Once more, I learned something new. I was used to gentlemen in the North who took your hand and led you to the floor. I told myself that I had come to dance, so my answer was yes. I had not thought about partners when we headed to this hall. All over again I felt shy and never wanted to go again. To this day, I do not know the gentleman's name, though he had asked what part of China I was from. Who had ever heard about North? Every time I said where I came from, it just seemed appalling to my questioners.

TWENTY-ONE, BUT ONE YEAR OLD IN THE SOUTH

I had just turned twenty-one, and the people in the office where I worked gave me a cake with candles on it. We gathered in the steno pool and everybody talked and laughed to each other while I stood in front of the cake, not knowing what to say and feeling very shy. I tried to look at each one of them and wondered how many knew that Inuit don't celebrate birthdays, that we don't reckon growth in terms of age. And I also wondered what the reaction would be if I were to speak in that direction. Instead, I thought about the trouble they had gone to, to make my day happy. All these important people were taking the time to stand around me for this day. All I could say was thank you, and I thought to myself that I was now one year old here in the South, an anniversary which no one seemed to remember.

According to the office manager, I was now able to take ten days' holiday. I decided to go home and see my parents.

Arriving at my home was unforgettable. Everything looked small but so familiar. It was so peaceful. Nobody was hurrying or looked like they were carrying a load. There were no red and green lights to think about while walking, no looking twice before setting out, no keys to remember on entering a tent, no meal rules to follow. Even the clock, which I looked at first thing in the morning and last thing at night, no longer seemed important.

I THOUGHT I WAS A QUEEN

My first day at home was a lot of handshaking and lots of attention. I felt very important and noticed that what I said was listened to. I attracted that kind of attention for a couple of days, at least I tried to. On the third morning, my bubble burst. My grandmother had not changed. She was still the same and most of all, still had her own rules. Her attitudes towards me and my brother remained: that we must get up as soon as we wake, dress and go out and look at the world.

I felt very confused, outcast, and most of all, unwanted. According to my grandmother, I was no longer a lady. She told me that my mouth had grown too much, that I was lazy and too spoiled, that I was like an icicle which would break if I was given orders. I had to join in the chores, clean the tent, get pails of water, cut wood, help my brother to look at the nets in the water, clean the fish, pluck the ducks, make bannock, do washing, heat the water on the fire—many, many things I had not done since I went to the South. When bedtime came, my muscles ached, and sleep was not hard to find. I became a queen again, only in a different sense that was familiar to my people. I was praised for the chores I could still do. Our visitors were amazed that I did not forget my language and that I did not turn up my nose at my chores, that I did not ignore people, and most of all that I could still touch sealskin and eat seal meat, or anything raw. Nobody had the right to put me back in my place but Grandmother— which she would never do, as she is too wise and too strong in the mind.

CAUGHT BETWEEN TWO LIVES

When I left for my holidays, I was given a choice by my chief: I could stay at home, or I could come back and still have my job. Though my grandmother ran my brother's and my life, my father always had a say in what we did. But there were many complications to such a decision, and four other people involved.

At the time of my birth, a young man had been chosen to be my husband by my father and the mother of the young man. It was known all over our community that it was to be so. Both Grandmother and Grandfather had let this go on, much against their will, in order to keep peace with Father and between Father and the parents of the young man. I am sure that being older and wiser, they knew all the time that it was not meant to be. When I think about it myself, the relationship had never been as strong as it should be in such arrangements. I was never allowed to be alone with this man in my growing years like all the other girls in the same situation. When I sewed things, he was never mentioned, nor were songs sung for me, that I would make him a good wife. It seems the whole arrangement was rather artificial. Nobody dared talk about the real reasons, as it involved who would gain the most out of it economically. Customarily, the agreement between the mother and my father formed a bond never to be broken, though in actual fact it could be, with good reason.

The parents of this young man came from their camp when they heard that I was home from South. There was so much tension among my family and the parents of the man. The young man himself did not come. His mother announced that he was waiting for me at the camp. In the tent sat my grandmother, acting very cold towards our visitors. She bothered to serve tea only because it was our custom, but I could see that her heart was not in it. My father also sat, looking very troubled. He knew Grandmother was against the marriage, yet he was very fond of the parents of the man. And there I was, causing all the tension and having no say about it. Finally, the mother asked, "Are we taking Mini with us? You know she is long past the age of our promise." No one spoke. My brother and I looked at each other, he making funny faces at me, with teasing gestures all over his body. Finally, Grandmother spoke, but very fast: "Mini has work to do; she is going back to South." I could sense that this was not really her wish, but her way out. She had always observed that this young man was too lazy and never went hunting, and if he did, he was never successful. According to her, I would have starved. She had always commented that my knowledge of caring for a home was too much for him. Nothing was said again, at least not in front of me. Altogether, the whole thing appeared forgotten, but the mother never accepted it. She said later that her son would wait no longer and declared him free to marry anyone he wished. The bond was broken.

I was feeling caught between two lives when my father told me that I could stay if I wanted, or go back south. To this day I do not know how he was feeling. I knew that he always believed that his children should have a chance to learn different things and about different people. I felt very helpless and very much alone. I had to make my own choice. Suddenly, all the things I had learned about choosing on my own began to come back in my mind. I began to analyze my situation. If I stayed, I would never see all the nice shops again. I would have no freedom, nor, most of all, a private life. On the other hand, I felt unwanted by my family. I told myself that they did not care about me anymore. I even asked myself, why did I ever have to go south? If I had not, I would at least still have my parents. I was blaming them. I was feeling so sorry for myself that I did not have time to see that it was all my fault.

I went back to South excited, but very much alone. The Terrace seemed empty. There, nobody cared what you did, but people did care in my home, about every little thing. That day I became "southernized" in my mind. I told myself that I would just have to be two people. Here in the South, I mind my own affairs, make up my own mind, care for my own chores. But when I go home, I have to involve myself in other chores and mind my elders. It was never true that my family did not love me or that I was unwanted by them. Today, they are most happy to have me and I enjoy my visits, as long as I remember that I have to adapt. I went back to the routine of the South and accepted it without wondering and without feeling confused.

A HOUSE IN THE AIR

During my stay in the South, I learned that there was another North besides where I come from, which is James Bay. I was born on Cape Hope Island—originally Weetaltuk Island—founded by my grandfather, George Weetaltuk, during his nomadic travels in the late 1800s. Never in my early years did I know that there was another North until I had a chance to see maps of the world. I have heard and knew about the areas surrounding my home. On the maps, I saw Frobisher Bay, Cape Dorset, Lake Harbour, Coral Harbour and so on.

One day, my chief came to me and asked if I would like to go to Frobisher Bay. I had heard about Frobisher Bay, but I was not sure about its inhabitants. I could not believe that there would be any Inuit in a place with a qallunaat name because at home, I was used to Inuit names for places with Inuit inhabitants. As I began to get ready for the trip to Frobisher Bay, I began to hear bit by bit that Inuit live there. By this time, I would have gone anywhere where there were Inuit, so I took the trip.

This was also my first trip on an airplane that looked like a house—at least, that's how I described it to myself when I entered. I had been in airplanes before, but not enormous ones such as this. My feet did not make a sound, just like when I entered the Governor General's house. The cabin was carpeted and had fully finished chairs, not like the ones I have sat on in little airplanes. One could even walk in this one—people were smoking and eating there too. The plane even had a waitress, like in the restaurant, but she was dressed beautifully in navy blue. Every now and then, a voice would speak and tell us how high we were and how far it was to Frobisher Bay. The plane even had a lavatory and a bed. I told myself, this is a house in the air.

Much, much later, I was told the plane belonged to the Minister of Northern Affairs, Alvin Hamilton. When I come to think of it, he was in the plane too at the time. My shyness suddenly came back when I was told that I flew in the Minister's airplane. If I had known who it belonged to, I would never have taken the trip, and the trip wouldn't have caused the return of my shyness, my worst enemy in me.

HE WROTE ONLY FEW WORDS

I had thought that I had seen everything until I learned that there are many kinds of contests in the South. A girl came to me one day and said that I should enter a Miss Northern Affairs contest. This one I just had to see, and it had a challenging ring to it, so I entered. As soon as I arrived at the building where the contestants were meeting, I felt so sorry that I did enter the contest.

There were so many people and judges and over thirty-six contestants. We each had a number—mine was seven. We stood in a line-up. When the first number was called, my heart pounded. I could see what the first girl was doing. I just could not walk like that, nor could I smile on my own. For the first time since I came south, I asked myself, "what am I doing here?" I had gone too far. Before my number was called, I had to make so many little decisions. I told myself that I will just have to be myself. I would feel funny if I tried to walk any way other than my usual walk. The sound of clapping hands came from the other room. By then I was shaking. When I heard my number called, my mind argued by itself. I have to go ... I have gone too far... this is no time to be shy ... I see most of these people every time I go to work.... Out I went. My smile was no problem, a smile can hide many kinds of fears. I could not help smiling at all those people—but I was so glad when it was all over. I was told that I would have to wait until all the others had done the same. I waited and my number was called again. This time there were only seven of us. I was told that I had to do it a third time! When it was over I had come second to Miss Northern Affairs.

What does one do, to come second to a queen? I met a photographer and a man who wrote only a few words. I had never seen anyone who took pictures like that. The photographer worked hurriedly and he kept putting some little gadget near my face and he clicked just as fast. In the meantime, another man was writing while he was asking so many questions, but he wrote only few words. How was I to know that he was trained for his job? I told myself that he must be careless. My qallunaaq had come to the contest and could not wait for the paper to come out. As usual, I did not know what she was talking about. I met my qallunaaq after work and we went straight to the newspaper stand. We found a bench on our way home and began to read: "ESKIMO GIRL SECOND IN CS BEAUTY CONTEST. Mini Oadla, 29, of Old Factory, became possibly the first Eskimo woman to place in a beauty contest with white women here today." It went on and on, where I came from and what I liked. My qallunaaq was horrified by the mistake in my age and told me that I should get them to correct it. I could not be bothered about that. I had had enough for one day. But it was no wonder the writer had made mistakes—he wrote only a few words. He did not even spell my surname right—he wrote it "Oadla" when it was "Aodla."

MY FEELINGS WERE HURT

How did I allow myself to get into the things I did? I never understood until I was in the middle of them. I found myself one day in a building with a lot of big cameras, wires dangling down from the ceiling and a man walking around with a great big machine. A lady took me to a room of mirrors and began to paint my face. My skin felt gooey, sticky and stiff. My face looked like I was hot all over, like I had been running endlessly. The lady called it make-up. Well, I was all made up. Then I was made to put on a parka in the middle of July, when the temperature outside was eighty degrees. It would not have been so bad inside the building, but up I went, right to the roof, where the sun beamed down. A man made a movie of me while I drank ginger ale. I understood that I was advertising the ginger ale.

Seeing my picture on the back of Pure Spring Ginger Ale trucks made me feel funny and odd. My feelings were hurt, especially when girls I knew would come to me and say, "Who do you think you are? Why did they pick you? Why does it have to be an Eskimo?" Prejudice was something I was never allowed to practise, no matter how different people seem, either low, middle, or high class, and especially whatever nationality they were. I was only to respect them. Grandmother would say, you look very unhealthy if you practise prejudice, and if it's pointed at you, it's because you created it. I began to notice that some I considered to be friends would not have anything to do with me, and that others seemed to be proud just to know me. I decided that I would rather keep my friends than have my picture behind a truck, so I refused the next time I was asked to advertise. The man who talked to me about it told me that I should do it to make extra money. I started to cry because I figured he did not care for my feelings. He repeated that it was up to me, so I refused. He said that I was odd, that other girls were just itching to be televised, that I should be proud to be chosen. To this day, the man does not know that I had to put up with insults and dirty letters. How can people waste time and stamps to send such letters?

VISITING A MINT

What is a mint? The only kind of mint I knew was a candy flavour. One day my qallunaaq said, "Let's go see the Mint today, it's on our street and not very far from here." We walked to the Mint, and on approaching, I felt a little afraid. There was an RCMP standing at the gate. The building was surrounded by many harpoons—at least, that's what they looked like to my Inuk eyes. I learned later that it was just a steel fence. Inside the fence stood the smallest house I had ever seen. Who could live in there? The little house was not finished according to my Inuk eyes, as it had holes all over. In fact, there was another policeman inside. He handed each of us a piece of paper with a number on it. Oh, no! Don't tell me I have to stand in front of many people again. I followed my qallunaaq. We went through a hallway and could hear a lot of noise, a lot of machines running. Money, money—I have never seen so many pennies. We went closer. There were many machines going, one sideways, another up and down. At one end, it looked like it was eating blocks of copper-coloured stones; at the other end, it was vomiting a lot of pennies. There were men who were picking them up and looking at them. Another man looked like he was counting. One was walking back and forth with little bags and putting them away into a box. I decided that was where the money was made and sent all over the world. "Mint"? Well, that is another mystery for me.

WE WERE NOMADS

I had never heard about West. I learned my geography by provinces, though I never really understood what they meant. Whoever heard of places that are divided up when they are so close together? Not me.

My work as a translator took me to the West one summer, along with a welfare worker. Once more, I was in a house in the air. Our first stop was Fort William, Ontario, where we stopped to change our plane. How did my companion know what to do? When we got off the airplane, she knew where to go. I just followed. She seemed to know my little mind, and from then on, she began to tell me many things. She showed me how to check my air ticket, how to find my luggage, how to find out when to leave and when we are arriving, where the bookstands were, where the lavatory was, and why these people are behind counters. She even told me we were not staying at Fort William, that we have to wait for another plane.

We took another airplane and arrived at Edmonton, where we got a place to stay that she called a Hotel. She showed me how to check in. I was so surprised to find my name written on a card in this hotel—I have never been here, how did they know my name? I asked her about it since she was so willing to tell me things. She said that she had booked it. Booked it? The English language gets funnier every day. She said that she telephoned this hotel. There are just too many ajugaitualuit! Things that are incredible, fantastic, magic, these qallunaat ways! I assured myself that I would just have to accept them and learn as I go on. We were both given keys. That was something I had gotten used to, having keys.

We went to the elevator and my companion pushed a button that said "Eight." There was something different about this elevator from what I am used to at work. It was much faster and my stomach felt tickles. For a moment, I wondered if it would always stay with me, but it was gone when we got to the eighth floor. When we got out of the elevator, my feet once more did not make a sound. I could see the whole floor was carpeted. I felt very elegant.

Once in our room, the first place I headed to was the window. *Aukataguluapingani!* was the word in my mind, which has many meanings: incredible, fantastic, tiny—an expression of a lot of surprise. The houses and cars and people I could see looked so tiny. But the sky still looked pretty high. Everything in the room was very elegant. It even had a television, a telephone and its own lavatory. It seemed that my companion had made all kinds of arrangements before we ever got there.

The purpose of our trip was to visit patients in hospitals and homes having anything to do with the Inuit. The next day we went to Charles Camsell Hospital. It was very sad to see all these Inuit. Some had children in the North whom they had not heard about since they came here. So many worries and yet they were just like me, accepting their surroundings without question. I felt a bit useless in my job because I had never heard the Western Arctic Inuit language. I tried to speak with some but could not understand. They didn't understand when I spoke to them, and yet they seemed so happy to see me. All I could do was return my Inuk smile to let them know that I felt for them.

We then moved on to Clearwater Lake, Manitoba. We travelled by a little airplane, which was familiar to me, but I had never had such a trip. Flying over mountains, we went up and down, and I felt very afraid. I could picture myself falling down below. I told myself that the pilot must know what he is doing, so my being afraid lessened, and I did not want to think about it. When we arrived, we both felt very lost. My companion had made arrangements for somebody to pick us up, but there was nobody there. She telephoned someone, and not long after, a doctor came and took us to a hotel. We seemed to have gone from one extreme to another. In Edmonton, we had stayed in such an elegant hotel and had our luggage carried for us. Entering this hotel, we could not stop laughing—not at the hotel, but at the situation we were in.

We checked in. The man behind the counter did not seem to care whether we stayed or not. He was not in a hurry. It seemed he had no time to follow or rules to go by, which made him look like an odd qallunaaq to my Inuk eyes. He was completely at ease. To me, he was just too natural to be in the South. My companion asked about our luggage, which the doctor had brought in. The man told us that we had to carry them upstairs ourselves. I did not care—I had carried heavier loads than my suitcases before. There was no elevator. I went hysterical from laughing. I was following my companion. With her suitcases in her hands, along with her coat, camera and purse, she took hold of the bannister head and started to ascend. When she stepped up, the bannister head, being yanked, almost came off in her hand! She sort of placed it back, and we managed as best we could. All the way up, the stairs squeaked.

We entered our room, and I went to the window; on moving the curtain, I began to sneeze and dust was flying around me. I looked out and saw old papers lying about, and the grass was just too natural. It looked like some part of my home; it was growing long and wind-swept. But it was dead-looking. My companion and I just sat for a while—we were tired, mostly from laughing so much. I could tell that I had not had a good laugh for a long time because the muscles in my stomach were aching. The floors in the room were all bumpy and there was no carpet. It did not bother us; after all, we were nomads.

We then got picked up by the same doctor to visit Inuit patients at the Clearwater Hospital, five miles away from our hotel. This time, I could understand the patients and they could understand me, though their language was still a bit different from mine. I noticed every time I asked "hanuipit?" (how are you?) they said "qanuingilanga" (I am fine), where I would say "hanuingilanga." I decided that they spoke baby talk. We stayed for a few days, and by this time, the patients began to look familiar, and I supposed we began to look familiar to them. One of them told me that I spoke baby talk. Both of us had no knowledge that there were different dialects in Inuit language. I learned much later that there are many different dialects in Canada alone—not even counting Alaska and Greenland.

THE FISH LIKE TO BE DRESSED UP FOR

Our stay in Clearwater fell on a weekend. Anybody that we wanted to see was not around. It was on the Saturday that one of the doctors asked if we would like to go fishing. I was all for it—fishing I have known since I was very little. We travelled quite a way by car to a lake. There was me, in a pink suit and high-heel shoes, catching fish by the dozen while my companions were not getting any. They were dressed for it in jeans and old shirts and flat shoes. Who thought that I would get a chance to go fishing while visiting hospitals? I had no such clothing with me, so I went in my suit and best shoes. My companions began to joke and tease me that maybe the fish liked to be dressed up for.

HOSPITAL VISITS

Our next stop was Brandon, Manitoba. By this time, I began to realize that there were so many Inuit in the hospitals. I felt very sad, knowing what they were missing and what worried them. Most of these patients were mothers and fathers. How were their homes managing with all the work that had to be done, especially the provision of food and clothing? In the North, everybody is too palangaungittuk—not loose, not free to really help out in such motherless and fatherless homes. I learned from talking to them that some had been in hospital for two years, some for

one year and others for six months. Some had not heard anything about their relatives for a long time. Some did, and had had bad news about a relative having died. I wished that I was many persons so that I could take their places so that they could go home and enjoy their families. The job I was doing was not very pleasant for me.

We then went to St. Boniface, Manitoba. Entering the hospital, something struck my mind that was rather familiar. I braced myself, trying to remember what it was. Finally, I could see that there was a crucifix on the wall and that nun nurses were walking around in the building. It was just like the school I went to in Fort George. I felt warm to see something that was a little bit embedded in me. I felt somehow that I knew these people even though their faces were not the ones that I knew. We saw only one child there who had forgotten his language completely. It was also sad. How will he communicate with his parents when he goes home? My companion was a very understanding lady. She seemed to know what made me sad and always brought me out of it. When she was not busy with her writing, phoning and making arrangements, she took time to tell me a lot of little things. She even taught me how to handle a knife and fork while eating properly, as she called it.

Our next visit was to a hostel. There we met people who were waiting to go home. The house reminded me of the hotel in Clearwater Lake. It was even worse because it had the smell of a human who has not washed for years. The Inuit looked like they had not been out for years. They were so pale, not like the skin I am used to seeing on Inuit—wind-burned and sun-tanned from always being outside. They were on the second floor, and outside the house there was no room for them to be able to go out. Their lavatory was horribly messy, dirty and smelly. And these were the people who were waiting to go home after hospital care? It would be no wonder if they went right back to the hospital. The lady who had opened the door for us never came upstairs, and that was that. She did not seem to care at all.

As long as I can remember, my parents have lectured me never to look at people on their exterior side. But I could not help but notice the woman who opened the door. She had on a low-necked black blouse, and her hair looked not very normal: it had black roots and on top was dried, fussy-looking blonde. She looked like she had two big red apples on both sides of her nose, and her lips were smeared with the same red, red colour.

She fascinated me in a funny sort of way and I wondered why people take the time to ruin themselves. I do not know which appalled us most—the smelly upstairs or the lady downstairs. My parents also taught me never to make comments on anything I saw or heard as long as I was with anyone older than myself, so what I thought was unsaid to my companion. But it was obvious that she did not like what she saw either, and she wasted no time in going back to the hospital and telling the doctor about it. I told myself that the people in the hospitals may not be so saddening after all—they were at least in good care.

It had been a month since my companion and I started to travel. We finally started back to where we belong. It seemed every time I returned from a trip, my adopted home just got sweeter and warmer. Even my qallunaaq seemed to get bigger than life and so good to see when I came back.

Some months later, we visited hospitals in Quebec. It was much different from what I had seen in the West. The patients looked so much happier and were well-informed about how and what and why they were in hospital. Some even knew the date when they were going home. But the things that saddened me just seemed to get worse. I had never entered a mental hospital, though I had looked after a mentally-sick man. This was to be my first visit to such a hospital. The building itself was standing inside a steel fence, like the Mint. It looked so empty inside, and it seemed that every door had a steel fence. The Inuk man we were to visit happened to be my cousin, one of my uncle's sons. I had often wondered where he went to. The last time I had seen him was at Moosonee Hospital, and at that time, he was waiting to go home.

My father had written later that he was home and then wrote again that he was back in the hospital for a reason that could have been avoided. Bluntly, he said that my cousin had many mental worries. I could feel in the letter that my father doubted that I would understand what he meant and so explained no further. But his teachings began to ring a bell. Never, no matter how much you are hurt with your feelings, even if you feel like retaliating, don't ever terrorize anyone, or you will be the cause of the person's mental state. That was too deep for me to understand, so I always had put it away through one ear and out the other. I never put much thought into it. Who is capable of practising such a thing unless they are very sick themselves? And here, I was seeing clearly my father's Inuk beliefs.

I wished that crying was not so embarrassing in front of people. I could hardly hold on to my tears when I saw this man amongst men who did not seem to notice anything and who looked at me with blank faces. When I spoke to him, he seemed to remember; in fact, he asked who I was and I told him. He repeated my name just like he remembered it. I felt so much pain, especially because we were children together, knowing his parents, and most of all knowing that his mother was dead and that all his sisters were grown up and married and having their own children. I especially felt sad because I knew his reasons for being mentally sick. I do not know his reasons for being sick medically, but our Inuit beliefs as to why he was sick were well-known at home. We believe that people can go mentally sick from severe treatment and qiilingunik—sadism. There was another Inuk man, about his age, who used to enjoy teasing him and playing tricks on him. This man played terrible tricks, like putting traps in his bed. He scared him while in a canoe on their travels. He dressed up in a terrible made-up face with soot on very dark nights. He made up stories that he was having affairs with his sister. This was his endless treatment and he was very much outcast for his condition. Still, today the villain is very much an outcast, and what is worse punishment than to be ignored by the whole community? My cousin is now home with what is left of his family. But how sad that his life was ruined by another man who was a lot sicker than he at the beginning.

NEWSPAPER OFFICE

So far, I have met newspaper men and women and know they ask many questions and write only few words. I have often wondered how they get what they write onto this paper that looks like it requires many, many people to finish. It was a very hot day when I was walking home alone. I decided to take a different route than my usual one, when a lot of noise distracted me. I stopped walking and tried to figure out where the noise was coming from. It did not sound at all like cars or trucks that I am now used to hearing. I followed the noise. It came from an alley where many cars were parked. The building where the noise was coming from looked very calm as I looked up at its full height. As I entered the alley, the door of the building was wide open. There I stood and saw the newspaper being processed on big machines. There were only two men working on the machines, and not many, many people as I had pictured it before. I wanted to ask the two men many questions, but I was afraid to even enter the building.

I did not have to ask anybody about this after all—at least that's what I thought the day when one of the girls I worked with showed me a duplicating machine. It was like the big printing press, only it was smaller and the copies had to be made by hand. When I learned to use it, I told myself that it was only the other, bigger machine that had a mind of its own.

BUTTONS COUNT A LOT

One of the things that bothered me most was the heat in the South. I had long hair and it began to irritate me when the days were hot. I asked my qallunaaq to cut it for me. She said she was afraid that she would make a mess of it. Then she told me about hairdressers. Who are they? How do I see them? Where do I go? She said she will go and make an appointment for both of us. I should have known—it is not a place to go any time when the heat of the South is killing you. We went together. So, that's what those were. I had seen them while walking on the street.

I felt just like I did the day I entered a restaurant for the first time. Will I? Me? Be served like that? Get my hair washed by somebody who I have never seen? Will they really put curlers in my hair? That is not minding your elders: they are minding me. Me? When we entered, the elegance struck me, as usual. The lady behind the counter asked for our names. Her long fingernail fingered through her black book and said: oh yes. She motioned us to come further in. We passed women wrapped in plastic bibs, some with wet hair, some with curlers on, some in a process of being combed. One that I passed gave out an odour that was strong and stung my nostrils. One was having gold-coloured wet paint rubbed into the black roots of her hair. The woman in the West with the red, red apples on both sides of her nose flashed into my mind.

The ladies were so helpful. They did not seem to mind at all what they were doing for other people, especially washing their hair. I was feeling very awkward getting served like that. When I had finished getting my hair washed, I began to feel even worse because the hairdresser was combing my hair and began to put curlers in. I wondered if I would be here all day with my hair all wet and in wires.

When she finished, the lady motioned me to another room, and there, I saw other women sitting. There was something over their heads making a blowing noise. The lady sat me down and fitted my head under one of these blowing things. I felt very afraid. The sound was even worse after she clicked something. Suddenly, I began to feel heat all over my head. I wanted to get out, pull out the curlers with all my might and get into the outside air. Then I saw my qallunaaq being brought in and put under one of these noisy things. I assured myself that if she could sit like I am doing, it must not be frightening. I looked at her and smiled just like I had nothing, not even fear, on my mind. She smiled back—I kept her smile in my mind to feel secure. Every now and then I would hear a click at the back of my neck. It was making me very curious about what was making that noise. I was afraid to move. Nobody else was moving, so I did not dare.

A long time later, the lady finally came back, felt my hair and said that I was ready, and she motioned me back to the other room. When I got up, I wanted to stretch and yawn. My whole body was not awake. I wanted to take the curlers off as fast as I could and then scratch my head with all my might. But my surroundings would not let me, so I ignored what I wanted to do. I made sure to look at the thing to see what had made the clicking noise. The thing had numbers and a button. I decided it was like an automatic washing machine. I assured myself that all the machines that I have seen had buttons and people just pushed them. Yes, of course, just like I push the buttons of elevators.

My hair was combed and the lady made me look in a little mirror all around my head when she finished. What was I supposed to do or say? She sort of expected me to say something. I looked at her and said something that came naturally to me: "Thank you!" She was pleased. My face looked big and bare and my hair was all curly. Though I felt strange, when we got out, I felt cool and able to take the heat a little better. My qallunaaq said, "My, those hair dryers can get hot." So, that's what they are called, I said to myself.

MY FRUSTRATION

During my childhood, I knew only three eating utensils—plate, cup and ulu, a knife that belongs only to a female. Its blade is shaped like a half moon, and it has a good gripping handle. It can be sharp as a razor blade. This knife is very important to an Inuk woman. Its rounded edge shapes its way to whatever kind of skin or meat one is cutting. It can be sharp as a razor blade. In our traditions, one has to be a female to own one. Though I have learned in school what knives, forks and spoons are, I owned an ulu at home. Nobody used it but me, as every woman has one of her own. It is only with this that I ate, along with my hands and teeth. I have gotten used to knives, forks and spoons, but there were times when I really wanted to enjoy my meals.

I learned about different kinds of food while living at the Terrace. Every day there was a menu posted at the door of our dining hall. By the time I had been there a year, I had learned the names of the foods. Sometimes we would have spareribs and chicken legs. I used to get the urge to eat my own way, to pick them up with my hands and really enjoy the meal. My surroundings would not let me. Only Henry the Eighth seemed to have been allowed to do it in public. I felt too shy. If I did, I would have to get up and go wash my hands, and by the time I got back to my table, my tray would be gone. It was very frustrating not being able to eat with my hands.

FEELING CRUSHED

One day, I was on my way to visit friends that I had made since I came south. I had just gotten off the bus when I heard a noise that I never heard before. It sounded like a truck that was having a hard time moving. I looked back across the street. I had not seen this kind of truck before. It had writing on it which said: "Keep Your City Clean." Then I understood something that I had been wondering about. Looking at the city from high buildings, I used to wonder where all the people in these houses put their rubbish. Maybe they do not have any, I used to think. That is impossible because even my little room somehow produced some rubbish, yes, and what about all the rubbish I saw in the cans in my office? They were emptied each day, but I did not see piles of it outside the building. This truck I was watching, with men picking up cans from outside the houses along the street, answered my wonder. I watched a man throw in the rubbish from a can and the truck began to make a noise. There was something rotating inside and all the rubbish began to be crushed and I grimaced and felt crushed.

JUST CLOSE YOUR EYES AND EAT

Having been to one restaurant, I thought they were all the same. But I have learned there are many kinds. Once my qallunaaq and I decided not to take our lunch at our residence but to have lunch in a restaurant. When I met her, she said, "Let's have some Chinese food." I had no idea what Chinese food was. I have met Chinese people; in fact, I have been taken for one so often that I was beginning to think that I knew them.

The place we entered looked very colourful inside. In one corner were two doors with something written on them. It looked like someone had thrown black paint at the doors and the results were these funny shapes. We were given a menu. As usual, my qallunaaq was completely oblivious to my wonders, so I simply followed her. I ordered what she ordered. That is Chinese food? It looked like the stew my grandmother used to make for pups. "I have not had any for ages," my qallunaaq said. Do not tell me she ate it before and did not turn piusirluttuk—retarded. If she had had it before, it must be edible. I will eat it. Scooping it up and getting ready to put it into my mouth, something went back and forth in my throat. When I finally got brave enough to eat it, the taste was not so sickening as it looked. It took me some time to like this alurassak—this prepared dog food, but today I am crazy about it and call it by its respected name— Chinese food. I even look at it while eating.

GOOSE PIMPLES ALL OVER

By this time, after about a year, I had met many people. One of them asked me if I would like to go to the museum. Where is that? What is that? I followed the lady.

When we arrived, the huge doors of the building made me feel so tiny. I could not believe that they actually opened. (Strange that nobody met us when we arrived; I was getting used to being met at the door. One cannot just walk into any house like I do at home when visiting.) We began to walk around. It did not look like a store or any other building I had been in. The lady seemed to know everything. As we went on, some of the things I saw were strange, others looked familiar. Everything looked so old. They must be pimmarriaaluit—treasured. The lady went on and on, telling me that these animals lived in Alberta at one time. Alberta? I have been there and it's not so far. I decided that this building is where the qallunaat gather old things. Yes, it must be old things—even Inuit do not have boats like that today. Yet some of the animals I saw still existed where I came from. I felt very confused. Looking at all these big animal bones, I began to picture them alive. All over me came goose pimples.

HE READ BACKWARDS

In our traditions, children are not allowed to ask questions: asking is considered an adult affair. Asking my elders questions was one thing I got scolded for. One day, I went into a restaurant on my own. Sitting at the counter, I noticed the man behind the counter was reading some kind of newspaper that did not look at all like it was in plain English. From a distance, it almost looked like Inuit syllabics. I got very curious. I sized him up—he did not look at all like he would scold if I asked him about the paper. He also did not look like a plain qallunaaq. I said, "That is your language?" He said, "Yes." He said that was his newspaper from his country that was written in the Arabic language. He even showed me which way he reads, and he reads backwards.

Then he asked me if I had a language, and I said yes. His eyes got round and so big that I thought he was going to scold me for asking so many questions. Finally after staring at me, he spoke: "Yes, yes, you are the girl on television drinking ginger ale—Eskimo girl. It's cold where you come from? It's hot outside, is it not?" I thought for once I was going to do the asking and just get answers. Maybe it would have been better if he had scolded me. But I valued this man's point-blank guess very much—for once, I did not have to be Chinese, Japanese or Hawaiian.

My drinking ginger ale, I suppose, helped him a lot. I realized too that I have missed a lot by not asking enough. I think now that asking more questions would have saved me from a lot of wondering about the South and its inungit—its inhabitants.

LIFE OR DEATH

One day, I decided to go for a walk on my own. I convinced myself not to think about the clock or my stomach. If I got hungry, I would go to the restaurant. The street I was walking on suddenly became bare, with no buildings anywhere. I felt a sudden release from something that had been keeping me from freedom. In fact, I felt I was coming out of a tent, free, and there was nothing there ready to crush me. There were trees and nice grass that was growing so even. I could not believe that it grew so neatly. I have seen some places that looked like this at home, except there were always stones or twigs. It felt so quiet and I felt so free that I wanted to run and jump all over. I began to gorge in my mind on this beautiful freedom. I had not realized how much I missed the peace that I knew at home with nature. My whole body began to relax.

Suddenly, out of nowhere, someone was screaming, "Hey, you!" over and over. I looked around and there was a man coming towards me. He looked like a policeman. My little heart was jumping all over my body—at least that's how it felt—and my knees got weak. I did not know what was going to happen or what he was going to do to me. When he got close, he asked if I did not know or read English; I said I did. I guess I was so lost in my freedom that I never noticed a little sign that read "Keep off the grass." I had just passed it by like a piece of stone or twig. I said that I was sorry, that I did not see it. He became very understanding and told me not to let it happen again.

On my way back, I talked to myself all the way. Qallunaat are suna-tuinnangitualluit—particular. The whole thing was crazy to me. I did not understand. Atummaqai?—I suppose it is necessary? The man made it sound so important and got so worked up about walking on the grass. It made me wonder what qallunaat do when it's very important. I have never seen a man at home who got all worked up unless it was a matter of life or death. I did not see that I endangered anything. Who is free? Not me, as long as I lived in the South.

SO MANY AND SO QUIET

My qallunaaq and I decided one day to go to the library. I knew what that was—we used to have one at school. I pictured the one we were heading to as just the same as the one we had in my school, in the corner of the classroom. When we reached the building, the picture I now had was disappointing. The big house was only for books? The lady behind the counter was very quiet; she actually whispered. I could not make up my mind about whether she was playing at something or if that was her natural voice. This was not the kind of voice that I was used to. Then I turned around and there were many people standing and sitting. I could not believe that this many qallunaat could be so quiet. I learned later that I too have to be quiet at the library. It was another qallunaat rule that I have had to accept and use.

I HAVE SEEN MANY DEATHS

At my home, I have seen many deaths and have kissed many dead people before they were buried, ever since I was only a child. Our tradition for the dead has always been to mourn for one year, and close dead relatives have to be visited often at their graves. The family of the dead has to wear black clothes for a year. If one wears bright clothes, one has to have a black strip around the sleeve of the garment. Our belief is that no one really dies until someone is named after the dead person. So, to put the dead person at peace and to prevent their spirits from being scattered all over the community, we give their names to the newborn. Not until then do we believe that the dead person is spiritually at their grave. The minds of the people do not rest until the dead have been renamed. It is a sense of responsibility that the dead should rest and be in his or her place. Otherwise, it is like leaving the dead dispossessed and deprived of their rightful rest.

I had never really stopped to think about death. I accepted it like any of the other losses we experience in the North. I guess the ritual we followed was created for that reason, so that we would not think about death itself. For one year, the close relatives cannot go to festive activities or dances, nor are they allowed to make jokes. I had never really realized that death meant a loss of life, even though the last thing our ritual demands is that we touch the dead before burial, to make us understand that the person will no longer respond.

I had come to know a man whom I worked with. He told me about many Inuit who exist in parts of the North besides where I come from. He had shown me maps of the world. He also spoke my language and used Inuk manners when he approached me. He was the one who drove me to the Terrace upon my first arrival to the South. When one feels very alone, one always finds some reason or other to depend on someone either physically, mentally or for moral support. That was how I was beginning to feel about this man. It was because of him that my work was meaningful. It was because of him that I struggled through this fascinating, strange qallunaat world. It was because of him that I fought through the daily routines which were so hard for me to get used to. When I often stopped to think how lonely the world of qallunaat is, it was him I thought of and I no longer felt alone, because I knew there was someone I struggled to make my life meaningful for.

Now he was dead. His death was my first realization of what death means: he was gone forever, never to be seen again. I went to see him at the funeral home, which was also my first visit to such a place. The building itself made me feel so very sad. I had kissed and touched many dead relatives, but my surroundings would not let me follow the ritual I was brought up to follow. Looking at him in the casket, in the suit which I had often seen him wearing while walking, sitting and talking and responding, it suddenly hit me that he was not doing all those things. I felt very upset, cold and hot all over my body. My eyes were aching but I had not one tear. I wanted to get out and be on my own and nobody to touch me or talk to me. I thought about my mother, who had been dead since I was three years old; I thought about my grandmother, on my mother's side, who died when I was ten; I thought about my grandfather, who died when I was sixteen. I thought about all my little cousins who died during a measles epidemic at home. This man had taught me about the maps of the world and he had taught me the sense of loss at death.

I AM IN THE MIDDLE

In 1958, my job as a translator took me to Frobisher Bay, Baffin Island, Northwest Territories. Because I was a working girl, I lived with a qallunaaq woman whom I saw from 5:00 p.m. until my bedtime. Our conversations were simple: good morning and good night. It sounds unbelievable, but we did share a bunk bed. Because I was from somewhere else, Inuit were strange to me and I was strange to them. The qallunaaq whom I worked with accepted me from 9:00 a.m. to 5:00 p.m.; socially, I did not exist. I was friends with qallunaat as long as I made parkas and translated for them. My surroundings were familiar, but I could not reach either Inuit nor qallunaat, even just to converse, like I could with Inuit from my home or when qallunaat were in the South. I should have been sad all the time, but I had no time. I was too busy studying people around me. Inuit were in the middle as well, like I was.

The Inuk man was caught between his desire to go hunting and the clock, which was at one time never important to him. He would be late for his job and get fired. His mark became unreliable, so he would go hunting and feed his wife and children on the seal which he had luck with. Eventually, the weather would not allow him to go hunting again or the money that was left from his last pay was all spent on ammunition and grub. But there was always an answer for him—he went on relief for a few months and tried hunting again. If he was successful with his hunting, the strong beliefs of his tradition to share amongst his neighbours would not allow him to eat it alone with his family.

He then begins to visit his friends and relatives, which he has not seen since he started working like the qallunaat, and somehow he borrows money. In the meantime, his problems and worries are swelling up in his mind. His wife no longer looks up to him with happiness when he used to bring in seal—she is too wrapped up herself with the problems that have arisen in her home. She is doing a lot of visiting herself, trying to get food for her children. The husband finds some friends who are making homebrew or who have bought from the qallunaat, at five to ten dollars, a bottle. He finds this drink very intriguing and it makes him forget his problems. So now he sleeps in the day and gets up at night when his friends are available.

Then, one of these nights, someone in the group remembers a card game, which his ancestors learned from some explorer or Hudson's Bay man. Instead of playing it just as a game to pass time, as it was played by his ancestors, he turns it into a gambling game, and now money is involved. He manages to win now and then, and when he does, he buys all the ingredients to make homebrew. Instead of going to his friends, he begins to make the brew at his own home. He then gets very popular with others who are in the same situation. His home begins to be their regular meeting hall. His wife, who is terrified (in some cases) of people who drink, is no longer amused by her regular visitors. The rules that were given to her by the qallunaat to have the children in school are no longer an obstacle. She has a greater obstacle to overcome: her drinking husband.

The children no longer listen to her words. They realize that the language they have learned is much stronger and has more impact. So now, they tell her to be quiet and to shut up. She has heard them in earlier times using such words with each other. She feels very tired; she does not get enough to eat; she loses a great deal of sleep and can hardly keep awake during the day and falls asleep while her younger children are running around, going in and out without proper clothing. Then, one day, a mysterious machine of the qallunaat comes around, the ajjiliurrutik—machine for taking pictures, X-ray. Not very long after, she is told that she has to go south to the hospital. She does not know for how long or why—she guesses that she has tuberculosis, one of many gifts her ancestors have received from the qallunaat. She no longer sees her former problems but worries about them while in the southern hospital. Her children are now under the care of their grandparents. They can no longer answer back and find their grandparents are much stronger willed. Now they are having to grow up a different way.

Because all kinds of people fascinate me, I also studied the qallunaat in the North. They are also in the middle between their jobs in the North and their authorities in the South. In the North, they appear knowledgeable of everything. They give out rules that they understand. When asked a question by the Inuit, their favourite replies are "maybe" and "will write to South." In the South, the ones receiving the letter remember the occasion when they had visited that community. To them, the Inuit did not seem to have that problem. They remember their smiles and handshakes and recall that the schools, offices and recreation affairs looked very well at that hour of their visit. Their siallaat—servants—had followed their orders. Everything was working according to plan.

The letter has quite a trip itself. It has been in the hands of the receiver, receiver's head, head of the head and finally third head's head. Everybody now has something to do. The letter even went through a machine and was made into several copies. It has been some months since the letter arrived. By this time, the Inuk who had asked the question will have sorted it out himself. A reply is sent finally to the original writer, telling the Inuk that those in the South will write to the people who have something to do with the question. Inuk again sits and waits—to him, it sounds as if they are doing something about his problem.

Perhaps his question becomes very pressing in his mind and he decides to write himself. His letter goes to one of the heads; the head sends it to the head of the translators. The translator head sends it to the translator. The translator is very upset on reading the letter. (I know because I have translated such letters. Most of us translators lack many English words, having gone to northern schools. I say this only because I have seen the schools in the South—they are not quite the same. They are much more responsibly run. The most different thing about the schools in the South is that the reports are given to parents on how well their children are doing, in what way the children need help, and the parents can go and see the teachers. I have not seen this done in the North.) The translator then puts the letter into English; somehow, it does not sound as pressing as it does in Inuttitut. Altogether, it does not sound very important to the receiver because we translators lack many important words in English, though we know them in Inuit language. Here is one example that has upset me many times: "Qittungara anniakuvimmut aullalaursimajuk suli tusangilara naningimaat tusarumavunga iqaumainarakku isumaalugillugo"—my child is gone to the hospital; I have not heard where he is. I would like to hear as I think about him and worry about him. It is a human, worrying, and pressing sentence from the writer in his own language. He had expected to get a reply about his worry very soon. I am still learning many things, but I have learned that the qallunaat language can be just as pressing as the Inuit language. So I will translate the sentence once more the way the writer had intended to express his feelings: "Some time ago, my child went away to be hospitalized, but I have not yet heard of his (or her) whereabouts. I would be pleased to hear as I think and worry about (her or) him a great deal, and my mind does not rest from worry."

I have also learned that one cannot translate word to word with the Inuit language; for one, we do not have words for her or him, and sometimes, our sentences can be only one word. For example, "tusaruma-vunga"—this word will depend on the context of the situation: "I want to hear," "I would like to hear," "I would be pleased to hear." And by adding another "a" at the end of the sentence—"tusarumavungaa"—it would become a question: "Do I want to hear?"

One day, the qallunaaq in the North decides to go with the hunter and his dog team. On the whole, he enjoys it all—the freedom of not having to look at the clock for once. He sees igloo building, harpoons being used, stalking of seals, dogs being harnessed, the whip being handled. He sees how an Inuk can handle a mass of dogs with few commands, how an Inuk can get out of ice chunks when stuck with his sled. That was all too interesting. He does not really care for the coffee breaks—it takes too long to be made, and everything he had taken to eat was frozen. When he finally gets his coffee, it is full of piluit—caribou hairs, which fall off the outfit he is wearing and also went into the grub box. What can he do? By the time he picks them out of his cup, the coffee will be too cold to enjoy. He just has to gulp it down like an Inuk man.

For the first time, he sees the Inuk as a capable person. In fact, he is very amazed by what the Inuk can put up with. He begins to invite him to his home. While talking with him, he begins to find out a lot of things about how the Inuk lives in his own home, and what kinds of ways he uses. He begins to understand the full meaning of his language. He asks him to carve for him—the carving has a meaning itself and the Inuk explains what the carving is doing. He realizes for the first time that the carving speaks like the art work in the South. Bit by bit, he begins to collect. From among his collections, he begins to give his relatives in the South carvings as gifts for Christmas. At the same time, he realizes that his job no longer deals with "just Inuit." To him, the Inuit are human after all, with feelings, ways, affections, able to think, capable of a daily life which he would never choose for himself. His ways of approaching the Inuk begins to change; he no longer talks fast, no longer feels like giving rules that only he understands, but explains in a way that the Inuk will understand. He now takes longer to explain his dealings. His manner changes towards the Inuk—he no longer hurries, and even his posture is no longer like a stiff, frozen seal. It has become thawed, warm, and the Inuk realizes he too is human after all.

In the South again, the qallunaaq is very friendly—he no longer walks like he is carrying a heavy load. He even has time to speak with the Inuk in the South. Sitting with his colleagues, he listens to their big plans for the North. There will be a new runway for aircraft, a new school building, a new administration building, new quarters for the qallunaat who are employed there, a new home economist to teach Inuit how to be clean and to show them how to wash and prepare meals, new ways to bring the Inuit children in to the school, to have soup served during the lunch hours, new community affairs, a survival course for the new qallunaat who are to go north. There is no mention of a new way to teach Inuit how to cope with their changing lives, how to cope with liquor, how to cope with a working husband, how to plan their spending now that he is no longer a hunter. There is no mention why Inuit children have to be taught the English language, or why there is income tax.

So many things the qallunaat have introduced to the simple Inuk. Though the qallunaaq man who had begun to understand Inuit had so many suggestions to make about how to cope with Inuit, he cannot even mention one idea in front of his boss. He feels very withdrawn after having to listen to his boss's big plans. He wonders how his boss will understand him if he makes any comments on how to cope with Inuit. He becomes very quiet and cannot bring himself to try and explain the things he has seen happen when other new ways of the South are being put to work in the old North. What he says will affect his job, which he cannot afford to lose. He lets his colleagues and boss dream on with their big plans, and he agrees to them. He is trained to respect his heads—what they say is always right, what they say has to be the way. No matter how he feels and how much he understands the Inuk way, he chooses to be quiet and to sit back and listen. He is now "Inuk-washed."

Being in the middle, I also studied the young women in the North. At one time, it was Inuit tradition that a young woman's parents chose her husband at the earliest age so that she may have less pain and easy childbirth—and mostly to prevent promiscuity. Now she is also in the middle, between the Inuk man and the qallunaaq man. In her changing community, she has seen qallunaat women who are attired in pretty frocks and wear make-up. In her eyes, they choose what they want, wear what they want, ditch and pick husbands. She finds that the qallunaaq man is friendly towards her—in fact, he notices her looks and tells her so. On the other hand, the Inuk man would notice what she can do and not what she looks like. But the qallunaaq man speaks loud and makes it all so exciting for her. The qallunaaq man does not know how to approach her for what he needs. He arranges some meeting place where there will be more privacy. He then invites her and gives her an intriguing drink. He gives her more than he takes. Anything he says is now agreeable to her.

The meetings go on and on until she is discovered by the police. The qallunaaq man knew the rules all the time—that he was not supposed to mingle with Inuit girls at that place. Somehow, he gets out of breaking the law, in spite of the promise he made when he signed his contract to work there. The girl is now in the hands of the police. She is asked many questions. "How did you get in there? Where did you get the drink? You are not supposed to go there! What is the name of the man you were with? Who does he work for?" She knows that she will suffer a great deal more if she tells on him. She lowers herself and feels that she is not important enough to get the big, important man into the hands of the police. She is warned not to go there again, not to drink or she will go to jail. It makes her afraid, but more so of the qallunaaq man whom she is afraid to report.

Then, one day, she has funny pains and an uncontrollable itch; she now carries one of his gifts—venereal disease—so now she has to go back and forth to the dispensary and get many needles to cure it. If she has not received that gift, she may find herself pregnant. Now the community sees her condition; she is suffering in her mind and it affects her family. The Inuk man, whom she had rejected, rejects her for carrying a qallunaaq child. The qallunaaq man has disappeared, or if he sees her, he avoids her and acts like he had never been intimate with her. She has to carry her problem alone. After the birth, her parents become very understanding again—they have gained a grandchild, and they know the child did not ask to be born on its own. They also know that the new mother has paid enough for her promiscuity, through the rejections from all around her and by having endured the pain of giving birth. The Inuk man who had some interest in her before all this happened now sees what kind of mother she makes; he convinces himself that it is all too unwise to reject her. The baby may not be his, but he can learn to love it just as much. Not all marriages in this community started off or ended like that; that is only another thing that involved my little mind, while I was in the middle, in my one-year stay in this community. And, of course, it does not happen only in that community—it has happened in the four corners of the world.

"LIFE-OR-DEATH" HAD A REASON

Back in the South in 1959, my qallunaaq and I decided one day to go and see a tulip show. I had learned by then what shows were and why qallunaat follow this custom of having them. I had never seen so many tulips in so many colours, nor so many people among the flowers. My weakness for watching people pulled me away from my qallunaaq. There were people taking pictures, bending down to smell the tulips. Then I saw someone who looked familiar—it was not the same man, but the uniform was the same as the one worn by the man who had got all worked up when I had walked on the grass that day. I decided that his reason must have been this, to make the grass grow for tulip shows. Why did he not tell me that? Really, qallunaat have many laws which they have no time to explain to a little Inuk like me.

I AM CRAZY ABOUT IT

There is one that I have not seen, and that is a woman's fashion show. I am crazy about this. I have only seen a fashion show once on television. Because I like sewing, I am crazy about fashion. I have also decided that fabric stores are my favourite shops. Every time I go shopping I have to go into these stores, even if I don't buy anything. I could spend all day in there if I had the time.

LANGUAGE WAS PULLING

I went to visit a cousin who was living in Quebec City. I had taken a train that made many stops. Along the way, the names of the towns began to change to French names. Having gone to a French convent school, I could understand some of the signs I saw. At each stop, the train became heavier with people who spoke only French. I felt that I was the only person who spoke a strange language. During my visit, my cousin took me to many places, and everywhere we went, the people spoke French. Even in the shops, cashiers said, "Oui?" Walking along the streets and talking, my cousin and I seemed to be the only two who understood each other. After two days, I began to feel that there was a cellophane shield all around me. I could see the people, I could hear them, and yet their sounds were unreachable.

On my third day, I was on my way to catch a bus to visit the citadel. Among the crowd, I gradually began to hear a welcome voice. It almost sounded strange because I was hearing other voices that were not the same. The couple I could hear seemed to me to be sticking out like the voices of snow geese amongst many voices of Canada geese. Their words were familiar and yet odd among the others I was hearing. I looked around to try to pin down the couple. Their sound fascinated me very much, and yet the language they spoke was the language I was used to hearing, English. I just kept my pace with them because their sound was comforting—I was not the only one who spoke an odd language. Their language was pulling because I understood the sound. I forgot my own destination. Without being aware, I got lost because I was following this couple and they were going somewhere else. I asked myself: Suruaaluvit?—What is wrong with you? I had to turn around and find my bus stop all over again.

SILLY CRY

My qallunaaq and I celebrated our birthdays on the same date. In our first year as roommates, we gave ourselves a party. By this time, she and I could talk to each other about our problems, sorrows, wishes, dreams, and our female-to-female secrets. We got along very well, only because I did not argue or disagree with her wants, suggestions and plans. I went along with everything she did and enjoyed it as well. There was never any situation where she had to force me into whatever we decided to do.

Someone had given me a pair of baby-doll pyjamas for my birthday. They were the new fad that year. Every girl was daring to wear them. They were beautiful. Because I was brought up by my grandmother, I inherited some of her idiosyncrasies. She treasured anything that she thought was beautiful, no matter what it was. When I got into her trunk or suitcase, I would find one old necklace bead, an old, broken ironstone plate with flower prints on it, an old dress she picked up from her neighbours, a brand-new ashtray with scenes on it, a brand-new slip that she had put away because it was too pretty to wear. It had been sometime since I was given these baby-doll pyjamas. I kept them in a drawer among other things that I treasured. They were very pretty to me and too pretty to wear. My other reason for not wearing them was because of my shyness.

My qallunaaq and I shared one dresser and one closet. She used one side and I, the other. Every time one of us opened our drawers we saw the other's things. Both of us knew about everything we owned. She went to bed in baby-dolls and I went to bed in my long-legged flannelette pyjamas. Neither of us really noticed or mentioned to the other what we wore to bed. It was something that was not important, so we took it for granted as one of our habits. But one evening, while she was sitting at the dresser attired in her baby-dolls, combing her hair and looking in her mirror, I opened the drawer where I kept my treasures. Whatever I needed at that moment was not in that drawer. Seeing my baby-dolls, it dawned on her that I had never worn them. "Do you not like those? How come you have never worn them? They are too beautiful just to leave in a drawer. Are they too big? Are they too small? Why don't you try them on?" What could I say to all her reasoning? She would not understand my reasons anyway, and besides, they were not important. I followed her suggestion. I knew that if I argued my side, it would become a worked-up affair, so I tried them on.

I felt very naked, very flashy. To me, she became many, many people instead of being one. She got all worked up just the same: "Oh, how beautiful! The colour just suits you! You look so cute in them! I don't think you appreciate the girl who gave them to you! I think it's terrible just to leave them in the drawer! Why don't you wear them? Are you shy? I would give anything to have nice brown skin like yours! Are you shy about your legs? Look at my legs, and I wear baby-dolls!" Phew! I began to cry. When I began to cry, she got all the more worked up. "How silly of you to cry, it's so stupid! Whoever heard of crying over baby-dolls?"

We both got very quiet. How could I explain that I did not cry over wearing the baby-dolls? I wanted to tell her my feelings, but I could not. I wanted to tell her that I treasured them because they were too pretty to wear in an old bed, that I was afraid that they might get all wrinkled, and that I did not want to wash them, for they would lose their prettiness. I wanted to tell her that I did not wear them because I appreciated the person who gave them to me all the more, because I believed that if I did not wear them, they would last that much longer. I wanted to tell her that I was not brought up to show off my body, that showing off one's body where I come from is described as anguniattuk—fishing for a man, the word also used for dogs who are in heat. Where I come from, to be considered a lady, you do not show off what you have, you do not show off what you can do, you do not show off what you know in your mind, and you do not speak loud, especially in front of a man. He is supposed to show you what he has, what he can do, what he has in his mind, and most of all, he speaks to you. A woman's reaction tells him everything—at least, that was the way at one time.

My qallunaaq finally broke the silence by saying, "I did not realize you were so shy. I did not mean to hurt you. I am awfully sorry. You don't have to wear them if you don't want to. After all, they are yours." I wished she would just keep quiet about the whole thing and stop being worked up over some unimportant matter. I cried because she gave me too much attention and she insulted my baby-dolls for not understanding that they were my treasures. That was the first time my qallunaaq and I had had unhappy feelings since we met. It was the first time I stood up for my beliefs without following hers. It made me wonder how many times we would have had unhappy feelings day in and day out if I had not followed her and if instead I tried to explain my beliefs to her.

Sometime later, I asked my qallunaaq if she would like to come home with me during our summer holidays. She was very excited and wanted to come very much. Her first question was, "how much is the fare?" The figure appalled her, and she said that she would have to save and save. We both had six months to save for our fares and to buy all sorts of items. Her list included new clothes, a new purse, a new suitcase and a camera. My list consisted of presents for my family—fabric for both Grandmother and my stepmother, guitar strings for my brother, wool to make socks for my father, baby powder for my new baby sister. I wanted to tell my qallunaaq that she did not need all those new things, but the memory of our unhappy feelings made me hesitate. I imagined her getting all worked up if I told her that she would need only what is suitable for my home: rubber boots in case we have to walk on wet grass or for getting in and out of canoes. I cannot tell her that she will need low-heeled shoes, because her high ones will never get her to move where she steps, as it's all earth where we walk that it would be better to bring slacks instead of a new dress so that she, being a qallunaaq, would be warmer; that she will need a comfortable, warm jacket in case we go on a trip by canoe; that we can share a suitcase—hers being old does not matter at all. Camera? Well, that is her qallunaaq way, to take pictures. It is her belief and goes with her traditions, so I did not give it a thought. I wanted to tell her to take what she usually takes when we go to her farm home, but I dreaded our unhappy feelings just thinking about what I would like to explain to her. I kept my mouth shut.

I decided to give fabrics to Grandmother and Stepmother, knowing that there is not much choice in the store where they are. I bought guitar strings for my brother because he had written to ask for some—there were no such items in the store at home. And I bought my baby sister powder because I thought it would be easier for my stepmother. Where I come from, mothers usually have to gather rotting wood. It has to be at the point where it breaks like powder when squeezed with fingers. It has to be kept near heat in order to dry into flaky dryness. When it is flaked, one has to look for the old roots and take them out. Sometimes, mothers will wrap this rotten wood in a cloth and hammer it against two stones. Again, one has to look for the roots so the baby will not get splinters. In the winter, when everything is covered with snow, it is not easily available; if it is, it is very wet and takes longer to dry. Mothers then have to use soot from the wood stove. It also has to be flaked into powder but mothers don't care for it as much, as it is messier. One has to be careful to handle it so it will not make everything go black when the baby suddenly kicks up and spreads it all over. For this reason, I brought my baby sister baby powder—I thought it would make an easier time for my stepmother.

SECOND LOOK

I often wonder why people look at me twice and almost always from the top of my head to the tip of my feet. I could ask a few questions about it. Maybe what I am wearing seems to people to be out of place, because I am wearing qallunaat clothing when I look like I come from somewhere else. I have been taken for many nationalities. (Probably their eyes would pop out if I were to walk around in caribou skins in eighty-degree weather. That would be phew! too hot for me.) Some people ask, "What are you?" Some try to guess. Some take a long time to come around to the question. Some open up a subject about their world travel and talk on and on about China. At one time, their questions started getting way out. They asked me what I thought of the Vietnam War. I did not know what to say about this because I had never known war. The only enemy we have in the North is the bitter cold winter—or even some summer weather, which can suddenly turn on us and prevent our fathers from going out hunting and providing us with food. What I had read of the Vietnam War and the pictures that I've seen made me wonder for what reasons the people were fighting and what about. I thought about the families who were involved, little children who did not understand why their mothers and fathers were suddenly gone, the fear and suspense that were involved. I suppose there will be a time one day when I will find out why people have wars. Maybe that's why people give me a second look, wondering why I am not in my country when it is at war. Whoever heard of Inuk in the South anyway? Not the people I meet.

INUIT IN THE SOUTH

I do not know of any other government department, other than the Department of Indian Affairs and Northern Development, which brings Inuit to the South. I only know that there is not much done for them, for their comfort. The Department has programs for qallunaat employees who are to go north—they call it a survival course. In this program, the qallunaat are taught how to build igloos, how to meet the hazards of the cold and some Inuit language. Everything is done through the Department for their comfort while living in the settlements of the North. Houses are made available. The qallunaaq does not have to live far from wherever his job is to be. His food is taken care of before and after he gets there. His house is usually equipped with a washing machine, running water, a refrigerator, a stove and furniture. Besides his salary, he gets a northern allowance. In the building where he works, he has a telephone, along with a list of the people he can call on. All the comforts he has known all his life are there. The only thing that is strange to him are the faces of the Inuit. I have met people over and over who are amazed that the Inuit have survived in the North, and so far, the qallunaat have survived it as well, thanks to the precautions taken on their behalf.

I do not know of anything that has been done for the comfort of the Inuit in the South. The Department has taken families from North to South to employ as its translators. Before coming out, the family had no training whatsoever or any kind of program on how to survive in the South—though they do not forget to tell the Inuit what time to come in to work, where to sign their names in their black books and how to fill out an income tax form. There are no homes made available to couples who have children. There is no program for them to follow to be able to find out where, how and what kind of living quarters are suitable, where and how to shop for groceries, what kind of entertainment is available to them, what to do when one of them gets ill. They are expected to know all this for themselves as soon as they step into the interior of the South.

The Department is so anxious to tell the Inuit how to clean their houses so that the houses won't wear out so fast. I have never forgotten a speech that was made by one of the heads of the Department when he arrived at the settlement. The Inuit had expected to hear something fantastic since he had come such a long way especially to talk to them. The speech went something like this: "I am very glad to be here and enjoyed my visit to your homes. I am very pleased to see that they are. so clean." One old woman came over to me and asked if he was really the head of the Department, and if so, why he did not have the intelligence to tell us something that we do not know, instead of telling us what our houses looked like. We lived in them every day and we knew what they were like. How could I tell my elder that he did not think the Inuit have intelligence? He had nothing to say, as his visit to the community lasted only a couple of hours. He should have been amazed, especially if he were to live in the conditions in which Inuit had to live, with no running water, no flush toilets, no refrigerators and some with no electricity.

When anybody goes north, nobody can miss these wonderful houses put up by the Department. They are most colourful—blue, red, brown and some even orange. One would think the Inuit had a choice of colour, which they did not. The material for housing arrives by ship, already painted, to the communities of the North. There are no questions asked about where the Inuit would like to have their permanent homes erected. The Department does all the choosing. When an Inuk puts up a tent or an igloo, he does not put it where it will be most colourful. He has to think about the wind and be very careful which way his door will face. He examines the ground so he won't sit in his tent sinking everyday. I have been in these colourful houses which were put up without consideration of the weather. My parents have lived in them. In the winter, during snowstorms, the doors are piled up with snow which has entered through the cracks of the door, and the door gets stuck, iced in from condensation which forms all around the walls. In the mornings, before the stove is turned up high and before the bodies warm up the rooms, one could skate around the corners of the rooms. By midday, it begins to thaw and water is all over the house. Some communities put up with this anywhere from three to eight months of the year. It is too bad that the heads of the Department do not visit the northern settlements at these times. I wonder if it would make any difference if they did visit during the harder times of the year. What would the Department heads do? Go back to sit and write about their visit, of course, to say how wonderful it was, how interesting. To them, everything looked rosy and cozy. It is a bigger wonder why the Department does not choose for the Inuk in the South where to live. There, the head has a greater right to do so, knowing the South with its conveniences and all its countless laws.

THE SITUATION WAS FAMILIAR

One day, I was asked to go over to another building to meet an important man. When I got there, there was a photographer and this so-called important man. On the table was a carving shaped like Inuk woman, and beside the carving were savings bonds. The important man shook my hand and asked me how I was. He did not wait for my answer as he seemed rather excited over something. He directed me to a desk and positioned me there; behind me was a map of the Northwest Territories. The man showed me how to hold the bonds and look at the carving and to have a big smile. Instantly, the photographer took the picture.

When I went home, I told my qallunaaq about my picture being taken. She asked me right away, "Does that mean your picture is going to be in the paper again?" I did not know—I was not informed why my picture was taken, least of all for whom, what or where. She decided to get a newspaper. We began to turn the pages. Sure enough, there I was, big as life, holding savings bonds against my chest and looking at the carving with a big smile. The story read: "Eskimos now buying bonds, keeping up with progress," some remark like that. I felt sick. I had no idea what bonds were. My parents had never even heard about them, let alone afford to buy them. Today my father still has no idea what bonds are, though he has been working with Northern Affairs for the last thirteen years. I felt sick because I was being used to show the qallunaat in the South how well Inuit are treated in the North. I recognized the whole set-up because I had grown up with the great politicians of my people and had known, seen and experienced their way of handling the community.

Grandfather Symma always led the group when we moved to Old Factory. Whenever Grandfather could not come, one of my older uncles led. Both of them always stepped down as soon as we joined Weetaltuk. As I grew older, I began to notice and hear more about what these three men would do. Whenever problems began to arise, it seemed they were started by Weetaltuk. He slowly began to doubt his own ability to lead, and the fear that the community would not follow him anymore was his constant worry. He showed it by not sharing the animal that was killed, when sharing was the usual, traditional way. If someone reminded him to share, he would innocently say that he forgot. When he did not forget, Weetaltuk would divide food into very small pieces to bring suffering to his intended prey. Of course, the whole family of that person would suffer, not because of the small portions, but because this treatment by the leader seemed to be enjoyed by everyone else in the community, who would probably have liked to do the same thing to that particular person for one reason or another. But it was different when this was actually done by the leader, especially when the leader was supposed to know his own limits. No one is allowed to take part when the leader is ostracizing someone, for those who take part will have no trust left for the leader. If people ostracized others amongst themselves, it could become a massive situation and could therefore get out of hand.

Even when an ordinary person did not take part in a leader's attempt to ostracize someone, there were always some people who stopped communicating with the person who was being treated in such a way. The leader would be so involved with his political game that he would fail to see when it was getting out of hand. The ostracism would grow in the community, and the family that it was pointed at would be completely ignored for some time, because the people had joined in with the leader silently. What is the best way to make someone suffer mentally in the community? Withholding communication and ignoring that person. Some men would even unset another's traps. Some men would "innocently" forget what they borrowed from another person, or they would bring the item back but just put it down anywhere, giving it a chance to be ruined.

I do not know what my picture was doing in the paper, posing with bonds. I only felt and began to learn that qallunaat too had politics. That, of course, I had been raised with ever since I was born, and I knew well to keep away from it when I looked at my picture. I became very apprehensive after that when someone phoned, asking to interview me. I felt I could not be a part of something which was not really happening to my people.

WEETALTUK DIED
AND THEY BECAME WEAK

Five years had passed since I had seen my parents when I had visited them while they were still residing at Old Factory River. During that last visit, a boat had arrived from Great Whale River. In this boat was an administrator from the Department of Indian Affairs and Northern Development.

Along with him was his translator. I had met this administrator in Ottawa where I worked. Sensitive as I am, I felt somehow that I was in his way. It seemed to me too that he felt awkward around me. After a long silence, he began to talk to his translator about moving the Cape Hope Islanders to Great Whale River. I told myself that this would never come to anything, that the Cape Hope Islanders would never think of moving anywhere else. They had resisted before—this was the third time that they were being asked to move.

It was in the early 1890s that my grandfather began his travels along the coast of Hudson Bay and James Bay, coming all the way from Belcher Islands and ending finally at Charlton Island. At one time, he named the Belcher Islands Weetaltuk Islands, after himself, but then ended up calling them Qirqirtat, the Islands. To this day, they are called this by the Inuit in Hudson Bay and James Bay. During his stay on Charlton Island, he met Robert J. Flaherty, who made the film *Nanook of the North*. Flaherty had travelled northward from Moosonee, Ontario, looking for mineral deposits. In the course of their conversation, Weetaltuk told him of an island with iron-rich rocks, so Flaherty took along Weetaltuk with his family and another family, that of my other grandfather, Symma, the father of my father. In the year 1913, Weetaltuk navigated the boat, the *Laddie*, bringing Flaherty to the islands. He then travelled back to Cape Hope Island and settled there. Again he named the island Weetaltuk, after himself.

Here on this island, he made his family. The three eldest sons had been married when they had come down from Belchers. There were three other sons and three daughters, two of whom he took with him, and one he left at Great Whale River. One of the daughters that he brought with him was my mother. He travelled all the way down the coast of Hudson Bay and James Bay. At Cape Jones, Symma decided to go with him again after their year together on the Belcher Islands. While in Belchers, he had chosen wives for his two eldest sons. And while he was passing Fort George, he chose a wife for the third eldest—she was half Indian and half Inuk. For this, she was called "alla"—stranger, the word also used to describe Indians on account of their origin.

On Cape Hope Island, Weetaltuk built his house, and so did his three sons and my father's parents. In 1935, one of his daughters, named Malla, married my father—or in those days, they came to be in a trial marriage.

A trial marriage has to be tested, taught, advised, and finally approved of by the parents of those on trial. In 1936, I was born to them as their eldest daughter. The tradition is always for the only son to stay with his parents, so my mother automatically moved in with my father's parents. During this time, Grandfather Weetaltuk sent a note to Great Whale River, by the ship that passed Cape Hope, to have two particular women and a man brought back; he knew these people and had chosen them to be the wives for two of his sons and a husband for his last single daughter.

On Cape Hope Island, he was the leader of the people, his sons and daughters and in-laws. He chose where the seasons would be spent. He performed the church services, did baptisms and burials, and divided the animals that were killed to be shared. He did the burials when there was a death. When freeze-up came, he was always the first one to test the ice to see if it was safe to travel on. His supply of qallunaat goods—sugar, tea and flour—were never nil. It was his habit to bring out these goods while waiting for freeze-up, when everybody else had run out from the last trading, which had been the last week of August, and when there would be no trading again until early December. His house was the centre of every activity: dances, church and feasting. He lacked no equipment of any sort, whether Inuk man's tools or qallunaat tools. All his furniture was handmade by himself. On Cape Hope, he built a sawmill and a steamer to curve wood to be used in building boats and canoes. To this day, his youngest son Pili builds boats at Great Whale River. Today, there are still two boats running, which he and his sons and in-laws built—one is owned by the Roman Catholic mission and the other was bought from the RCMP by the co-op in Cape Dorset, NWT. I was in Coral Harbour, Southampton Island, NWT, when this boat was being transferred from Rankin Inlet to Cape Dorset in 1971. All the memories of Cape Hope Island surrounded that boat in my visions, and my heart felt warm to think that I should see it again, a boat that was built right in front of the house where I was born. It outlived its builder, as Grandfather Weetaltuk died in 1957 at the age of ninety-eight.

Though all of his children were grown, Weetaltuk's house was never without his grandchildren. With each child, he had particular sayings and ways of noticing them. His way of noticing me was always to measure how fast I was growing, standing me up beside the legs of his chair and telling me how tall I was getting. He would do this no matter how often I went to see him during the day. Then, one day, Grandfather Weetaltuk no longer measured me. Instead, he asked me if I needed scratching. This started to happen after a measles epidemic hit Cape Hope. He and I were put in a tent so that we would not spread the measles. He spent his time scratching me with a potato sack rag to ease my itchiness. From then on, he asked me if I wanted him to scratch me and I would just qaqajuk to him—show off with babying gestures.

Weetaltuk did not run the lives of every individual in the community. Family heads had to do that. I can remember the big trips he decided on and then made because they were always so exciting to everyone, and everybody talked and knew about them. I guess he had planned to die right there on Cape Hope Island, and that is where is he buried. After his death, the group became disengaged and drifted apart—one could tell there was no more strength left among them. They could no longer fight back the intruders who were so anxious to relocate them; they became weak and reluctantly moved to Great Whale River, where many promises of jobs and better housing were made. When I visited them at Great Whale, not one Cape Hope Islander had a job, and as they had not been allowed to bring their canoes, they had nothing with which to survive the strange surroundings that they were adapting to. My father had never been idle in all his life, and there he was with nothing to do. He was not willing to go and get handouts from the welfare people, so he sat at home doing nothing but feeling quite helpless. All the Cape Hope Islanders were living in tents, which they warmed with wood stoves using what little wood they could get. Their move had really gone backwards.

While I was there, I went to see the administrator from Northern Affairs and told him about my father and what he was used to doing, that he had always navigated boats in the summer and managed stores and built houses and repaired watches. I don't think he believed me, as my father is one of those people who do not show their capabilities. He is withdrawn, shy and does not waste many words. The administrator gave him a job as a janitor at the school. Every able-bodied person from James Bay was set back by this move. They were taken advantage of when their leader died.

MY INUK WAY THAT I WAS BORN INTO

It never occurred to me that I could survive in this hard, fascinating world of the qallunaat. Though I can now take much for granted—like its inhabitants and daily routines—and live by its laws, I still see many things, moments and happenings that I will never really understand. Maybe that is because I was not brought up to live with its rules? My culture has rules too, but I learned them when my bones and brain were soft, so they were easily embedded and put there to stay. I keep telling myself that I have been born twice, once to grow and learn my own culture, and secondly, to learn qallunaat culture. Once, I was asked which way of life I preferred. I said that I did not really know, and that it would take years to explain my choices and preferences from both cultures. They both have bad and good, wonderful and sad, easy and hard times. I do not think that I would choose to live twice in either way. Now I am arguing with myself, because I could not possibly live twice. Is that funny or what?

But it is very nice and exciting to remember my own ways. My mother was dowered to my father on the day she was born, which is one of our rules. For this, each called the other "angilissiak"—waiting-for-you-to-grow-up. No well-classed Inuk woman can marry a poor-classed man. But a high-classed man can marry a low-classed woman, for the poor-classed woman is believed to make the best wife, because she will surely need and serve him well. He, in turn, has good reason to pamper and spoil her without really spoiling her mentally. It is the well-classed woman who would be spoiled in this way and therefore have a greater chance of taking over the man's manhood—he would end up the laughingstock of the community. But this kind of thing happened very seldom, perhaps when a young man had made his own choice for a wife, for it is Inuit tradition that parents choose wives and husbands for their children. Both my father and mother followed this tradition. I was born to them as their eldest child when they were both seventeen. In our society, a young man will have learned his duties as a man, though he has just begun to learn how to bring up children. His own parents and in-laws are there to guide him, which is the case for the new mother also.

Before I was born, my mother had to decide who would be involved at my birth. During her pregnancy, many people came to ask for her consent to attend. Customarily, such decisions are based on a number of considerations. People who have asked for consent have to be considered by close relatives and immediate in-laws. Those who are believed to have wisdom of life, who are successful economically and socially, are usually favoured. The first person who has to be there is a midwife, man or woman. In my case, it was my grandmother. While I was being born, she had to study how I came into the world. According to her, I moved all over, which she took to mean that I would be in strange lands one day. Ironically, here I am in the strange qallunaat world. Also present at my birth was the person I was named after, my other grandmother. This automatically meant that I would never call her "Grandmother" and she would not call me "grandchild." Instead, we called each other "sauniq"— namesake, bone-to-bone relation. This brought my parents and I that much closer to her. I was now their security against in-law problems.

Then someone had to dress me in my very first clothing. It can be a man or a woman. Since I was a girl, the person who dressed me has to call me arnaliaq—bringing-you-up-to-be-woman. This person, for the rest of his life and mine, has the heaviest responsibility. Just how I turn out to be as a woman is his job. He guided me to have knowledge of the ways of people and taught me how to know myself. He lectured me on how to approach different kinds of people. In other words, he brought me up to have a sense of responsibility with my mental attitudes toward our daily life. He was responsible for shaping my mind. As long as I remained a child, he brought me presents on special occasions such as his hunting successes, or on the first and last trading trips to the Hudson's Bay store in the fall and spring. In return, I called him "sanariarruk"—he-forms-me-into. All the things that I make and do for the first time go to him as long as I live.

The most serious part of my birth involved another child. By an arrangement between my parents and his parents, we too called each other "angilissiak"—waiting-for-you-to-grow-up. Eventually, I would be expected to marry this man. This understanding cannot be broken unless there is a good reason; for instance, if he is considered to be lazy and not a good hunter. That is how the Inuit child is born. But, I did not end there. With all these people to guide me, I began to grow. Now, I remember....

I REMEMBER

I was barely four years old when ice was just beginning to form on the sea. My father and mother had gone camping with another couple, and I had been left behind with my grandparents. When my father did not return from the summer camp near Cape Hope, it began to cause worry in our settlement. Two of my uncles and their families had not returned either from Old Factory. They had gone to summer there, waiting for the return of their schoolchildren from Fort George mission school.

Taking me with them, my grandparents decided to search for my father and his party where they had said they would camp. It was a terrible trip by canoe for both Grandfather and Grandmother. The paddling was strenuous, having to break the forming ice on the sea. Grandfather was paddling and poking the ice while Grandmother steered at the rear. After hours and hours, we finally sighted the camp. As we came nearer, nobody was in sight. No one met us as our canoe docked, yet we were very noisy. No doubt misfortune had overtaken my father and mother—it is traditional that arrivals are not greeted when something serious has happened. I felt by the actions of my grandparents that there was something wrong.

I walked beside them across the stony beach area, up towards two tents at the edge of the trees. I was out of breath, trying to keep up with Grandmother, who was holding my hand. My four-year-old legs were trying their best to avoid falling, my eiderdown outfit felt heavy and I was so hot. There was a strong smell of skunk as we came near to the tent entrance. We entered. The whole atmosphere was sad. There lay my mother, looking very thin and barely audible when she spoke. She gave me love sounds that mothers made and told me not to come near. My baby brother was sitting beside her, looking very lost. Father was sitting down near her. He reached for me and gave me a long caress with his nose.

The couple that were with them had also had misfortune. There was a lot of snow on the branches of the nearby trees. Apparently, their only son had been throwing rocks up into the trees to bring down these chunks of snow. They were hard and a lot had fallen down on him, injuring one of his eyes.

We did not wait another day before my grandfather decided to travel to Old Factory where there was medical help. Three canoes made the treacherous trip, including a dog that had been sprayed by a skunk. I think every Inuit and Indian and even the odd qallunaaq came down to see us on our arrival. The priest was notified. With all this happening, my brother and I were taken to our aunt's tent and fed with warm food while our grandparents pitched up their tent. I must have slept for some time because I next remember great daylight. It was a beautiful sunny day, but everyone was moving rather sadly. I was not even reminded to go out and look at the world, just fed and dressed. It seemed that every person that came to our tent shook my hand and gave me a hug with gestures of sadness. To my mind, there was certainly something missing, and I knew what it was. Usually, there is a lot of news exchanged and gift-giving; people make verbal relations with each other, binding it stronger; children, like me and my brother, are told how much we have grown, how smart we are with our chores. But people did not seem to be in that mood. I learned a few years later that it was this day that my mother died. I do not know if anyone tried to explain her death to me and I do not think that I would have really understood. I did not miss her at that age, but today, I often think that I would have liked to have known her.

IT WAS A STRANGE WINTER

After Mother's death, our time at the post seemed so long, and yet it was only early fall. My father and my immediate family dressed in black clothing, the symbol of mourning, for one year. It was at this time that my father began to encourage me to learn the Cree Indian language. I already knew a few sentences—come here, let's play, I am afraid, you are terrible—but to my father, that was not enough. He repeatedly told me to learn to speak it fluently. He would point out some Indian children playing nearby and ask me to join them. For some reason, it seemed important to him that I should learn the Cree language quickly, instead of the way Inuit have done over the years—slowly and through frequent contact with the James Bay Indians.

Every James Bay Inuk learned it and communicated with the Indians. None of the Indians seemed to have learned our language except the word "kamiit"—sealskin boots, which they vitally needed. They would swarm around the Inuit tents in the fall, ordering a pair from every available woman who could sew sealskin in the fall before they went to their inland camps.

When fall arrived and winter was showing its way, we did not move to our usual wintering site, which was usually on Cape Hope Island or the area nearby. All the Inuit had gone except my family. It seemed that my father had to work for the Hudson's Bay in the coming winter. It meant that we moved to the other island in Old Factory River, right amongst the Indians. Not that they were many during the winter, as most of them go inland to catch beaver and don't return until summer. The importance of learning the Cree language became clear: I was now having to play with Indian children.

I remember only sad and strange things about that year. Our tents were pitched near the Hudson's Bay store. There were two tents facing each other in order to make extra living space for my father and his belongings. On the other side were my brother and I, Grandfather and Grandmother. Other than us on the island that winter were the Hudson's Bay store manager, a qallunaaq, his Indian assistant Thomas Mark and his family, the Anglican missionary and his Indian wife. The rest of the Indians had gone inland for the winter. On the other side of the river were the Catholic missionary and a brother, and a retarded Indian man who managed the Frères stores, his sister and her family.

Nothing seemed meaningful and nothing familiar. It was an odd and strange winter. Even our routine had no purpose or feeling. Every day, Father would go out and return only for meals and at bedtime. Grandfather did the same. My brother and I had nothing to do except help Grandmother get pails of water and cut wood; while she cut wood, Brother and I would place them neatly near the doorway for easy reach. She did not allow us to go any further than the water hole on the river ice. She allowed us to visit the assistant manager's family only when she went. Even the weather seemed very cold and dark.

Then, the sun began to stay longer, and every now and then my father would burn something and discard items. Grandmother would announce that he was slowly coming out of his mourning. What he was burning and discarding were the things of my mother. One Sunday morning, I watched him pick up a gramophone record and place his hands around it and crack it ever so gently in half. He put it in our wood stove and watched it melt while his face grimaced with deep sorrow, like he was asking himself, "Why did it happen?" The record was my mother's favourite reel. He looked up and saw me watching him. His face changed to the loving, ugly face I knew and he gave me love sounds with deep sympathy. According to our tradition, he was not supposed to practise any more sorrow over the death of his wife but to accept it and let her rest. Surely, if he kept his sorrow going, he could easily go mad—that is the belief in my culture about people who have lost loved ones through death. He knew the tradition, but it seemed that he had to do it one last time. Afterwards, I never saw him again practise sorrow. That summer, one of my aunts had a baby girl who was named Malla, after my mother. My brother and I had to call her "our Malla," though the ending of the name was changed with "apik," which means "smaller" or "not the real one." My mother was now considered not floating without place but resting in peace.

Finally, one day, my brother and I were sliding around our tent area when we noticed a movement in the distance, at the mouth of the river. There was not just one, but a whole trail of them. I yelled towards our tent to make sure Grandmother heard me: Allaaluit!—Indians! Over and over as loud as I could. They were coming back. My whole inside was bubbling with excitement while Grandmother stayed calm. I was not excited by the Indians but by what would follow them: Inuit, those familiar faces. There would be so many to play with in my own language—other than my brother—who played dog sleds, hunting and fishing.

I WILL NEVER KNOW ANOTHER SUMMER LIKE THAT

Before I knew it, the whole little island was covered with tepees and white, white tents, and the smell of branches was in the air. There were constant visitors, shaking of hands, comments being made about how we had managed so well without our mother. Then, when the month of June arrived, the Inuit came. It was so good and exciting to see familiar faces. Our tent was packed with relatives and again, comments were made and bonds were strengthened. My family moved back to the other side of Old Factory River with the Inuit. To me, the whole summer seemed all sunshine after such a long, lonely winter. I was able to visit with whomever I wanted and do my duties without feeling that I was trespassing on somebody else's land.

Most of the Cape Hope Islanders were now at Old Factory except Grandfather Weetaltuk and his youngest son. They usually never moved during summer except to come to the post and trade. Men began to put fish nets into the water and visit them daily, and they began to hunt geese and ducks. Women began to arrange themselves to begin berry picking and to see who would get a canoe from her husband. Some days, we would leave in the early morning and return in the early evening, at least before the men came back—otherwise, no one would be home to pluck the geese and ducks or scale the fish. Arriving back was always so hectic, especially for me and my brother. We had to put everything away, bring the grub box back to its place, bring the oars to the safe place, carry to our tent the wood that we had gathered while we were out, get pails of water, get the wood ready for tonight and for the next morning, pull the canoe up where it was secure and turn it upside down so it would stay dry inside.

Of course, my brother and I did not do this in a peaceful way. We spent most of our time fighting verbally, comparing who did the most and who did not. By the time we were finished, one of us would go home crying. Neither of us would get sympathy. In our culture, if one is sympathized with, one will grow up with a mixed-up nature, aggressive and respecting no one, but wanting respect for his or her aggressiveness. That kind will surely end up with no respect at all from the community. So if one of us cried our way home, it was a waste of tears. We had to forget the whole reason for crying. But anyone would forget to cry on approaching a tent that has a successful hunter living in it. Before one gets to the door of the tent, one smells a goose or duck cooking, and one enters and women are in the process of serving the meal, goose boiled with dumplings with lots of gravy, and fish and blueberry salad. I will never know another summer like that.

TRADING WAS A CHORE BUT NECESSARY

The Hudson's Bay Company supply ships arrived, along with other ships that belonged to the missionaries. This occasion used to cause a lot of excitement among the whole community. Everybody was curious—what has arrived, what is new among the goods? The most popular item was fabric, and the women just seemed to race for it. Grandmother would make a big discussion about whether she should get some for me when she got her fabric. Did I need a new dress? Or did my brother need new pants? And always, both of us got our new clothing, and both of us were expected to look after them and wear them only for Sunday best.

Then the Catholic mission boat arrived, and everyone would want to see the bishop, even the strongly-professed Protestants. The whole dock area would swarm with people. Bishop Belleau was the most fascinating man who arrived yearly at James Bay. Though everyone was fascinated with his outfit, beard, and his knowledge of the Cree language, there was something else about this man that attracted both Inuit and Indians. He ignored no one. As soon as he stepped out of the canoe he would be in the crowd, shaking hands and taking time to show his ring to those who asked to see, and greeting people by their names. His attitude was most unusual and very kindly. He was not like other big qallunaat who came to count how many of us were left, nor was he like the ones who seemed to be afraid to be too near us, as if we were full of incurable disease. (I'm sure most of us carried such disease, but then, it originally came from them.) When the bishop gave the church service, the whole community would go, even the Indians from the other side of the river. He would cause the biggest conversation among people for weeks after he had departed.

The Catholic supply boat arrived soon after, the one that always brought sadness to me and my brother. For this was the boat that picked up our father, as he was the only man who knew the way to Fort George, where the water was deep and where it was shallow. He would be gone for one or two weeks and sometimes passed us altogether and went on to Moosonee. He would be there until the schoolchildren began to be picked up from Moosonee, then on to Fort George, and home again. He would be home only until the boat had to go back to Moosonee to anchor for the year. Without him, I always felt so lost and daily tasks seemed meaningless. When he finally anchored for good, he always had presents for me and my brother, always something useful. Before he had even had a chance to do his summer hunting, the season would be gone and we would have to get ready to move to another camp for the fall, usually to a spot where my grandfather thought there would be plenty of game to sustain us before winter set in.

The Indians would slowly disappear inland, and the Inuit too, after having supplied themselves with dry goods sufficient to last until the ice was safe to travel on sometime in the first week of December. While waiting for freeze-up, people took time to get acquainted again and to catch up with what individuals had gone through during the summer. Women began to sew winter clothing for their families. Games were played in different homes, and children were noticed for their behaviour, growth and talents. This always seemed an indolent time for the men, for they took time repairing sleds, harnesses, whips and all the other winter gear, the summer gear having been put away in safety. By the end of November, everybody, including children, would be walking around in new winter clothes: parkas, kamiit, mitts, and I, as always, in my new eiderdown pants.

At this time, the men decided who was to go to the trading post at Old Factory. There had to be at least two teams of dogs, enough to bring back supplies for the people who placed orders. The day before trading travel, Grandfather Weetaltuk would do his yearly testing. This ritual has always been memorable for me. I can still see him walking out of his door, all dressed in a new outfit and harpoon in hand, to test the safety of the ice. Feeling with the harpoon, stepping where he felt, he walked slowly and did not look back. Finally, he would stride, without making himself lighter like one trying not to wake up a baby. Then everyone could see that he was now walking with his normal walk, slowly becoming smaller and smaller until he had no shape, but looked like a moving object. Then he became bigger and bigger and more recognizable, until he was again entering back into his house. In no time, the news would be out that the ice was now sikuttuk—solidly iced. There would be no doubt that the traders for the community would leave the next day. This was the one night of the year that the whole community would go to bed early.

My sleepy head would hear, "Mini, you are the only one who will miss the qallunaaliattut"—traders to the post, or literally, going to where the qallunaat are. This was Grandmother's way of getting me up fast. This was one morning out of the year that I would forget that the wood stove was not yet lit. This was the one morning that I ignored the cold, crispy air in the tent and would leave my cozy eiderdown sleeping place, for I dressed so fast and out I went to watch the dogs being harnessed. The morning was so crisp that footsteps were making grinding sounds on the snow.

One could not really see the people who were moving around; only their shapes were recognizable as the sun was not up yet.

When every necessary item for the travel was latched up on the sled and each man had sat himself in his place, the pituk—the string that holds the sled anchored to the ground—would be loosened, and away the teams went. At first, the dogs would run tirelessly. After a while, their tongues would hang out and they would trot at their normal pace. The man would sit, his breathing making smoke from the crisp cold, concentrating on the dogs and the horizon around him, getting up now and then to take a few steps to keep warm and encouraging his dogs with command words that he had taught them to understand: "errah" for left, "auk auk" for right, "uit uit" to go, "how how" for come here, "aha aha" for even pace, "auu auu" to stop. This kind of trip was made with a grub box, sleeping bag, a harpoon and a gun for each man. With seventeen to twenty dogs and so little on the sled, and the snow being so crisp, the travellers would reach the trading post towards evening provided there were no problems, such as dogs becoming tangled too often, or surmiq— soil coming off the runners, or bad weather.

In the meantime, there was anxiety at home for their return, as some families had run out of tea, sugar, flour, coffee or oats. Borrowing a bit here and there had started some time ago in the middle of November. This was also the time our grandmother, without fail, would remind my brother and me how different things were from the days of Father's childhood, when he would come home from woodcutting and ptarmigan-hunting with tea and sugar that he had stowed away to surprise his mother at this time of the year. Everyone seemed to be restless, especially children, and we would be sent off to nasik—to look to the horizon for the traders, thus giving time for the wives to have the tent warm and hot tea ready just in time for their arrival, and plenty of wood cut so the stove would burn without end until bedtime. This time also was the earliest bedtime for the whole community, for if the traders did not arrive tonight, they would certainly be here late tomorrow afternoon. There I would be, trying to wait up for them, but constantly being reminded by Grandmother: "Mini, you are the only one who will miss the arrival of the traders tomorrow because I will not spend time trying to wake you." Who wanted to miss the arrival of the traders? Not me! And into bed I went. "Mini, undress or you will walk in your sleep." I am sure Grandmother had eyes in the back of her head.

The next morning, there would be no way anyone could keep me in bed. This was one morning that I did not count my stockings, as Grandmother called it. Usually I made an effort to put my stockings over my toe, over my instep, over my heel, halfway up my leg and finally over my knees. The time that I spent dressing seemed so long to my grandmother that some days she would wake me by saying, "Stocking counting time." The whole process seemed to be an ordeal because I would rather sleep. But not this morning; this morning, I did not even drink my hot gravy and out I went to nasik—to look to the horizon in search of traders.

Finally, some child would come running home, out of breath, calling at the top of his lungs: "Qimmussiit, qimmussiit!" Dog teams, dog teams! Someone would ask, "nani?" Where? An adult had to go and look to make sure. She would return and announce: "Ajjiliqut"—they are coming. Children would start running towards the traders and get a ride up to the camp. Such an exciting sight to see the dogs, now running faster after having scented camp. One would hear the commands to the dogs and finally "auu auu"—stop. Nothing would be unpacked until each man had all his gear put away and his travel clothing tended and hung to dry. His parka had to be hung and the snow and frost brushed off the fur. His mitts would be turned inside out and hung to dry. His boots were also turned inside out and all his socks changed to dry pairs from damp ones. He had to have hot tea and a meal if he needed one. There I would be, struggling at the side of Grandmother, trying to turn one mitt inside out and Grandmother complaining how slow I was: "Mini, your future husband will not get very far, you are so parqpaaluk"—slow with clumsiness. All I could think about was what we got from the trading post. Finally, when all this was done, everyone got relaxed and all the goods were put into order, which belonged to whom. All night, there would be exchanges back and forth, from house to house, as some of the items got mixed up along the way, and there would be children like me, bringing gifts to our sanariarruk—our builder. It sure was a chore, but it was necessary to trade.

THEY CAME BEARING GIFTS

There was no more travelling that winter except for the men who went hunting. We stayed on Cape Hope Island all spring and summer and followed our normal spring season activities. But we had very unusual visitors that summer. A small Peterhead boat arrived with passengers I had never seen before. I had never seen qallunaaq other than missionaries and Hudson's Bay traders, and I did not regard the missionaries as qallunaat, for the ones we knew had Inuk names. Besides, they spoke my language and had black hair. I can still see myself running like mad towards our house when I noticed that these men had blond hair. I went inside and headed straight to the little window, pulled over a box to climb on and watched these two qallunaat.

There were two barrels near the house where my grandmother kept her seal oil, oil which we used for qullit—seal oil lamps. One of the men reached down into a barrel and picked up some fat tissue and sniffed it. I started to giggle because he put it down so quickly that I could see the oil splashing up on his face. Just as I was getting down from the box, Grandmother came in. She had been visiting, probably trying to find out who these people were. She understood what I had been doing. "How embarrassing! How dare you peep like that! That is tirlianik—hypocrisy. You are embarrassing!" I tried to tell her what I saw. "Suva? What? Splashed by oil! Well, they looked for it! I hope they felt embarrassed!" That episode always stuck in my mind, for I discovered two things. One, Grandmother had a great sense of embarrassment over little things that I thought were normal and funny. Two, somewhere exist strange blond people.

The two qallunaat stayed with Grandfather Weetaltuk for some time. I know it was a few days because I was not allowed to go in and out of his house. No child was ever allowed to run around when there were strange visitors who were considered special, as it was considered embarrassing for the child and parents suffered from the outcome if the child interfered in such an important occasion.

After the two qallunaat left for Moosonee, Grandfather Weetaltuk began to bring out old army clothes, old pieces of broken chandeliers and old thread-snapped Victorian beads. He shared them with each household. Even I got one bead from Grandmother to look at and admire. I would hold it in my little hands, examine it, turn it, and look through its hole. To me, it was so pretty. It had a white background and different-coloured spots all over it, and it was shaped like a teardrop. I kept it in my sewing box, which Grandfather Symma had made for me out of dried grass. It was decorated with animal shapes on top and around it. Inside it was a needle on a cushion Grandmother had made for me out of qallunaartak—qallunaat material, fabric. It was also decorated with the syllabics of my name. There was also a thimble which my sanariarruk had given me from one of his fox pelt trades at the Hudson's Bay Company store. All the rest of the contents were little rocks that I had picked up along the shore of our settlement, and which I thought were pretty.

Grandmother used to hate these stones—to her, they were just extra weight. To make me get rid of them, she used to tell me that I was making the rocks laugh. And when I made the rocks laugh, it meant that I created evil around me, that the rocks enjoyed my creation and made evil laughs. So I used to get rid of them real fast. But somehow I always forgot about their evil laughs and started collecting all over again. Each year I grew bigger and a little stronger, and the rocks that I collected grew bigger too. I would come home from rock hunts weighed down with rocks that I was carrying gathered up in the front of my dress. I would puff, barely able to walk, and drop all the rocks in front of our house. Grandmother would hear them drop and yell out, "Ainnali"—Not again! She did not like them where I dropped them because they were in the way and caused people to fall over them. Scaring me about their laughs would start all over again. I would puff and puff and try to put them out of the way as best as I could. Then I began to carry rocks on my back—even bigger ones. In the evenings, when she was straightening our sleeping platform, she would find one or two long, black rocks which I had pretended were my dolls. Her final word was, "Tusanngituaaluvutit"—You are definitely hard of hearing. I would get scared, not because I was hard of hearing, but because the sound of her voice told me that evil laughs would definitely happen pretty soon. The sound of her voice also told me that it was final—or she would find another way to stop my terrible habit.

At that age too, I was terribly anxious to copy the older women. Most of them were carrying babies. I began to carry a pillow. Grandmother did not like me playing with the pillows because it made extra work for her when the pillow burst or tore and the eiderdown scattered all over.

She would warn me that the pillow would tickle me to death. It was a belief that a person who laughed for a long time could die, which we call "aattuq"—catch a breath and not come out of it and therefore stop breathing. This is believed to happen when a person is tickled endlessly. That, of course, scared me, so I did not carry the pillow on my back.

Grandmother also received a piece of chandelier glass. That was her treasure. In her childhood, as she always put it, she used to be allowed to play with a piece of iceberg and look through it. Now the piece of glass had taken its place, and it did not melt when it was brought into the house. When she was a child, Grandmother used to lick a piece of ice and it would shine and look like a glass. If you looked through it, she said, you could see funny forms. Children in my grandmother's time would spend hours looking through ice. In the evenings, when there was nothing happening and when my brother and I were bored before we went to bed, Grandmother would get us ready and tuck us in and lie between us, giving each of us a turn to look through this piece of chandelier glass towards our qullik. We would spend hours looking through this glass and see many forms of our qullik with dancing shines all over it in different pretty colours. We would eventually fall asleep and would not think about the glass again until Grandmother brought it out from her sewing bag made of loon skin. She never allowed us to touch it unless she had nothing to entertain us with.

That summer, some of the men walked around in army pants and coats and some in army hats. Most men did not go for these clothes, and their wives used them to wipe their feet on before coming into the house. I did not like them either because the men I saw in them looked overpowering and strange. The smell of the clothing reminded me of the odour of the Hudson's Bay Company warehouses when I went with my father to pick up a sack of flour, and I did not like that smell. That was not the end of the strange people who came bearing gifts.

THE WORLD WAR IN THE QALLUNAAT WORLD RUBBED ON US TOO

Every summer when a ship arrived, Grandfather Weetaltuk would receive a parcel from somebody. From one of these ships also came the news that there was a big war in the qallunaat world, that the fighting was so great that many people were being killed. Grandfather Symma would tell Grandmother of the news after we had gone to bed. I would lay awake listening—though I did not know what to make of it all, I took it all into my head. Sometimes, I thought that Grandfather was just telling a story as he always did to Brother and me. Grandfather would go on: Jamaniaaluit—Germans, wanted the whole world, that was why they were having a war. I would never picture the world as round as it is on the maps; I would only picture the enormous area on Cape Hope and wonder why the Germans would want the whole world. That would be my last thought and it would be gone out of my mind the next morning, all erased by the coming day's chores.

We did our usual summer chores. My family did not move to Old Factory, and we just stayed around Cape Hope. Some men went to trade. Ships passed and some stopped. The news was still the same, that there was a war in the qallunaat world. One particular man went to Grandfather's house—more news came and a lot of guns that did not look like twenty-twos, three-o-three or double barrel were being distributed among the men. They were told to use these guns on qallunaat who wore clothing with the swastika sign on it. A picture of a swastika was drawn and it was called Jamaniaaluit. The guns had arrows mounted on the barrels, and the bullets were big and pointed. I watched the men examining them; they could not get over the size of the guns. One of them commented, "Shoot a seal with this, there would be no skin left on it." Everyone put the guns away where they could not be seen, and we all lived in fear for a long time. I saw the guns only when the men cleaned them—they felt responsible for them because they belonged to the qallunaat.

We began to hear big airplanes, especially at night. When they were heard, everybody would turn their lights off. Some days, we could see them far off on the horizon. When planes were heard, some would say, "Alalungai—just listen, this is the one that's going to hit us." Everybody would freeze at the thought of it. Then, one summer, the men were told that a man named Hitler may have come our way, that we should notify the post if ever he was seen, that he too wore the swastika sign. We were mystified as we were not told why we should look out for him; all we were told was to report any man with a swastika sign. People wondered and called him "hiallak"—habitual crier, as the name sounded like the word cry: Hitler—hiallak.

My crippled uncle was the only man who could not go hunting on all day trips, so he used to stay around in the community. He had a great sense of humour and always teased the children lovingly and always stopped to play with them. He began to make airplanes out of paper for us children. He would put the swastika sign on them with a pencil and throw them in the air and say, "Here come the Jamaniaaluit!"

I began to think that Grandfather Symma was not just telling stories. Men no longer went out alone and the women were not allowed to go berry picking on their own. Symma would tell us, "This is what Henariaaluk—Big Henry—used to talk about, that the qallunaat will have wars, that the future will be worse, that one day our land will be full of qallunaat, that no one will know the other, that there will be unrest among Inuit." Grandmother would ask him, "How would that be possible?" He would go on, "Maybe not in our time, maybe in Mini's and Miki's time and maybe in their children's time." Though it hit me very hard at the moment he was talking, I would forget all about it the next day. Whoever he was, Henariaaluvinik—the late Big Henry—had not been lying. Nobody ever talked about him, just about what he had said. I know he was not an Inuk because Henry is not an Inuk name; in fact, people who have the name Henry in my community originate from this Henry. All I could tell was that he was very respected, that people called him our dear Henariaaluk—like the Great Whale River people called Big Harold, our son-in-law. Everybody called him that because he was liked and had a special place in the hearts of the people. They had a special name to welcome him, as he was an accepted qallunaaq. Harold died only a few years ago from old age.

Today, I keep thinking about those predictions that I thought at one time were just stories. There may be no war in Inuit land and there may never have been one, but I begin to see that there is unrest among Inuit. Certainly qallunaat are becoming many in our land and the Inuit are beginning not to know each other.

DID THEY REALLY
PAMPER THEIR EYEBROWS?

Grandfather Weetaltuk would receive more army clothes, more chande-lier pieces, more beads and carpenter's tools which he could not get from the Hudson's Bay Company. There was a hand saw, file, screwdrivers and lots of nails. Later, I found out that he used to make furniture for some qallunaaq and would ship it out. No doubt he received these gifts from and made furniture for qallunaat whom he had known from way back, before I was born. As long as I could remember, his house had had glass in the windows, which he must have received from a qallunaaq friend. That was probably how it began, how the qallunaat came to rub off their materialistic nature on the simple Inuit of Hudson Bay who had depended on nature alone.

No wonder Inuit call them qallunaat. I said at the beginning that qallunaat means "people who pamper their eyebrows." But I am not sure anymore if that's what it means. It was never explained to me by any of my ancestors why the qallunaat were named that. I know for sure that it does not mean "white man"—there is no meaning in it at all pertaining to colour or white or man. I know for sure, too, that it was the qallunaat who named themselves white men, to divide themselves from other co-lours, for it is surely them who have always been aware of different racial colours. Inuit too are aware of different races, but not of colour. I have never known or been taught to identify another race by skin colour.

To come back to the word qallunaat: I have turned the word inside out to try and find the meaning. First of all, the word qallu can mean eyebrow; by adding an ending one has qallu-naaq, meaning one qallunaaq; qallu-naak—two qallunaaq; qallu-naat—many qallunaaq. The word implies humans who pamper or fuss with nature, of materialistic habit. Avaricious people. Qallu is also the beginning of the word qallunartak, material or fabric or anything that is manufactured or store-bought. It can also mean a rag made of material or fabric, or any material other than a material from nature.

Somehow, I cannot see how the Inuit would have been impressed if the qallunaat pampered their eyebrows. I cannot imagine the qallunaat pampering their eyebrows when they did not care how they looked in the middle of the Arctic; even today, they do not seem to care how they look. They are so busy making money when they are in the Arctic, they don't seem to have time to pamper themselves, let alone their eyebrows. Furthermore, when I see pictures of the first qallunaat who went to the Arctic, they always look so dishevelled, with overalls, plaid shirts and heavy-looking sweaters, their faces covered with beard and their hair uncombed-looking, at least in summer pictures. Pictures during winter do not look as if they had any way to pamper their eyebrows, with caribou outfits from head to foot and their faces frosty-looking. For those reasons, I do not understand why the qallunaat would be called people who pamper their eyebrows. I definitely believe it was meant the other way—qallunaaraaluit, very respectable, avaricious, materialistic, humans who could do anything with material, or those who fear for their capacity to manufacture material. All those meanings are in that one word: "qallu," the beginning of the word qallunartak—material or fabric (man-made); "naa," avaricious, who flaunts, who is proud to show his material, who lures with material; "raa," respectable, fearing, magical; "luit," many, human. ("Luit" can also mean they or them rather than us.) I do not know which word was formed first, qallunaat or qallunartak; I know for sure that they go together. I was born too late to witness the naming of the first qallunaat arrivals to the Arctic who could have possibly pampered their eyebrows.

Inuit, too, gave themselves an identity. To me the word "Eskimo" does not mean anything. It is an Indian word—"escheemau"—that qallunaat tried to say at one time. It is a Cree word: "Escee," yagh, sickening, can't stand it; "mau," human. At first encounter Cree Indians got sick at the sight of the Inuit eating raw meat (and Indians do not eat raw meat). Today, the Inuit still eat raw meat and it's still yam yam as far as I am concerned. When we lived in Old Factory amongst Indians, we had to be very careful that we did not eat raw meat in front of them. When people ate raw fish or any meat that we eat raw, we had to keep looking if the Indians were coming so that they would not see us—not because we were ashamed but so that we would not sicken them. Inuit differentiated themselves from the animals of nature, not from other races. "Inuk" means one human; "Inuuk" means two humans; "Inuit" means many humans. "Inuk" can also mean alive as opposed to dead. Today, of course, the Inuk identifies himself as Inuk, different from any other race he has encountered since the days when just he and the animals of his land lived in the North.

OTHER FEARS EMERGED

With all this news coming to us from the ships, my grandparents began to revive stories that they had heard from their parents and also some stories that they had experienced. Because there was so much fear in our community because of the war news, other fears began to be told, like that there used to be qallunaat seen with funny boats, with pointed ends both front and back. Henry's name came up often, and what he had said would be repeated—about how qallunaat in faraway places had wars. The story about qallunaanguat, the phoney qallunaat, was revived, and it was said that their boats used to be seen only when it was foggy.

On Cape Hope Island, when it is foggy, the fog hangs around very close to the surface of the sea, and there would be patches where the fog broke. These qallunaanguat did not come near the Inuit but were seen when their boats darted through the broken areas in the fog. When their shapes were seen, they had pipes in their mouths. They would only come at night to kidnap little girls. For that, they were called "arnasiutit"—women-kidnappers. When my grandparents first moved to Cape Hope, these sorts of people used to be seen. A cave is believed to exist on the west side of the island, and these arnasiutit were seen coming from this cave. These men used to hide around the settlement areas. Their inik—nest-like places made in wooded areas down on the ground—have been found. There was one such area at the edge of trees not far from Grandfather's house. That was an area where little children seemed to wander off because there were a lot of raspberries growing there. This inik was very noticeable because it was very different from other places that ended up looking used by other people.

These arnasiutit—women-kidnappers—used to shake hands with little boys and men. One of my aunt's little boys was believed to have shaken hands with such a qallunaaq; he ran home saying that the man who shook his hand had long white hair, was dressed in rags and was very tall with blue, blue eyes. That boy became very sick after that handshake, and he died from some kind of delirious disease. All the others who had died in that way also had handshakes with the strange men in the woods. One Indian girl in Old Factory who had been kidnapped and then released also died from such an experience. Though little children were allowed to play outside, they were never allowed to go off far, especially near the wooded areas.

IT WAS A TIME OF
JOY AND A TIME TO LEARN

We wintered on Cape Hope Island, and the men hunted, but during the middle of winter, we moved to Charlton Island. It seems Grandfather had made some arrangements to meet some Indians from Eastmain for trading. Two men arrived right in the middle of a great celebration. Grandfather Symma had gone on foot, looking for seals. He had walked quite a distance when he discovered some trapped whales, apparently very many. As he was on foot, he managed to kill one whale and brought back only mattak—whale skin, a delicacy for us—one of the luxury foods during summer. Everyone was so excited about the whales. Our tent was packed while the men came to discuss the trapped whales with Grandfather. The poor Indian visitors who had pitched their tent near ours did not get their usual attention, though they were not completely ignored. Their presence just did not seem exciting, not when all the men were discussing how they were going to go about the whale hunt. The next day, there was not one man left at our camp—even the two Indians left for Eastmain, saying they would return later.

During the day, one of my aunts decided to move her tent a little bit further away from the trail, as every time the dog teams arrived her entrance was sniffed by excited dogs. To do this, she stripped the tent from its original foundation, removing the chimney from her wood stove. The stove remained, still burning. She planned to keep it going while she pitched her tent, so she would not waste precious flames and the tent would not take longer to warm up once she put it back in. Suddenly, there were the sounds of dogs barking. Everyone just looked at each other, as it was too early for the whale hunters to have returned. Every head was out of the tent. One could see the dogs, all excited, and a man fighting and rolling a child who seemed to be on fire in the snow. Every person went toward the scene. There was my father, who had just arrived from Old Factory all by himself. Just as he was arriving, he had seen this little two-year-old cousin of mine on fire and had stopped to put her out. By this time, everyone knew what was happening. The little girl was burned all around her chin, right up to her forehead and all her beautiful, long, braided hair was gone.

The mother tended to her, and my brother, Grandmother and I helped my father undo his sled. Grandmother told him of the news about the whales and Indians. We sat in the tent and joined Father in a meal. I remember that part, so cozy. It was so nice to see Father. Frères stores had let him go to hunt. He had left Old Factory that morning, stopped a few minutes at Cape Hope and then come on to Charlton. Our tent was so warm with the wood stove crackling and our bright lamp burning. Sitting with my father was rare for us. It seemed he just worked so hard for the Hudson's Bay Company and Frères Stores and on the ships since our mother had died. It was also rare for Father to talk and ask questions, as he was very quiet.

The whalers must have arrived very late, because when I woke, my grandfather was talking to my father regarding news at the post and Cape Hope Island. Outside, there were already some women tending the whale meat, sinew and skins. There was so much whale that no one bothered to divide it up for each household. Everyone just helped themselves from the pile sitting on the meat racks outside.

Before long, every woman had whale skins hanging up to dry in the sun, as it is used to make soles for kamiit. The skin turns white while drying and whiter still after it has been chewed to soften. There was no shortage of the material, and even little girls like me were given skins already cut out so that we might learn how to make boots. Of course, it had to be little pairs. I decided to make a pair for my brother, but while I was in the process of making them, Grandmother pointed out that I had to give them to my sanariarruk. Like all children, I cried because I wanted my brother to keep what I made. But customs are customs, and when I finished, I had to walk down to my sanariarruk's tent and give him the boots. He hugged me and gave me all the praise that I wished for. It encouraged me, so I went home and asked to make another pair for him. But no, it had to be something else. It was only the things I made for the first time that went to him—such was the promise that had been made when he had dressed me when I was born. My grandmother then said that I could make a pair for my brother. Like the first pair, I chewed the skin to soften it, and Grandmother made me patterns for the sole, instep, heel and the leg pieces. After cutting the sole into proper shape, I then had to cut the instep and the heel into shape and fold them in half so that the edges were even, and then put them in a container to soak for a while. This part is tedious as one has to be careful the skin does not soak too much, otherwise it will go right back to its raw stage and become hard to handle.

I sat near the container, asking Grandmother every few minutes, "Namasivaat?"—Are they ready? Finally I took them out, handled one and put the rest under a canvas so they would not dry out. While I was waiting for them to soak, I made ready the sinew to use as a thread and found a good needle. It cannot be any old needle. The length and the shape of the eye has to be just right so that it will not be hard to pull through or cause the skin to split. The thread is tested by running it between the teeth and feeling it with one's tongue to find any broken or weak parts. The strand has to be the shape of a carrot; the narrow end is purposely shaped so that the very small eye of the needle can take it, making the tiniest, waterproof, strong stitch around the edge of the skin. The sole has to be pleated so that it comes over the instep part and is shaped like a moccasin slipper.

Having sewn the instep and heel together, one has to go right around to put the sole on. When that is done, it has to be turned inside out and reinforced by sewing in the instep piece, which is protruding about one-eighth of an inch around. When that is done, again one sews big stitches with a knot on every stitch to secure and shape the heel. Again, turn them right side out and soften by rolling them between the hands, back and forth, and stretch them with special stretching equipment made of wood and shaped like the boot. Then leave the boot in the air to dry properly. While waiting for it to dry, the leg piece is cut, shaped and sewn. One has to be careful with this part. The legs are made of sealskin fur. The fur for boys and men has to run downwards. It can be decorated by sewing different colours, black and white, running down the front. The fur for girls and women runs sideways and can be decorated sideways.

At this point, the women usually take a break or do something else while waiting for the feet to dry, or they make strings for the legs which are threaded in and out through little holes that are about an inch apart all around the top part of the leg. Each end of the string is crossed over the other; when you pull them, the whole top part of the leg pleats and prevents snow from getting in. The foot parts are then sewn on to the leg parts. Finally, the boots are finished. The experienced women can make a pair in a day, but it took me three days to finish a pair that fit a four-year-old. Around that time, all the little girls of my age were making boots; there was so much material around. It was indeed a joy and a time to learn for our future so that we might take care of our husbands and children.

TO LEARN IS SOMETIMES PAINFUL

The Indians arrived back as they promised; this time, they got more attention on their arrival. The purpose of their coming was to trade goods or money for boots, mainly spring boots, which are even more tedious to make than fur ones. One man wanted three pairs and planned to stay to wait for them. His partner dealt with families other than my grandfather's. Every woman and girl was chewing skins for the next couple of days. There was Grandmother chewing and reminding me endlessly how to do it properly: "Mini, do not chew without interest, think about partridge berries and your mouth will wet more and you will finish chewing that much faster. Hold it this way and go back and forth alternately, turn it on the other side every so often. If you chew without attention, you will only tire your jaws." I had to learn so many things that year, probably things I would have to know for the sake of my future. I had to give up so many things that I preferred doing, such as going into the woods with my brother, hunting ptarmigan, putting up snares for rabbits, gathering spruce gum and looking for the tracks of the foxes, and carrying babies on my back for the other women. To learn is sometimes painful, not being able to do what one wants to do.

JAMES BAY ROBBERS

Then the wiskitchan began to arrive. These birds are a nuisance. Their name came from the Indians, and I do not know what it means. At this time, my brother and I would be reminded not to leave our mitts or scarves outside; if we did, we would never see them again. These birds were very hard to see, not because of their colours but because of the swiftness of their movements. They pick up anything that they could possibly carry. They can be the cause of much labour amongst women, for they have to remake what the wiskitchan have stolen. If one of them is seen, then it is quickly shoo-shooed away. Usually, little boys are given the job of chasing them off. For some reason, they are not allowed to be killed, but I have never had this explained to me.

IT WAS PEACEFUL

By the beginning of April, the men were talking about moving to a good goose-hunting area. Grandfather decided that the whole camp should move because we had to move anyway to get back to Cape Hope Island before the ice got too thin on the sea. At that time, Charlton Island was the best goose-hunting area known by the James Bay people.

After spending time on the south side of the island, we moved to the northeast; there, it is hilly with rock, and some parts mushy with partridge berry patches, which are impossible to reach because of the swamp. It is here the geese come to feed and nestle and get fat. Men have to take chances to shoot them while they are flying in order to avoid the swamp. It was here that my brother shot his first goose, which I got thoroughly excited about. Excitement always made me forget about traditions and customs. My brother and I may have never gotten along peacefully, but whatever he did for the first time was always so lifting for me. That is when traditions and customs fell on me and seemed to punish me for being so mean to my brother, because I do not remember ever keeping what he brought home. Whatever he killed for the first time always went to his sanariarruk—his builder. That surely brought my dignity right down to the ground. It would take me a couple of days to get over my disappointment at not being able to enjoy my brother's hunting success.

It was a beautiful April month; the sun was shining, beating down, doing its job to quickly melt the snow and thin the ice on the sea. Men never seemed to sleep now—they just watched the geese. My father would sit for hours at the point, not far from camp, dressed in dull-coloured clothing so he would not be spotted by the birds. My brother and I would take turns bringing him tea during the day. But by the time he came home, we would be asleep. Waking up the next morning, the aroma of fresh goose cooking would hit my sense of smell. I would pop up my head to see who was up, and there was my grandmother, already plucking more geese.

No matter whether she was sitting with her back to me or sideways, she would know that I was awake. "Mini, you will bear unhealthy children if you stay in bed any longer. Go out and look at the world." My imagination would really go to work, and I would picture my unhealthy children. But I never did picture a baby of my own; always it would be people I knew with some kind of handicap. My uncle, who was crippled, would flash through my mind; one of our dogs who had one small eye; an Indian man who walked with twitching movements. (It is only today that I understand what my grandmother meant by "unhealthy": those who are spoiled, lazy or unkind, liars, stealers, cheaters and hypocrites.) How could I form those kinds of children just by staying in bed a few more minutes? Customs and customs, so I had to get up and look at the world around me; it was peaceful.

NO MORE BABY HAMMOCKS

The goose hunt could never last long—the thinning of the ice always pressured us to move before it got too dangerous to travel on. But before we left the area, the men had to get seals, which by this time were basking on the ice. My father decided one morning to take my brother and me.

As we left the camp, with nothing on the sled but the three of us and a grub box, the dogs just shot out after their long wait for freedom. My brother and I sat behind our father, hearing every command he made to the dogs. It was all such a new experience. This was the first time we had ridden on the sled without being put in the uqugusik—the hammock-shaped baby place. It made me realize that we were being treated as growing-up. It was very different and much more strict for us, not being able to move or talk too loud. For in uqugusik, we were always able to play and talk and move any way we wanted. Our voices did not disturb the working dogs as we were muffled by canvas and blankets. I found it strenuous just sitting on the sled, not able to fool around, but it was something else that my brother and I had to get used to.

Finally, our father turned around for a minute and asked us to scan the horizon for the seals. This was also new knowledge to be learned. Then I saw something dark quite far away and poked my father on the back and pointed to what I saw. He looked and then turned back at me and said with a very loving voice: "Old woman," which meant it was no seal at all but a dirty-looking piece of protruding ice. How silly I felt! Suddenly Father stopped the dogs and directed my brother to keep the dogs quiet with the whip. He started off to stalk a seal, slowly, stopping now and then until the seal put his head down. Here, I was feeling very tense. All the alertness that I was taught to have was working very hard. I wanted to watch my father, but my brother and I had the job of keeping the dogs quiet. Not all of them were willing to rest; a couple were very alert and kept making anxiety noises. My brother said, "Keep ready to jump on the sled; when the dogs hear the shot, they will not wait for you." I pictured myself being left behind and not ever catching up. That made my tense body even more tense. My brother just seemed so relaxed. I stood near him and wondered, is he not afraid? Will he be able to handle the dogs? This is also his first trip out, but maybe it was natural for him—after all, he will grow up as a hunter.

I think it took ten or fifteen minutes for Father to get within shooting range of the seal he was stalking. That is a long time to try to keep dogs settled. Bang! The dogs got up all at once and it was one mad scramble—some dogs were too fast for the others, some were caught on the legs by traces, and one was so doped with sleep that he was dragged and his trace slipped under the sled. There I was holding on to my brother's arm without success—my hand began to feel for the rope that was lashed to the sled for us to hold on to, but none of it seemed to be loose enough to get hold of, as my mitts were bulky. I was still trying to make myself comfortable, puffing and trying not to drag my feet, when we reached my father and one dead seal. There was one mad scramble all over again—the dogs were so excited and began to compete to see who could get closest to the seal and who could lick most of the blood. A couple of them began to fight, just like they were telling each other, "How dare you lick on my side? I was here first!" And out came the whip, not really aiming at one dog in particular. Father just cracked it over them all, but the two never stopped fighting until Father pulled one away by the trace. Then he had to quiet them down. He said that there were two seals at this hole, by the looks of the area where they were basking. He more or less told himself that, as he probably felt that we were not adult enough to hear such news.

When the dogs were all settled, he motioned my brother toward the seal breathing hole. I could hear him saying, "The seal will soon come up for air, and this one you will harpoon." My little heart jumped. How cruel of my father to burden my little brother with such a responsibility! I watched him showing my brother how to hold the harpoon; instantly, I could imagine my brother being pulled away by the seal down through the hole, never to be seen again. I began to whimper, and tears came down my cheeks. I had been very warm from all the excitement, but I began to get cold. All I could think about was my little brother harpooning a seal. I could hear Father: "Before his nose appears over the water, aim." Splashing sounds could be heard and there was my brother, holding on with all his strength. I pictured a very big seal, but when he began to pull after some struggle, out came a little seal. The very first seal of my little brother. "Nassiputit," announced my father to him. "You have got your first seal." It hit me then that my brother had begun to be a hunter—the very old tradition and way of survival that my people have carried for centuries.

Father said that we would have tea, also our first. Our grandmother had not allowed it, believing that it was strictly an adult affair to have tea. We had our tea, which I liked only because of its sugar content. Father looked at the little seal and said to my brother, "You again have something to bring to your sanariarruk." What could I say to that? I held my emotions once again, which was too much. When we got back, I did not bother to help unharness the dogs; I did not even pick up anything to take to safety. I just got off the sled and went straight to our tent. Nobody noticed, as everyone was standing around the scene of our arrival. In the tent there was no one, they were all down at our sled. I cried and cried. I never even saw the seal again—it went straight to my brother's sanariarruk, skin and all.

I stopped crying when everybody came and did the usual arriving duties. I guess I panted and acted so isolated that I finally caused an argument between my father and grandmother. Father said: "You know the rules; when are you going to teach her that there should be no ugguanik [sorrow seeing something go, through stinginess]? It is time to start now, or we will have problems, and she will suffer when one day she has to leave us." Today, of course, I know he was not angry or blaming Grandmother, only enforcing our rules on how to bring up children. Indirectly, he was talking to me; that way I would surely change because I did not enjoy the unpleasant argument between the two people I needed most. Inuit parents have long used this technique to straighten children; it is the best weapon, and it saves direct constant scolding, which children can begin to take as a challenge. It worked on me. I had to accept our rules and traditions. Pleasing others was so pleasant after that. My brother and I were out of the baby travelling hammocks—though we still had to be in them on long, long trips—but I would rather stay home and tend the sealskins after that kind of educational travelling.

THE DOLL LASTED MUCH LONGER ON THE WALL

The thinning ice finally forced us to move back to Cape Hope Island. There, we waited for the ice to break up. And, of course, the trading season came. Only parents who had children in school went and stayed in Old Factory—there, they waited for their children's return. Summer passed, and some children went back to school, and the parents returned to Cape Hope to wait for the freeze-up. Winter arrived again, but this year there were different plans for the men. Three teams of dogs went to Moosonee, Ontario to trade.

It was very exciting to the whole community, as Moosonee was considered to not be lacking anything. I was even told that I would get a doll, a real one, not made of rags or stones. I was given the doll, but I never got to play with it; my grandmother's idiosyncrasies would not allow it. She kept the doll hanging on the wall, right above our qullik, our seal-oil lamp. To her, it was too beautiful to play with, so she treasured it. I was allowed only to look at it. I used to climb on the table, trying not to knock off the qullik, to feel the doll, but I was always caught by Grandmother. She never really scolded and only encouraged me, saying that I will have it that much longer. I used to think that since I am going to have it that much longer, then I should play with it and she can hang it when I have had it for a long time. To me, the wall had it and I did not. But I know now what she meant at the time. Still, the way I took it was that the wall would give it much longer life and I was not going to.

NATURE CAN BE MEAN SOMETIMES

The following summer, after that trading at Moosonee, life went on, but the men were visiting each other more than usual, discussing something quite serious. I felt in my bones that something was happening. The women were sewing much more than usual—our old tent was repaired, even though it had already been put away for the winter. I even got a new pair of heavy eiderdown pants made. There was something happening.

The following winter, three teams of dogs left Cape Hope Island, travelling towards Moosonee. Grandfathers Weetaltuk and Symma led two teams, and my youngest uncle, with his wife and new baby, led the third. The rest of the Cape Hope Islanders, five families, were left behind. I cannot forget this trip as it was so sad for everyone. It was not at all like the other big trips that were exciting, with everybody knowing where and how long it will be. It was so sad and different. On our route between Cape Hope and Charlton Island, a terrible blizzard came up and we had to stop. We could not see anything, not even the other people with us unless they were very close. Even then, they were a haze, but we knew by their shapes and by their manner of movement who they were. We stopped and tried to make camp, but everything was blowing away, and our tents could not stand up. All the men could do was try to put up one tent over and over. Finally, after the men had fought strong winds and blowing snow, all three sleds were put upside down to hold the edges of one tent. In this one little tent were six adults, two children and one baby. The dogs were not even taken from their harnesses, just left out there all curled up with one another. Though different teams of dogs can be enemies, they, too, seemed to understand that they needed each other to survive this terrible storm that nature brought on. It seemed rather mean, though it made a good hard surface on the snow, which enabled the three teams to travel that much faster. We would have gotten stuck in deep snow if it had not been for that storm.

GIANT BERRIES

The next day was just like pinguartuk—like fantasy. The sun was out, and not one thing was moving, not even the snow. The snow on the ice was crisp in the cold, dry atmosphere. Every move that was made by us or the sleds made a grinding noise on the snow. Everything was frozen crisp. The dogs were all covered with hard snow, and when they tried to shake it off, some of the frozen lumps just stayed on their fur. Some, too, began to realize the difference from the previous day and began to growl at each other, awaking to the differences of the teams. But they were all eager to move. Beyond and in front of us was Charlton Island. It was so big and so close, and yet we could not see it the previous evening. We had camped right within reach of its shore.

We did not stop at it. We passed an old cabin which we could see up amongst the trees. Grandmother said, "You used to live there when you were a baby." She did not actually tell me that. Instead, she made a remark that my little feet marks were up there near the cabin. A few years later, I asked her why my feet marks were near that cabin. "We used to live there, and in that cabin you learned to walk before you knew everything," as she put it. That was meant to be an insult, meaning that I asked too many questions when I should just listen. But I did not feel the insult as I was too busy asking questions.

We made many stops for tea, for relieving ourselves and to rest the dogs. Later, we arrived at Moosonee, right in front of the Hudson's Bay store. Our arrival was not known to me, as I had been asleep in the uqugusik. I woke to hear my grandfather making sounds for the dogs to be still: "auu auu auu." I popped my head out of the blankets, and I was facing Grandmother who stood before me with an apple and an orange in her cold hands. "Paungaaluit," she said, "giant berries." That was the first time I ever tasted apples and oranges in my whole life. I ate so many that I had a terrible tummy ache for a couple of days. They were indeed giant berries and they gave me giant pain!

GRANDMOTHER SOMETIMES NEEDED HELP

We put up two tents right near the ship and dockyard. On top of my tummy ache, I had a terrible cut on my forehead, made by me while trying to help cut tent poles with an axe. There I was, my head wrapped around like an Indian, right amongst Moosonee Indians. I did everything with my cut, scratched it, played with it, and examined it, until it developed into impetigo which covered my whole face. The word "naniasiutik" began to be mentioned often by my grandparents. It can mean medicine, nurse, doctor or a person who tends sickness. To me, it meant horrible, scary, painful and something that should never be met by a child.

Grandmother made two attempts to bring me to this horrible place. Each time, I ran right back home, taking long detours among bushes, along the sandy beach and up the bank to our tents. Grandmother, as far as I can remember, did everything in her power to make me do her wishes, and she always managed to persuade my brother and I. It was only when it got very impossible that she called on our grandfather to do something with us. For this incident, she had to. Grandfather just took a sheet off our bed and folded it into a triangle. He stood me on our bed, wrapped the sheet around me and turned his back, pulled me against his, then crossed the ends of the sheet around his chest and away we went to the hospital. Nothing was said. I could not even peep a word—I was too shocked. I even forgot all about naniasiutuk. The silence was too overpowering.

Entering the hospital, I panicked inside. The something that opened the door for us made me feel trapped. It had a long dress, a black veil and black stiff-looking stuff all around its face. There was also something hanging on its chest—that something looked familiar because I had seen it in the book my grandfather read to me every evening to teach me how to read and write. This thing that met us at the door brought us to a long corridor, up the stairs and into a little room full of beautiful bottles. There was another of these strange things in the room in similar clothing, but all in white. They spoke something strange together, but they spoke to my grandfather with the language I was used to hearing—Cree. Every now and then both insulted me saying, "Ipiaalu!"—Filthy! That's how it sounded to me, but all the time they had been saying, "Est belle." That was my first encounter with the Grey Nuns of the Cross. They and Grandfather helped Grandmother to calm me down, which she sometimes needed.

GRANDPARENTS SEEMED
TO HAVE MADE IT FOR ME

Though Moosonee was a strange community for me and my brother, we still got into a lot of mischief. Him and I used to take off for walks along the sandy beach. Sometimes, we just gathered junk that we found, which seemed to be all over the entire community. Moosonee was the dirtiest, most full-of-garbage area we had ever been to. No matter how often we were told not to bring anything home, Brother and I always came home with handfuls of old beer bottles, tin cans or whatever we thought was pretty to play with. It caused a constant worry for our grandmother, who thought we were taking things from people's homes. That is something we did not dare to do, as we were too afraid to go near strangers. Sometimes, we took a walk down to the dock area and sat by the bank of the river and watched Indians coming and going in their canoes. We just loved hearing their strange dialects of Cree. Though we could understand some, some words struck us as very funny and we would walk home, trying to imitate their words.

One of the things that seemed so exciting to the whole community was the weekly arrival of the train. The rail station would be swarming with people, but they did not seem to mingle with each other, even though they were all there for one purpose: to see who and what had arrived and to be amazed by the train. There would be a batch of qallunaat in one corner and a mass of Indians in another, and there we were in a little group. This was the time and place where my grandmother stressed that my brother and I be in our best manners or we would never come again. We never had a moment to be in bad manners as we were so struck by the enormity of the train, we were busy listening to the Moosonee Indian Cree dialect and, most of all, we were listening to the sound of the train. Before we could see the train, we could hear it. When it was heard, the excitement would mount and the mass of Indians would start pushing forward to be first in line. We little Inuit would end up behind them and could only see their backs and the roof of the train. Grandmother began to get fed up with this as it happened over and over, week after week. One day, she made a remark, "You little Inuit, because you won't always be here, should have the first chance to see the full length of the train. Therefore, we're going to put you up front."

She really wished for someone to say that, but it never happened. But one day, her preachings worked: "If you maintain yourselves and control your wishes without putting them into action with forcefulness, you will be blessed with them." One time, we were late getting to the station. We were just approaching the end of the rail where the train always made its turn to head back. The train was already making the turn when it stopped. The man in front had seen us, and he motioned to us to come over to the train. He let us onto the front of the train and gave us a ride as far as the station, where he stopped to let us off. Even though Grandmother always believed in not smirking, even she could not help at that moment, when she was getting off the train in front of all the Indians, to make another remark: "Now you can look at it all you want, but I had a ride in it." Even she put on airs sometimes.

I had not known the purpose of this move to Moosonee, but the following spring and summer of 1943, Grandfathers Weetaltuk and Symma and my young uncle started to build a boat. The boat was named *Notre Dame de L'Esperance* and was owned by the Roman Catholic mission. I have since been in this boat back and forth to Fort George and Old Factory River, going in and out of Ste. Therese School, which was run by the Grey Nuns of the Cross at that time. My grandparents seemed to have made the boat for me.

I WAS DUMPED

The boat was not yet finished when September came. We were still residing in Moosonee. It was the time when the missionaries gathered all the school-aged children to enter them into their schools. I was one of them, but my brother was still too young. The missionaries had already come around once to our tent. After that, I would hear Grandmother and Grandfather discuss school and me. Grandmother was very much against it, but Grandfather said that I had to go. It was just like him. He always preached that refusing people in authority can lead to a bad mark on the refuser. I would hear Grandfather explaining over and over that I would be home every Sunday in the afternoons and every summer. Grandmother would question him, "What is her reason for needing to learn qallunaat language?" I never found out how they came to agree, but they both crossed the river from Moosonee to Moose Factory and delivered me to Bishop Horden School.

The three of us were brought upstairs to a little room; sitting there was a great big man who made my grandfather sign papers. I still wonder today what the papers said. From there, my grandparents went downstairs and I was brought upstairs. Grandmother was crying—the first time I had seen actual tears in her eyes since I had been in her care. I did not cry. I was too busy looking around and examining the lady who was taking me up the stairs. She fascinated me. Because of her hair and red, red lips, she did not look at all human.

On the third floor, she brought me into a room with a tub of water in it, put me in, and washed me all over. Her hands fascinated me—they were so pale against my little brown body. All my clothing was changed. When all that was done, the lady brought me down to a huge room. There, it was very noisy, but the noise was familiar to me—the room was full of Indian children. The lady who was holding my hand stopped all the noise with a little whistle that was hanging around her neck. She called the name of Elizabeth Mark. I knew the girl—she came from where I came from. Elizabeth was the daughter of the Hudson's Bay store clerk at Old Factory River. Her parents and mine knew each other very well, and we children knew each other.

At that time, I was just becoming used to hearing Cree language. Though I could not put words together, I understood everything that was said. Elizabeth became my translator because of her dialect; the rest of the children spoke Moosonee and Rupert's House dialects. Every time something was going to be done with us, Elizabeth was asked to explain it to me. As time went on, all the girls were divided into two groups: junior and senior. I was in the junior group and Elizabeth, in the senior. I saw her all the time except during class hours and at bedtime, when I needed her most. The seniors went in a different classroom and went to bed at a different time, always later than us juniors. I understood nothing in qallunaat language, least of all reading, writing or arithmetic. I just loved it when the time came for artwork.

I soon got used to the strange routines that I had been dumped into. Some things I took very seriously; others I thought were just like playing house. I hated to face meal hours because I hated potatoes and turnips, and their bannock was terrible—it felt all gummy in my mouth. I forced everything down because I had learned not to leave anything—if I did, I was made to stay until I finished. A few times, I could not force myself. I would gather it all in my mouth, and out it would come with the force of a strong leak in a canoe, all over the floor. Luckily, I sat at the end of the table. I would be put to bed, my forehead would be felt and my temperature taken. That's when I felt most lonely, in this great big bedroom with two hundred beds in it. There, I began to think about my home, my food and the freedom out in the air. I never fell asleep until all the other children came up. With one hundred and ninety-nine Indian children, I was the only Inuk child, which made a total of two hundred girls. I was learning two languages at the same time, one with three different dialects.

I went home on Sunday as promised, though I only saw my family once. The next Sunday, when the principal and his crew brought me across from Moose Factory to Moosonee, my trained little eyes, knowing how to look over the horizon, noticed that the tents were gone. I wanted to point to make them realize, but I could not. I sized them up: they all looked so huge that I did not dare say anything. We kept on approaching the dock area and landed. Finally, one of the men noticed that the tents were not there. We did not bother to climb up the bank of the shore. We turned right around and went back to the empty school. All the other children had gone home for the afternoon. My little mind told me that my grandparents had not come to say goodbye to make it easier on me. They had warned me in the past that their tents would be gone some time soon, but it did not hit me hard until it did happen.

MY FEET WERE SMELLY BUT THEY WERE WARM

By Christmas, I had found my own playmates, and I had gotten used to some of the routines, no longer being afraid. Even some of the things I thought were like playing house no longer felt like it. But I still hated meal hours. My first church service was horrifying to me. Being the smallest of the juniors, I was always put in the front row of seats in the chapel, as in the classroom. The preacher seemed awfully close to me, his voice so loud, and his face mad-looking. I walked out of the first service because the preacher kept saying, "Mini, Mini." His glance toward me now and then and his arms waving all the time gave me the notion that he was telling me to get out. Nobody stopped me on my way out. Once I shut the door behind me, I did not know what to do. Nobody was around, as everyone was attending the service. I went to the girls' room. I climbed onto the lockers and entered the bathroom through an open air hole that was shaped like a window but without glass. I sat on the toilet for a long time. I wondered why he had sent me out.

It seemed hours before everybody returned. I could hear the girls asking and wondering where I had gone. Why did she go out? Where is she? Maybe she got scared? Maybe she felt sick? Poor little Inuk girl! With all that concern, I began to have a big lump in my throat. I could hear their feet swishing down the hall, eventually coming into the playroom. Finally, when all the girls had entered the room, our supervisor unlocked the bathroom door, which was kept locked whenever the room was going to be empty for some time. The supervisor talked and asked me questions for a long time. I understood nothing of what she said, though her voice told me that she felt very bad. I started to cry with all my might. It turned out the preacher had been saying "many, many" in his sermon.

Long after Christmas, Elizabeth and I got a letter from home. Hers was written in English from her father, mine was written in Cree from my grandfather. He knew that even if I could recognize syllabics, I still could not put them together, so he wrote in Cree so that Elizabeth could read for me. Along with the letter, a parcel came; in the parcel was a pair of kamiit—sealskin boots. Having been away from home for some time, the smell of the kamiit was awful. Some girls began to make comments and vomiting sounds, saying, "Eskimo, Eskimo." Elizabeth said, "Kachitoo"—be quiet—and made a remark that my feet would be a lot warmer than theirs.

I THINK I WAS KIDNAPPED

By springtime, I had learned to speak like the Cree children and had learned their Indian games as well as some qallunaat games, like numbers hopscotch. The food was no longer strange. I loved peanut butter sandwiches the best.

All the children began to talk about going home for the summer holidays and they gave each other their names and addresses. The dates were set for each child to return home. Funny—mine was not. It did not bother me, because I did not really understand what was going on. Nobody tried to tell me anything. I could not even remember what home was like, nor did I miss anything terribly. A group of children here and there would just suddenly take off by plane, or their parents would come and claim them back—at least the ones from Moosonee and Moose Factory area. Then, one day, I was completely alone. Everything seemed to be different. The supervisors that I had gotten used to with their rules suddenly began to hold me on their knees. I ate with them. They took turns taking me for walks and bringing me to the Hudson's Bay store. They even had me in their living room late in the evenings. I got very attached to one of them—his name was Mr. Lake. It was the same man I would meet in Ottawa at the young people's meeting many years later; he would recognize me, though I would not recognize him. He is now the Reverend Lake. Apparently, my bed was right above his bedroom, and when I could not sleep, I used to cry. He would hear me and come up to read me stories and lull me to sleep. He would come up in the mornings and bring me to the dining room, holding my hand. He took me for the longest walks and made mud pies with me, swung me the highest on the swings, and took pictures of me wading in the mud. I think I had been kidnapped, but they were pretty good kidnappers.

THEY CAME TO GET ME BUT THEY HAD NO RANSOM

Before I knew it, the schoolchildren began to come back again. Some were familiar faces, some new and strange. I never got home myself, and the new school year was beginning again. Some children began to ask why I did not go home, and because I was hearing their questions, I began to ask the same thing. The mystery grew and grew until it reached some of the supervisors. One child was told that all my family had died. I did not understand what it meant, though I knew the word death. I did not even ask about my parents. The older children had already accepted this reason for me not going home.

The winter came with the same routine and rules. I began to understand a little more about numbers, reading and the meaning of going to school. Playing outdoors was always something I looked forward to. My favourite spot was near the laundry, right underneath the window, where there was a hollow in the ground that made a nice little nest for me. Another reason I liked the spot was that the window was always open and the laundry matron would peep her head out and tell me how cute I was.

It was one of those days when suddenly, a group of girls came running, calling my name and pointing down at the gate. When I looked to where they were pointing, I saw two men coming. They came closer and closer, and when they entered the gate, my little heart jumped and a lump came to my throat. There they were, my grandfather and father. They had come to see me, all the way from Cape Hope Island. I am pretty sure they had come to get me out of school and take me home, as they had brought all my Inuit winter travelling clothing. All three of us were brought to the little room where my grandfather and grandmother were in a year and a half earlier. Then I was sent back to the girls' room and did not see them again until the following evening. I do not know what was said in that little room, but they never came back the next day, nor the next, nor the next, until finally I erased the memory of them out of my mind. I am pretty sure they came to get me out and bring me home, but I guess they had no ransom.

SO MUCH HAD HAPPENED WHILE I WAS AWAY

When the summer holidays came again, I went home to Old Factory River in a little airplane. It was on a Sunday, and people were just coming out of the church when we arrived. By the time I got to the shore by canoe (the plane had landed on the water), the whole beach, where the people of Old Factory River always anchored their boats and canoes, was packed with people. They looked so many, and I felt so shy. Someone brought me up to the bank and there, in a little group, were all my relatives, all supposedly dead. Grandmother was crying again. From there, on the little island of Old Factory, we went to the other side, where Inuit always left their boats on Sundays to attend Sunday services.

As it is an adult affair to give news about who has died and what has happened to other people, my brother began to tell me in his own way about who had died while I had been away. Two of my uncles had died. One had died from a bladder infection—he could not shoot his bow and arrow, as he put it. That expression was used to explain and to train little boys to pass their water. The other had died of a hemorrhage in the brain. My brother said that he went mad because he had too many things to think about. As children, we were always told not to think too much, because if we did, we could easily go mad. No doubt that was one way to think: to act but to forget too.

Three new cousins had been born to two different uncles and one aunt. The immigrant Belcher Islands had been married to a woman his mother knew in Belchers, and whose mother had asked to migrate to Cape Hope. She had arrived by ship and married the man. The little cousin, whom I had travelled with to Moosonee two years before, was now just beginning to talk and her favourite word was "niurrutissak," the items for trading. Niurruisagut, the traders for goods, was the name we gave to the Frères stores so that we could tell the difference between that side of Old Factory from the other, where the Hudson's Bay Company trading post was. This particular little cousin never moved from Cape Hope during the summer—her whole family stayed with Grandfather Weetaltuk. They came to trade at Old Factory every summer and went back to Cape Hope after a couple of days.

That summer, the mother of my little cousin had informed her that they were going to niurruisagut. At that age, she had no idea what that was and what they were going to do. As far as she was concerned, somebody by that name must be there. They arrived at Old Factory, and we met them down the beach where the canoes were docked. My cousin knew all the other Inuit but me. She thought she had never seen me—she had been too young to remember me. Her family pitched a tent not far from us.

When they were settled, my cousin asked her mother if they could go to niurruisagut and her mother explained that it was closed and they had to wait until tomorrow. But my little cousin insisted and cried and threw tantrums as she kept pointing at our tent. Her mother decided to take her visiting. She had planned to do this anyway, as it is one of our traditions to visit around with the people we have not seen for some time. They came into our tent: the little girl kept pointing at me and calling me niurruisak. Because she had never seen me or remembered me and she did not really know what the word meant, she has called me that ever since! The relationship between the two of us just stuck with that name even until today. My parents and her mother just laughed with loving gestures and her mother said, "She has no idea what it's all about" and gave her a long nose caress. My cousin looked so pleased when her mother pointed at me and said to her with love sounds, "Ee ee, that is your niurruisak."

Today, my cousin is married and having her own children. When I see her we both smile and strengthen our relation with that word, followed by laughter and gestures of understanding that we did not know any better then. Every time I see her, Frères Stores goes through my mind, and I remember all the trading events that took place there. I am sure they go through her mind too.

We stayed the whole summer at Old Factory River. The following fall, before the school ships came around, we moved back to Cape Hope Island. I was kept home that winter. It was so wonderful. Everything came back to me—the seasonal food routines—and again I saw Grandfather Weetaltuk testing the ice to see if it was safe to travel on.

SCHOOL IS NOT THE ONLY PLACE OF EDUCATION

That year, we wintered in the cove of Cape Hope Island. The men mainly hunted seal, while the women and children snared rabbits and hunted ptarmigan. I think this was the year I felt closer to my grandparents and father than I ever had, even though they were always away hunting. By the time they came back, it would be dark. There would be so much to do to attend to their gear and clothing. This was also the year that I heard many stories told by our parents. One evening, my brother and I and a cousin were sitting with my grandmother, who was sewing a pair of boots. My father was out visiting our aunt next to our tent. Grandfather was asleep. Grandmother began the story about inuppak, the giant. The giant was very thirsty for human blood. He had very long nails that were curved in so he could easily claw his prey.

There was this man who was very stingy. He was so stingy that he lived by himself, under his qajaq, so that no one would know when he had arrived from game hunting and he would not have to share his food. His neighbours had given up trying to get him to be kind. His answer was always, "You only want my belongings." Finally, he was warned that he would turn into a bloodthirsty giant and would belong to another kind of people who did not really exist. His usual answer was, "You only want my things." Then, one day, he went hunting on foot and secured his qajaq and his things so that no one could get at them. While he was away, something happened to him. He came back a huge man with claws that turned inwards. As he came near to the qajaq, he clawed the whole thing and pierced holes all over it. This man had become a bloodthirsty giant, or maybe the giant ate the stingy man himself. One of my ancestors who made the story no doubt tried to teach the people not to be materialistic, because it can be fatal not to be sharing.

Here is another story I was told when I was growing to be a woman. There was this woman who could not have a baby. She constantly blamed her husband and eventually became cold towards him. Each time he came back from hunting, she would be distant. Then, one day as she was cutting wood, she saw a worm, which she picked up and began to nurse. For a long time, she kept this secret from her husband. She even named it "Deed" because when the worm said anything, it would sound like "deed." She began to call it "My little Deed." She became warm to everything, even toward her husband.

Every morning, the woman made sure she got up before her husband so that she could hide the worm. She made sure her husband's sock was put back where he left it, because it was her husband's sock that she used to keep her "Deed" warm. One morning, she slept in because she was so tired from cutting wood. Her husband noticed that his sock was missing and began to look around for it all over the sleeping platform. Then he saw the sock right up against his wife's chest and he picked it up. He looked inside and not a minute more could he stand the sight. He threw the worm outside. When the worm hit the snowy ground, it said, "deed, deed!" twice very loud, and this woke the woman, who got up and saw her "deed deed" and the blood which her "Deed" had been nursing from her splattered all around her wood-cutting area. The moral of the story is that the way for a man to keep his wife happy is give her children.

Some of my ancestors were very good storytellers, and some did not have the knack of it. The stories were passed on verbally from generation to generation, as we did not have a way of writing. Everything had to be told from memory, just as we always memorized the landscapes of our hunting areas. Each generation had to carry them in their heads and tell them year in and year out. Sometimes, someone would invent a new one or tell the old ones over and over. Here is my contribution in the memory of my ancestors: a story that I invented as I imagined what they were like at one time—but a story that is not very delightful to pass on to my children.

Nakuk was sitting on the sleeping platform, enjoying his brand new son with his wife, Maviak. He was feeling very happy, as a son is very important, especially in his country, the Arctic. As he ages, he will have a helper and a provider when he can no longer hunt. Hunting is his only source of livelihood, as it is to his fellow Inuit. The main game they hunt is muskox. While enjoying his son, he conversed with his wife, dreaming that his son one day will be a great muskox hunter, chattering away that he will be a great dog-team and qajaq traveller, that he will have the best equipment for his hunting needs, even better than Nakuk's own. Maviak sat listening to him with an admiring smile; she could not help half laughing at Nakuk. She was thinking, "My husband has already planned for and equipped our son while his navel cord is still freshly cut-off." Though she was amused by Nakuk's dreams, deep, deep in her heart, she wished the same.

But, having a different perspective on having a baby, for now she only wanted to enjoy him, to cuddle and love him all that she wants. She was wise enough to know that this helpless child would not be helpless very long. And if he grew as fast as Nakuk was dreaming, she would no longer be able to cuddle and love him. This she had seen in her own family. But at this very moment, what she really had in her mind was a name for their brand new son. She finally spoke, saying, "Nakuk, what about a name for our future great hunter?" By this time, Nakuk was sitting up instead of leaning over the baby. He came out of his dreams and without hesitation said, "We will call him Malittak." He had not been dreaming all the time—he had been concentrating on the muskox, which had been rare during the last two years. He began to explain to his wife why he chose the name Malittak. Malittak means "he is followed." He said that maybe the muskox would follow the birth of their son, and the herds would be many again. His wife replied, "That is a big hope—it is his strength and good health we should hope for. He is only an hour old and we are already asking of him too much." "I am thinking about his strength and good health—that is why I hope the muskox will be many," retorted Nakuk.

Nakuk and his neighbours considered the muskox meat to be the best out of all the animals they hunted on their land. They could also turn the skins into many things: use them for mattresses, blankets, inner boots, and clothing, while the horns became their utensils, cups, knives, sled fasteners and charms. The daily tasks of Nakuk and his neighbours were endless: there was always something to be done with sleds that had broken on the last hunting trip, dog traces that snapped on sharp ice blocks, new ones to be produced to replace the ones that had worn out, new harnesses to be made for the new dogs that are ready to participate on trips. Skin clothing needed repairing, as it wears out on the seams and where the body presses most as it's worn, for a man moves a lot while manoeuvring a sled and paddling a qajaq. Boots had to be replaced often, as they wore out and shrank from being soaked and dried too often. A hunter needed many chores to be done.

They also had the occasional entertainment amongst themselves. Nakuk could still remember the entertainment that was given for him on the day he married Maviak. Now, he was thinking about having a feast for his newborn son. He went around to his neighbours, telling them the date of the celebration. The feast itself was very serious. It was not like the one that was usually given when an animal was taken, which was always gay, with everybody excited and laughing. Nakuk planned everything for this occasion, and he made it serious, more so because of his desperation for the muskox to return.

He chose five persons to take part in the ceremony. Each of the five had to bring a symbol. The feast started off with a gathering in front of these five people. Nakuk spoke as they came around, telling the people what the symbols represented. The first man had three muskox stomachs—he burst each of them and scattered the contents all around the ground. This meant that the muskox would have plenty to feed on. Second was a woman who had a bundle of muskox hair. She went about and scattered the hair—this meant that the muskox will know his place. The third was a man who had piles and piles of muskox bones. He held one bone and flicked every other bone with it—this meant that many will come. The fourth man had a whole carcass of a muskox. He buried it carefully—this meant that no waste should be made of the muskox carcass. The fifth man had bows and arrows made of muskox bones and tusks. He stood them in the ground with the points facing up—this meant that no hunter should kill any more than he needs, and above all never to terrorize the animal.

Everyone stood still. At this moment, Nakuk happened to scan the horizon towards the sea and noticed a strange umiak—a boat. He spoke: "Taku—look." Everyone turned. It came nearer and nearer and stopped in front of their camp. Nakuk spoke, "Do not move, I will go and see." He walked down and greeted the two men who had come ashore. The people on the hill watched and could see the three men waving their arms in all directions. After some time, Nakuk finally left the two men and came back up to his people with a very sad and disturbing stride. He returned to the spot where he had directed the ceremony and spoke: "Today, I had hoped to build strength for my new son. It is not so now, for today he is giving me strength to keep me human. The two officials from the qallunaat world have asked us not to hunt muskox for the next fifty years." He sat down, preoccupied with his private thoughts, while his people began to leave in remorse. He became aware of Maviak, carrying his new son wrapped in a baby muskox skin. That skin, he thought to himself, would maybe be the last muskox skin he would ever handle, and so he spoke to Maviak: "We are very fortunate that our son does not know and will never have to know how to hunt muskox, for he is fresh and will have the strength to be a great seal, polar bear, whale and narwhal hunter. Yes, he is very fortunate; for this we will name him Arlu—Killerwhale—the most feared and relentless hunter of the seas."

Besides being told stories, we also spent a lot of time playing games, such as string games, ajagaq and seal flipper bones, which is a long game. Monopoly is somewhat like it, only the game begins with two people getting married and gradually building a home, with all the first animals that the man has hunted and the woman eventually bearing children. The bones have to be flipped up into the air and should drop right side up.

Whichever bone turns right side up belongs to the player. The opponent takes a turn if one of the bones land right side up. The game goes on until all the other bones that are next in line to turn right side up have done so—if the player cannot get the ones that are next to turn right side up, they do not count, as long as they are not next in line. This game is very hard to explain in writing as it goes on and on until all the bones are used up (the game uses two sets of flipper bones). Every knuckle bone of the flipper is used. That year, I may not have learned more about numbers and the ABC's, but my learning went in other directions. School is not the only place of education.

PAIN, PAIN AND MORE PAIN

And the spring came again. For some reason, we did not go goose hunting but made a move to Old Factory before break-up. There, we spent the spring and summer with our usual summer activities. Then September came, and all the school-aged children were being picked up again.

Bishop Belleau asked the parents to come to the priest's house. Some parents initiated a meeting with him so their children could go back to school. My grandparents would not have anything to do with the meeting. The mission sent a messenger, asking for my father. Father went and simply told them that my brother and I had not been in his care since our mother had died. So, our grandparents were asked to come. Grandfather went alone, and as he was leaving our tent, Grandmother urged him to be strong: "For a change, don't let them take you over!" She knew him well, that he always gave in to what he called authority for the sake of keeping peace and to prevent bad feelings. He was gone for hours. When he came back, he announced that I would have to go back to school. The first thing Grandmother asked was, "What about Miki?" Miki means young sibling—that was the name Grandmother called my brother. Grandfather replied, "Him, too."

Grandmother had never shown any determination—at least, I have never seen her get strong-minded over matters on Grandfather's wishes. She just followed them in peace and with no complaints. Such was the tradition for women to follow that my ancestors created in order to ensure successful marriages. But this time, no one could change her mind—Miki was not leaving, not ever, not as long as she lived. She spoke over and over about her fears that my brother would grow to manhood while at school, that he would become a poor hunter, that he would come back (if he came back at all) spoiled, pompous, not caring, and without any sense of responsibility towards his land. It was too much for her to be left by us. But somehow, she had to give an alternative. She ordered Grandfather (which was also against our traditions—to order a man) that they would go back together to the mission. She gave all her reasons why Miki should not go to school, and she got her way. I had never seen her so determined—it gave me fear to see her talk so much all at once. Her alternatives were that neither of us would go at all or just I would go, but not my brother. She has managed this; today, my brother has never left Grandmother, even though he has his own family. Grandmother was still living with him and died in his house in January of 1974, at the age of eighty-nine.

Much later, I learned that her biggest worry was that my brother and I might get converted to Catholicism. Though she feared that, she decided to let me go to Fort George to Catholic school because it was much closer than Moose Factory, and besides, all my cousins were going to Fort George. But I think it also had to do with her past experience when I did not return home for two years from Moose Factory.

So, I went to Fort George with my three cousins and an Indian girl, whom we knew very well, and her three brothers. There were four other Moosonee Indian girls already on board. We were given all night to pack but had to be at the boat before six in the morning, the hour we were leaving. I wanted to cry so much, but I was not allowed to by my parents. This was something else that I had to learn to control. It was one of our traditions not to cry at departures, either for yourself or for someone else leaving. It is believed that crying for someone who is leaving means something could happen, such as a death while away—in effect, one has practised sorrow before it even happens that a person is never seen again. Of course, I feared that, and it is still in me so strongly that I always have to prepare myself to control my crying long before departure or before seeing a friend or relative off on a journey.

While on our way to the beach where we kept our motor canoe anchored, almost every Inuk came down. My father walked beside me all the way down, talking all the while: "You must be obedient—you will experience no punishment that way. Never tease the other children no matter how they tease you—just go away and do not retaliate. Don't touch other people's things. Just do what you are asked to do—you will find it much more pleasant. It will not be long before you come back. Do not waste your time being lonely for home, because you will learn nothing that way. If I hear any unpleasant news about you, you will have failed me and made me live with embarrassment. And you will not become a Catholic—if you are asked, you have to write to me." How my father knew that all these things would challenge me, I do not know. His last warning was, "I do not want to see any tears when we reach the boat." I climbed aboard the boat, and so did my father for a few minutes to give me a package of gum, a hug and a long nose caress. How hard it was to keep tears away at that moment.

A young priest supervised us to bed after a hot cocoa drink. Sleep did not come to me for a long time. I could hear every movement that was made, the water smacking against the boat and French language being spoken somewhere up on the deck. Before I fell asleep, all I could think of was my little brother, my grandmother, my home, and my duties. Every relative I have flashed through my mind. The hardest thing that hit me was that no one was lying beside me at my bed time. The last thing I felt was the motion of the boat and my stomach moving with it.

I had expected to be awakened at a certain time by our supervisor, but he let us sleep until we woke ourselves. We were already moving when I awoke, and I got very anxious to see if we were still anywhere near my home. I sat up and my stomach began to move. I felt so sick. Someone called, "She's awake," in Cree. The priest came down and asked if I would like to eat. I said yes when I should have said no. I forced everything down. Then I was asked to dress warmly and come up on the deck. I looked all around—nowhere could I see the settlement I had left. There was nothing but land in the distance and just water ahead of us. It was a brisk, cold, sunny day.

I sat down where the other girls were sitting. It seemed everything had changed overnight. There was nothing that looked familiar but the seawater. The whole crew I had never seen, the boat I had never sailed in, even though it had been built by my grandfather and all my uncles. The girls I had never met before. The cousins seemed familiar, but their attitudes were strange, and they spoke Cree language the whole time. Though I did not speak Cree as well then, I understood more. The eldest cousin began to encourage the rest to laugh at me by making comments: "She has decided to become good and go to our good school." That kind of treatment was most unfamiliar of all—for one thing, her parents were very strong Protestants and she never attended the Catholic church at home unless the bishop had landed at the settlement. Then she began to tell the girls how I lived at home, how I was never free from duties, that my grandparents were old and very, very Eskimo. The rest of the girls began to make vomiting gestures, and she looked so proud for having succeeded in her intentions. One of the older Moosonee Indian girls somehow was not impressed, and she told her sister, who was easily encouraged by the instigator, to shut her mouth. My feelings were so much in pain and so lonely that I kept hearing my father's advice. How he knew that I would need it—and so soon—I do not know. I have never told him what I went through and did not ever wish to, because I know what his answer would have been: "Do not bring home tattletales, it is ugly on you." That was something else I had to control many times.

During the sailing, I forced down all my meals. I am one of those people who feel like vomiting from seasickness, but with nothing coming out, which is very uncomfortable. The whole trip took from 6:00 that morning to 7:00 p.m. the next day. I kept as far away as possible from the other girls during the whole trip.

GETTING USED TO IT IS PART OF SURVIVAL

Arriving at Fort George was even more strange. The crew that I had begun to smile at disappeared. The nuns seemed to be so many and all looked the same, except for their heights. The girls I sailed with knew what to do and knew the school rules, as they had all been there before. All of them understood French and spoke Cree during playtime and English in class. I had a little Cree and English but no French but the phrase "Est belle" that I heard so long ago at Moosonee Hospital. I was hearing it again, now and then. Then the local schoolchildren came, some new and some old, all of them Indian children. All together there were fourteen girls, ranging from six years to sixteen, five boys, from six years to fourteen, two priests, four brothers, eight nuns, two servants and one janitor.

I slowly began to know who was who. Everything was routine: up at 7:00 a.m., wash and dress, make your own bed, and line up at the foot of the stairway by 7:30. Down we went to the second floor for morning mass in the chapel. At first, mass always seemed so long to me. I would get very hungry, and some mornings, I would faint and find myself in my bed. One of the girls would come up and get me after chapel to bring me down for breakfast. During breakfast, there was absolute silence. Anyone caught whispering was put to stand in a corner. Each child had a chore and stayed with it for the month, and then it would be changed at the end of the month. My first chore was sweeping the stairways from the third floor to the main floor. Two girls worked in the dormitory, one girl helped in the kitchen, two girls worked in the dining room, one girl helped in the dispensary, one girl in the laundry, and one girl at the Father-house. The rest of the five girls helped in the girls' playroom. I felt a bit insulted with my chore, as it was nothing to me, and there was no challenge. I found it very boring, but I did not complain. Each girl had to be finished before 9:00 and had to be released by their supervisors by then. When finished, we had to go to our playroom, where we washed, combed, took our aprons off and straightened ourselves, then lined up at the door to wait for the handbell which our teacher would ring from the third floor, just across from our dormitory.

In the class, we said a prayer, sang "O Canada" and "God Save the King." We memorized catechism for half an hour, and one of the priests would come up and give us religion lessons. Each of us had to stand up and say what we had memorized. Our teacher would then come back, and we would study history, spelling and arithmetic. All was silence during class unless there was such a time that we had to speak for our teacher. Other days, we would have home economics, such as sewing and knitting, learning ingredients and baking. Some days, we went for a stroll, and some days, we would have library day. Everything seemed to sink into my brain and stay there, but history I could never understand. The four continents or the nine (at that time) provinces of Canada did not mean anything to me. I had no idea what Canada was. As far as I was concerned, there was only Cape Hope Island, Charlton Island, Old

Factory, Moose Factory and Fort George and all the little islands that I knew by their Inuit names.

Our teacher also made certain that we learned the Cree syllabics, which were very similar to Inuit syllabics in that area. She announced that we may have an airplane coming by Christmas time and that we should write to our parents and should know our syllabics by then. That excited me, and for the first time since I had come, I thought about my parents. But I did not think about them long, as we were too busy. We never had idle hours except some Saturdays and Sundays or during holidays—we still had to do our chores but there was not so much routine during those times.

I do not know how we were chosen—maybe we put up our hands when asked—but four of us girls took piano lessons. We had to practise every day for an hour. I used to welcome this hour, as well as class hours, for from the time I was on the boat until my father came to pick me up, I was terrorized, teased, tormented and ganged-up on by all of the girls, no doubt instigated by my eldest cousin. Not one girl was allowed to play with me while we were outside. During skating, someone would push me; at bed time, someone would place a wet facecloth in my bed. If someone was caught talking while silence was in order, I would be blamed. When the teacher was not facing the class, someone would poke my back with a sharp pencil. Whatever chore I was responsible for would be messed up and, of course, I would be told that I did not do my job. If someone else was punished, actually caught by our supervisor, one of the girls would announce that I had told on her. I was not allowed to cry in case my tears were noticed, and I was warned that I would suffer more if I went near our supervisor with teary eyes. I had no choice but to suffer in silence. I was in pain every day with fear in my heart and mind.

Every night, I dreamed about horrible things. The dream that I remember most is when I was being judged by a nun and many children. I would be put on one of those Biblical weighing scales, and on the other side was a sack of potatoes. I would wake up just as I was lowering and lifting the potatoes on the opposite side. I was so alone—so many lonely moments when chores and classes were slack. Christmas came, and we had some holidays. It seemed so long before class hours came. I did my chores as long as I could and took my time either sweeping stairways, peeling potatoes, ironing, cleaning at the Father-house or at the dispensary. In any of those places, I could be me, the girl my parents had brought me up to be: happy, enjoying chores and most of all, free from fear and pain.

BAD PAINS HAVE GOOD REWARDS?

Although I have been surrounded by religion from a very early age, I still have a lot of questions about it. I know my culture had its own religion, but by the time that I was born, it was buried under other religions that were brought in by the missionaries from the South. There are things I strongly believe. For one thing, I have a very strong knack of foreseeing. I usually know when one of my children will be sick, whether for short or long duration. I usually know almost all of the outcomes of any situation I have been put into. When my husband is away, I usually know what physical and mental state he is in. Because I try very hard to ignore this—whatever I have—call it ESP or turnngak—guiding spirit, I also try very hard to question whatever religion I have learned about.

But I strongly believe that whatever bad experience a person goes through, which he does not seek or does not will himself to go through, there is always some sort of reward in some other way.

Sometime in the month of February 1946, one of the servants came down with a flu and had to be put to bed. Then one of the girls got it, one of the priests and one of the nuns. Indians began to come to the dispensary with the flu. There were four beds in the dispensary section of the school building, and every one of the beds was filled. Every morning, the girls that were up got fewer. The whole interior of the school was in chaos. Someone was trying to cook, someone trying to tend the sick, the laundry piled up, the school could not go on. All of the five boys were in bed. Around the fourth day of this chaos, our supervisor came with thermometers while we were still in bed and took everyone's temperature. After pulling the thermometer out of each girl's mouth, she ordered them: "Stay in bed." When she got to me, she said, "Up," and the rest were all in bed. The whole school got the flu except me. One of the nuns who was still up said that Sister Superior had decided to put me in a spare room so that I wouldn't get the flu. I did not believe this, as I expected to get the flu like everybody else. Every day I would tell myself that this was the day that I would be in bed with the flu. Every day I felt my head when I awoke; every day, when I went to the bathroom, I would look into my eyes and search, trying to recognize some sort of sign. But every day I looked healthier and full of energy. I even began to think that I would have such a bad flu because it was taking so long to get to me, but I never got it.

The nun who was almost the first one to take to her bed was gradually up and around. She looked pale and weak. I had to help her. She and I made food and brought it up to the sick. I emptied all the toilet pails at outdoor outhouses. Twenty buckets in all. Each pail would turn my stomach churning inside to the point that my tongue would hang out and my breakfast hurried to my throat, but nothing came out. By the time I got out of the outhouse, I would be blinded with tears, and the cold air would sting my eyes as I ran back to the school. When I reached the entrance, the bucket would clang noisily while I tried to open and shut the doors. This would go on all morning until all the pails were emptied, sometimes twice a day, as the sick were being given a lot of liquids.

In two or three days, another nun began to be up and around. One evening this nun and I headed down to the village to attend to the sick. On our way, I saw a man enter the Father-house. I was certain that it was my father. I tried to tell the nun, but our communication was terrible: she spoke nothing but French, very little English and no Cree (like so many other nuns did), and least of all, Inuttitut. I kept pointing to the Father-house, and she just looked at me. I repeated, my father, my father, pointing to the house, even though I was a little scared in case I was mistaken. Nothing was understood. I was aware that nuns and schoolchildren were prohibited at the Father-house unless it was cleaning time, so I gave up trying to tell her. As we passed by the house, I raised myself on my toes to check if I could see my father through the big window of the house. I was certain that I saw my father's head. I did not say any more.

Down we went, she with a bag of medicine and I pulling a sled, with medicine also. That particular evening was very cold. Our footsteps made a crunchy sound on the hard snow. She did not allow me to enter the houses and tents of the villagers. I stood outside and waited for her at each home. I was so cold and began to shiver. It began to grow dark. Finally, I could stand it no longer and started to walk back slowly, thinking that she would catch up with me. Now and then, I stopped and turned around to see if she was coming. But I got back to the school before I saw her coming. I just left the sled near the door of the girls' playroom, went in, and headed straight to the kitchen and stood near the wood stove. I slowly got warm. When I got warm enough, I went back to the girls' room and started to look out the window towards the Father-house to see if I could see my father or the nun that I'd left behind. But it was dark.

I heard the kitchen door shut and knew it was the nun that I had left in the village. I panicked, thinking that she would scold me for leaving her. I did not dare go and meet her at the hall. I could hear every movement she made, dropping her bag, taking off her coat, changing her boots and shaking her long dress. She came straight to where I was. I must have looked petrified, for she came over to where I was sitting and petted my back and said, "Pauvre fille, avez-vous faim?" I nodded my head and she took me by the hand and went into the kitchen. She fixed both of us a meal and put everything on a tray. She brought the tray into the girls' room and let me eat there.

While I was eating, the phone rang up in the nuns' living room, which was right above the girls' playroom. There was a netted square hole on the ceiling of the girls' room that allowed one to look into the room above. I could hear everything through that hole, which was right above where I was sitting. "Oui? Son père? Oui!" Her voice sounded excited, and so was I. She came down and told me that my father was coming. I could see she was not sure that I understood her. I understood every word she said. A few minutes later, my father entered. I wanted to cry with happiness, with sadness, loneliness, and over all the responsibility I was carrying alone. The lump in my throat was hard and the tears so hard to keep away. My father's teachings about crying stuck in my mind. He looked small and sheepish and looked like he was telling himself that he would break his rule for once, and he urged me to have a good cry. Once he gave me that privileged permission, however, I could not cry.

I sat near him just feeling close, while he gave me love sounds that Inuit fathers make to their children. In my culture, we have three levels of speech—baby speech, teenage speech and adult speech. I noticed that he was still talking to me in baby speech. He could not tell me how things were at home—that was an adult affair. He was not sure how much I knew of teenage matters, as I was under that category, according to our systems of growing. He did not realize how much I had been forced to grow mentally in such a short space of time. So, he sat there telling me how much I had grown physically, and he repeated all the advice he had given me in the past. He brought me a parcel with a pair of kamiit, a parka and a pair of black woollen stockings from Grandfather Symma. Surprisingly, I was allowed to wear them that winter. He said that he wanted to take me home, but I was not allowed to leave, mainly because the priest felt responsible for me. So I stayed. My father came to visit me a couple of times more and then went back home.

Some nuns got better, and also some children. Before long, everything was back to its normal routine. Even the instigator went back to hers, but somehow, I did not care anymore that I was so alone. I found little things to do on my own. I began to understand more clearly about religion—it was being drilled into me enough for me to be able to understand something that is outside of my culture. There was a statue of the Virgin Mary in the girls' play yard with a fence around it, which was referred to as the Grotto. There, I played most of the time. I began to talk to the statue, but I made sure no one could hear me. No child seemed to dare to touch or tease me if I stayed around the Grotto. I was simply ignored unless I moved somewhere else. Every day during play time, I headed there, just sat or stood and talked to the statue. I said whatever the other children were doing—if some were playing tag, I pretended that I was playing tag with the statue, or hopscotch or ball.

Then spring weather came, and we began to prepare for the concerts and stage plays that we put on at the end of the year. The whole village came to see us perform. The girls sort of let up on me because of the excitement. Everyone was wondering what she would be and what kind of costume she would wear. I wanted to express my excitement too, but I was instantly told to shut up. For a while, I was ignored when most of the girls were practising their plays. Opening night came. We had been resting all afternoon, and in the early evening, we put on our plays. I never enjoyed anything so intensely as I did the plays—the way they were put together fascinated me and the outcome was so challenging. After that, every time we had library day, I took out books on plays.

That performance marked the end of the school year. The routines still had to be followed—though not as strictly—and we still had a few little outstanding tasks to perform before all the schoolchildren disappeared back to their homes. We had a sale and exhibit of all the things we had made during the year. The whole school put on a sale of the clothing that had been sent from the South to this mission. The village was notified of the event. Every child was going back and forth from the warehouse to the boys' playroom where the sale was going to take place. I was going back and forth too, but alone, while most of the girls were in pairs.

It was a beautiful sunny day. I came out on my way to the warehouse, about my fifth trip. I took a short cut by climbing the high verandah, instead of using the stairs. I was just in the process of climbing when the father who was principal of the school came over. My left leg was still on the ground and my right leg was on the verge of gripping the verandah to climb up, but before I got on my feet, I could see his feet, with black shoes and the long black dress hanging over them. Whenever I saw him, he always had such a kindly smile behind his greying beard, and he always said something pertaining to what I was doing. But when I looked up, he looked so cross, and his face had a mask of deep pain. I realized that I had done something wrong, I was not supposed to climb the verandah. I said, "Hello, Father." He looked at me rather hesitantly, so I just kept going towards the warehouse where our supervisor was handing out the clothing for sale. Then he stopped me and spoke with his voice so shaky, "Mini, your grandfather Symma is dead! We just had a talk with the priest at Old Factory; all your parents are there now and your father is on his way to bring you back home."

I wanted to reach the priest to cry, but I controlled myself, as I was afraid that he might not allow it. I stood there on the verandah and cried. I think the priest went into the warehouse to inform our supervisor. She walked me back to the school and comforted me. It seemed I was spared from the pain of the flu epidemic but meant to suffer mental pain over my dear grandfather, whom I had considered more as a father since he and Grandmother adopted me the day my mother died when I was three years old.

A MOURNING TRIP

The parents of the local children began to claim them back. Finally, there were only ten of us, four Moosonee girls and a boy, three of us cousins and two boy cousins. Though the atmosphere of torment was not really erased, the instigator began to melt towards me. I felt neither compelled nor anxious to acknowledge her sudden friendliness. Maybe if she had been so earlier, I would have been delighted. I felt that I had gone through enough—nothing that happened or was said to me would hurt me again. This was the girl whom I so feared at the beginning of the year, and now I no longer feared or respected her. How odd that fear and respect can go together. But her sudden friendliness could have had many meanings. For one thing, if my father arrived to take me back home, she would have to wait another four weeks before the ship arrived to take her back home. It could have been anything, but I did not care to analyze it at the time, and nor do I now.

My father arrived and had a message that all my cousins were expected by their parents to come back home with him. The priest in charge felt very responsible for us and therefore asked the younger priest to accompany us on our way.

It was a beautiful June month. We left Fort George early in the morning. The sun was beating down, warming the air. Hudson Bay was so calm that one felt like walking on the water—it looked like beautiful blue ice. There was not a wave stirring, and all one could hear were seagulls fighting over a fish or sea-clam. We travelled in one motor canoe, and we towed another that contained our belongings. When the two canoes were all readied, we boarded, and my father expertly examined the motor. With a flick of his hands and one pull on the string, the motor started and off we went.

As we got further out, the familiar smell of the sea got into my nostrils. My mind was happy but my heart heavy-laden, as my father and I were in mourning. We did not stop until we had found a place to camp overnight. This I could not understand, because it seemed that it was only lunch time. I knew my father would have kept going to take advantage of such a nice day, to get as close to our destination as possible. Then I realized that he had a stranger amongst us, the priest, who was not used to travelling such a long journey with very little security. My father felt responsible for him, as he realized that the priest was entirely in his hands. Though the priest was not a stranger to his daughter, he was to him; therefore, he needed extra consideration—a practice my people have followed whenever a stranger was travelling with them. The priest was not aware of the consideration he was being given, nor would my father sit down and tell him about the responsibility he felt towards him. To me, the two men looked like two priests, one guided by God because of his profession and one guarding the other because of his sense of responsibility for a strange human being. I say strange because he was not used to such travels.

After our meal, the priest let us wade in the ponds and puddles. He was an avid photographer, and he took movies of the trip and of us children wading. When the tents were being pitched up, the priest had more items and junk than any of us. I have always remembered him whenever I have seen an anthropologist getting ready to go to the Arctic. They are the worst junk carriers that I have met—junk in the sense that the items they take with them are unnecessary. Sometimes they brought items that they did not even unpack for the whole year of their stay in the North. They cause the biggest sense of responsibility to their guides during travel. I know because I am married to one, though I have tamed him a bit about packing over the years.

The next day it was raining, so my father decided to stay put. Toward the evening, it began to thunder and thunder. It began to rain and rain. The lightning came down very low and boom! went the thunder in our ears. Sometimes it shook the very ground we were sitting on. The girls shared one tent with the priest and the boys with my father. All of us girls had been warned by our parents about shining objects during thunderstorms. Three of us tried to tell the priest to hide his cross and to cover his steel camera trunk, which was right between him and us. He, of course, did not believe us—like many qallunaat, it was to him just another folksy tale. For some time, it thundered and thundered. Finally, one of the girls gave up a blanket and covered the trunk. I woke up hearing the priest laughing with his little chuckle. All three of us put our heads up and turned to face him. He was pointing to the trunk that served as a divider between him and us and asked with a big grin on his face, "What is this?" It was too early for me to take up his challenge, so we made no comment and put our heads down again, despite his wish for us to get up now for breakfast. But we all reluctantly got up and ate with everybody. Outside, our tent looked like nothing had happened; the only trace of the rainy thunderstorm was the smell of the wet air. The priest was teasing us all day about covering up his trunk, so we told him that it made the thunder go away. Apparently, my father had been out most of the night checking and making sure that the tide did not carry away our canoes.

MINI'S PATERNAL GRANDMOTHER, EMILY AODLA (NEE CROW), AT OLD FACTORY, C. 1950.

MINI'S PATERNAL GRANDFATHER, SYMMA (SIMON) AODLA, AT CAPE HOPE ISLAND, C. 1949.

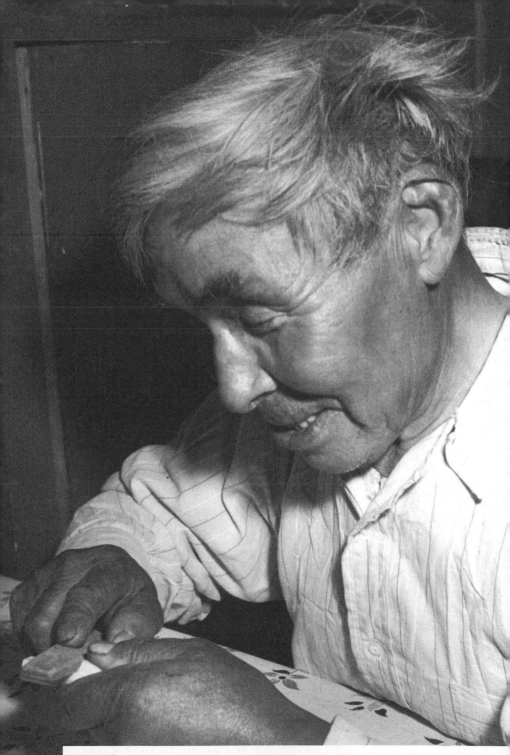

MINI'S MATERNAL GRANDFATHER, GEORGE WEETALTUK, IN HIS HOUSE IN CAPE HOPE IN 1954. PHOTO BY FRED BRUEMMER.

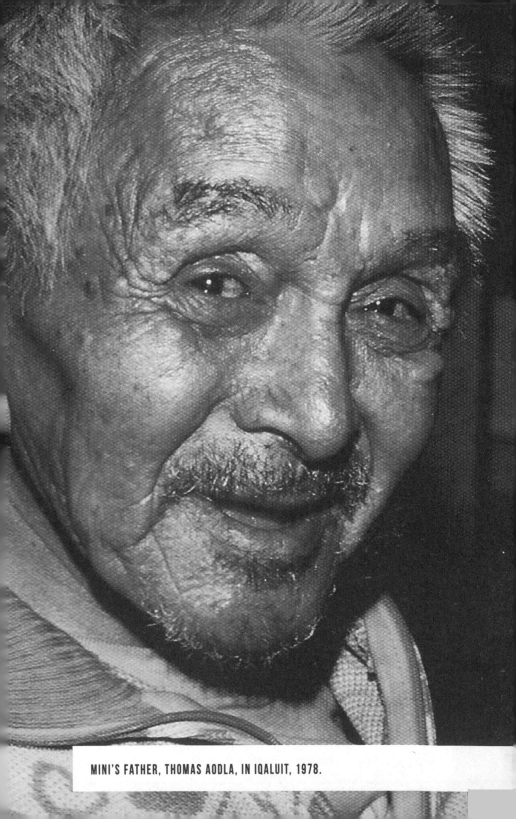
MINI'S FATHER, THOMAS AODLA, IN IQALUIT, 1978.

MINI AT HOME FOR THE HOLIDAYS AT HER FATHER'S SUMMER HOUSE AT OLD FACTORY, 1959.

MINI AT AGE 16 IN HAMILTON, WHERE SHE WAS INTERPRETING AT THE HOSPITAL AND TRAINING AS A NURSE. PHOTO BY MINI'S COUSIN, ANNIE WEETALTUK.

MINI IN 1958 IN MOOSE FACTORY, WHERE SHE WAS WORKING AS A NANNY. PHOTO BY KATHLEEN CARSTON.

THIS PHOTOGRAPH TAKEN OF MINI IN OTTAWA, C. 1959, WAS USED TO SUGGEST THAT INUIT WERE NOW BUYING CANADA SAVINGS BONDS.

MINI AND HER HUSBAND, MILTON FREEMAN, IN OTTAWA, 1972.

From Fort George to Old Factory River is about one hundred and fifty miles, not counting the fjords and points one has to follow to keep a safe distance from the shore. I know that a ship can leave Fort George at six in the morning and arrive at six in the evening, provided the weather is good throughout the trip. But with a little canoe and motor, it took us about a week and a half. As we neared Old Factory River, we began to see Indian camps. We had tea at one camp, only because my father knew them, and we got some sun-dried fish. How familiar the fish was! The Indians, always hospitable to my father, laid down a lot of fish in front of our tea fire. I had two fish and was ready to have another when my father said, "Mini, think. You have not had that for a long time—don't have too much all at once too soon." Gradual eating habits are practised in my culture—if one has not had a particular food for a long time, one does not eat too much at once as it can cause a nauseating sickness to the stomach which we call "kavalinniq"—turned right off from too much indulgence. (One can also kava—turn off—especially from boring types of people.)

After our tea, we proceeded on our way, until finally we went around the bend of a long point that cups the Old Factory River. Across that point, every scene was familiar. I had come to recognize that place after our year-in, year-out arrivals at Old Factory River—it clicked in my mind years ago to make me know that I had arrived at my summer home. All of us began to look at each other. I looked at my father, who was steering the motor. He smiled with that ugly, kindly, sun-tanned face but looked so tired and heavy-laden. I was filled with excitement, but also sadness, knowing that no one would come to meet me at the beach where we docked our canoes, which is our tradition when there has been death in the family. As we approached the beach, we could see that all the Indians and Inuit relatives of my cousins were all there. My brother and grandmother were the only ones missing. Once again, I could hear all around me the sympathies that I had heard so long ago when my mother had died.

My father told me to go on ahead, as he had to attend to the gear and see the young priest to his destination—right up to the priest-house—to relieve his sense of responsibilities towards him. Aunts and uncles walked along and pointed out our tent. I entered, and there Grandmother sat, crying, and Brother looking so sad. I could not hold my own tears, so

I sobbed silently. Grandmother no longer looked tall and proud as she always had. She looked so tiny and lost. Even her corner of the tent was very unorganized. Certainly the head of the family was missing! She was all in black—even her sealskin boots had black trim. When she realized that I, too, was crying, she spoke: "We will let him rest in peace." She stopped crying and soothed me. Then she turned to me and said, "We will see if your mind is as womanly as your body appears to be. My, you have grown into a woman!" Though I knew that she was complimenting me, somehow, it did not seem important how much I had grown womanly. All I asked in my mind was, "How are you going to do, Grandma?" I knew that, like all Inuit women with a quiet and reserved nature, she had always been the backbone of our family, and in that respect, she was strong. But I knew she had lost the companion that she had come to rely on morally since she was fourteen years old, and now, she was fifty-two.

My brother sat at the other side of the sleeping platform looking grown and sad. Grandmother ordered him to go and help our father with the gear. In a while, they both came back. Father dropped all his gear, which Grandmother later had to tend, near the doorway. He sat down and had his hot coffee without a word, still as quiet as he always had been. Only his face showed that he had sudden responsibilities ahead of him. After his coffee, he spoke to Grandmother: "I know it is hard for you, but they [meaning my brother and me] are both young, and we must try our best to erase the constant reminder of death among us." He was only following our tradition of not putting his children in an atmosphere of sadness. If only he had known how much my mind had grown in such a short space of time, to be able now to understand his silent suffering—the speech I could have made for him would have broken him into pieces. I let our tradition take its own course. But it took a week for me to realize how much I missed my grandfather, only when things were not done that were usually done when he was around, such as always having plenty of food and meat. Usually, by this time of the year, our fish nets were in the water, but they were still bundled up in a burlap bag, just the way he had put them away after mending and straightening them out, all set for the next use. It was indeed a mourning trip in every way.

DESPERATE CHANCE

It was not long after our arrival that my father became very sick—so sick that he began to talk while delirious from a high temperature. Everyone who had some kind of knowledge of medicine was asked to see him: the Catholic missionaries, the Hudson's Bay manager, the Anglican minister, the owner of the Frères stores. Father was so sick that he could not even take the shine of daylight, it pained his eyes. Our tent had to be covered with dark material and our stove constantly on fire, as he was shivery and cold. It was predicted that he would not live.

One of the constant visitors was the wife of the Frères store owner; no doubt, she felt she owed much to my father, as he was the one who took her to Fort George when she needed transportation and could not wait for the ships. He had worked for her family for so long that her three sons treated him like he was one of the family. She came in to see my father almost every day and looked desperate what to do. Then, one day, her visits gave me an idea. I knew that she lacked no spices, and I was certain that she would have mustard. My only problem was to get the nerve to ask her without feeling shy. But by this time, seeing my father suffer so much was agony to me. I asked her if she had any mustard, and she said yes. I began to tell her about the health and emergency lessons we had had in school—one of the medications we had been taught was a mustard plaster for pneumonia. A feeling in my little bones told me that that was what my father had, especially after that terrible thunderstorm we had lived through as we were coming home.

She was very eager and suggested that we go to her house to fix it, that I would have to show her how. We went up the little hill towards her house, the only qallunaaq-looking house other than the missionary's. The rest were all tepees and canvas tents. I had been in her house a few times—only by invitation from her daughter—and had never been any further than the porch, which was the Inuit custom for children who were visiting, unless one is invited any further. We entered her house, and I stopped at the porch while she took off her shoes. She then invited me into her kitchen where she laid out mustard, flour, utensils and thin cotton.

We went back to my father and warmed the plaster near our stove. We spread it where my father had the pain, right on his side above his left hip. Again, because of our custom that a child is not supposed to express knowledge towards elders, I waited for the woman to ask me how long it should be left on. I told her and explained what could happen if it were left too long. She came every day and asked if I needed any more mustard.

A couple of days later, my father began to be aware of his surroundings and his temperature became normal, though he could not sit up because of dizziness and weakness. He began to ask for food and drank lots of coffee, as was his usual habit. During one of the woman's usual visits, she asked my father if he was pleased that I go to school. He did not comment, but just gave his ugly face the twinkle-eyed, kindly smile that is his well-known expression of gratitude. He began to sit up, and our tent-hold began to go back to normal. For a while, Grandmother would call my father in the middle of the night saying, "Irningai? Irningai?" Dear son? dear son? She had been doing that out of habit for the last three weeks to check if he was alright. My father answered, "Ee, ee," Yes, yes. Hearing him answer without a pained voice let me know that I had done right, taking a desperate chance in using the mustard plaster on him.

WE ALMOST HAD AN INDIAN MOTHER

It was very hot that summer, so hot that the blackflies and mosquitoes never let up until late, late at night. Everyone had mosquito nets inside their tents, so one could sleep without being pestered. One of my aunts began to urge Father to sit outside every day and went out of her way to get the kind of food he was craving for.

One afternoon, I watched him sitting outside. He looked so thin. I wondered why he had never married again when Mother had been dead for all these years. Several trips had been made and letters exchanged with Fort George to find him a wife, as there was no one eligible in our community. One particular woman named Nellie was a high choice of Grandmother's. I heard so much about her, how sweet and kind she was, but that she did not want to leave her home. Her parents had already consented, but she did not want to leave. People said that she had even packed her belongings to leave but always changed her mind. I never knew what to think about the whole thing. At my young age, I did not see anything wrong, that my father had been a single man for all these years, until I began to hear people worry about it. Then I learned that it was not our way to have a capable man live alone for so long.

One day, we had a visit from an old Indian couple. They came to ask my grandmother if my father would like to marry their daughter. My father's answer was, "I would not know how to hunt beaver." They urged him, saying that he would be taught wisely how to hunt beaver. My father gave a polite chuckle to let them know that he did not mean to insult them, and told them that they had a beautiful daughter, but that he could not think of leaving his Inuk way.

My brother and I began to tease each other about having an Indian mother. "Naja—sister—is going to have an Indian mother," and I would retaliate that he was the one who was going to have an Indian mother. Neither of us considered that whoever married our father would be mother to both of us. As long as we had something to say to each other that was a little mean or ugly, that was all that mattered in our minds. How childish we were!

The summer got hotter and hotter while my father became stronger and stronger. His ugly, kind face tanned so brown, almost black, that one could see his white teeth without missing kukkik—some pieces of meat stuck in the teeth. He began to take short walks, and the first place he went was to see his motor and canoe down at the beach. No doubt he was anxious to travel again. He had never been idle for that length of time.

He did not navigate the boat for the mission that summer, which made my grandmother glad, mainly because she felt that he was not that strong. All summer, she kept worrying about him and constantly reminded him to wear a warm sweater other than his thin black mourning sweater for the death of his father. But it was so hot! He would start out with two sweaters and eventually take off both after a few minutes in the sun. That very hot summer passed by with our usual tasks: scaling fish, picking berries and finally, plucking geese. Then it was time again to move back to Cape Hope Island.

My brother and I were still busy teasing each other about having an Indian mother. But our childish teasing shows how Inuit and Indian cultures are different—otherwise, we would never have made such a big thing of it, my brother and I. Many people in southern Canada think that Indians and Inuit are alike. Maybe they share human form, but their customs, beliefs and their ways of living are very different. My father's reply to that Indian couple was not meant to be an insult, but it was true that he would have had to learn all over again how to hunt beaver, just as he had learned at an early age to hunt the animals that his own culture hunted. The background of the Indian couple was that of a very traditional beaver-hunting people, and my father had no doubt that he would have been taught well how to master Indian hunting skills. But that was not the only obstacle, as Inuit culture has many beliefs and systems connected to our way of life. My father knew this, and he realized that Indians did too. He was not about to begin a new way of life at his age. Brother and I used it for months and months to aggravate each other, but we never did get our Indian mother.

We wintered on Charlton Island where my grandfather Symma was now buried. Grandmother and I visited his grave a couple of times, as we camped quite a long distance from it. Again, we hunted goose the coming spring. My brother was the constant companion of my father. I could see Father aging very fast—he probably felt the heavy responsibility that was suddenly upon him. My brother and I got to know him better than we ever had—for one thing, he spoke to us a lot more, either to order us, lecture us or sometimes to tease us with loving gestures. One day, with a big smile on his face, he teasingly asked me if I wanted an Indian mother. I did not answer him because I knew very well he would never marry one, but not because he was anti-Indian or prejudiced against the different race. He knew very well too that the demand of their different culture and the role that he would have to play was something he could not begin to learn now. But my brother and I found it very useful when picking on each other. It was a long time before we ever forgot about that Indian mother, until we found something else to use to pick on each other.

FATHER KNEW HOW TO HOLD OUR TONGUES

The whole camp began to move back to Cape Hope. It was a beautiful sunny day when we hitched everything on the sled and set off. The middle of the bay was quite safe, but as we got nearer to Cape Hope, the ice became very thin, and there were potholes all around the coast of the island. We were about half a mile away from our cabins when I decided to walk along with our team. We had been warned not to step off our sled.We were never allowed to when we were travelling at this time of the year, as it is very dangerous because of the thin ice. It is not the same during winter when the ice on the sea is frozen solid. Everybody knew the rule, the different ways of travelling at different seasons—including my brother and me. We were being treated as growing children and were trusted to obey the rules, so we were no longer put into the uqugusijavvik.

I figured that my father would not know if I took two or three steps—I would be back on the sled before he knew it, or at least that's what I thought. Down I went! It was very strange that the dogs suddenly stopped themselves. Father turned around when our lead dog just stood there looking toward our sled. There I was, up to my armpits in the water, holding on to the edge of the sled. I was getting cold fast. My eiderdown pants were soaked, and the only dry spot on me was my parka hood. Grandmother was yelling, "Get her before she goes down!" No one stepped on the ice. Father crawled along the sled to get to the rear in order to reach me. I looked back at the hole Father had just pulled me out of. It was dark and cold looking! Though naturally I was cold, chills came over me and I shivered. Our sled had to be undone so tediously, without getting off, in order to get a blanket to wrap me up.

Here, my father had trusted me to stay on the sled during the whole trip. My brother and I had been taught how to persevere through discomforts on long trips during dangerous travelling seasons, such as springtime. We had been warned in order to prepare ourselves, since it was our first experience travelling on an open sled without the uqugusijavvik. My whole body urged me to get up and relieve discomfort. But it seemed I had to learn some other way, and that was the last time I stepped off the sled during spring travel. There was nothing else that could be done but go on. The land that was nearest to us was all rock and high cliffs straight down to the sea. There was no way Father could try to take our sled over those rocky hills.

I had seen Father in the past when he was a little bit irritated, when I did not listen to him right away. Now he was so mad that words were not coming from him. He turned to my brother and said, "I will leave you if you step off the sled!" That was his last warning, and we arrived at Cape

Hope without words, too stunned to take even a deep breath. No one else had arrived. There was no place I could go in to warm up. Grandmother took off all my clothes and wrapped me in drier blankets. I could see my father was still very mad by the way he was working, unlashing the sled and bringing our gear and belongings to the site where we would put up our tent. All kinds of feelings were going through me: fear, rejection, guilt, being useless and frustration at not being able to do anything. To cover these feelings, I scanned the horizon now and then, looking for the other teams, so I could announce when I saw them and make it known that I was being useful and helpful. But my inexperienced peepers could not tell dog teams from dirty blocks of ice, and icebergs fooled everyone, including me. I wanted so much to see the other teams first, but I think my father had already seen them when I finally spotted the teams. It was just not my day!

Our tent was up and our stove put in—usually a man's job—by my father. The inside-of-the-tent work and settling-in was the job of women, which Grandmother was doing. I was supposed to be in there learning and helping, but there I was all wrapped up in a blanket, feeling quite helpless. By this time, Father had disappeared to get wood for the stove. By the time he got back, Grandmother had the inside of our tent settled in, while my brother finished bringing in the rest of our belongings. While I sat in the blanket! I could also feel my brother's little anger, especially when he was having to do all the work. But he dared not complain out loud at me, not when our father was in that kind of mood. He was too stunned himself from the whole situation. But I knew that he would make it up when our Father was in a better mood.

The fire in the wood stove was eventually roaring, and Grandmother came out to bring me inside the tent. She already had all my spare dry clothes ready to put on. The smell of tea, gravy and coffee was in the air. The bannock was thawing near the stove. In a while, we all sat and had hot tea, coffee and gravy with bannock. I looked at my father, who was sitting on his own side of the tent. He became aware that I was looking at him. I must have looked rather sad, because in his eyes was a twinkle full of love that lit up his ugly, affectionate face. Forgetting and forgiveness were in the air, and my brother and I slowly let loose with our tongues.

HOW GRANDMOTHER
GOT FLAT FINGERS

The rest of the teams arrived, and every woman and child came in to warm up and have tea. The biggest news was that Mini had fallen through the ice, thanks to her disobedience. Should I speak for myself? Scream? Laugh? Show humiliation? No, I must control myself—that is the custom I am growing up in, so I sat there taking it all in.

It was a beautiful, wonderful, idle time again, as it was spring. This was the time again when everybody got to know each other over and over while the ice was in the process of break-up. Again, people were lending and borrowing from each other the store-bought items that were getting low. The sun began to stay longer and made everybody look brown and burned, while glistening snow caused snow blindness to those who were careless with their eyes. Then we began to get ready to move to the trading post, to Old Factory, as usual. On our route, we stopped at a little island to pick goose and gulls eggs and also to make tea. Everyone took a walk to find eggs. Some brought little pails; others just used their caps. Everyone enjoyed the tea, even more so because of the eggs. I never cared much for goose and gulls eggs—somehow, I connected their taste to rabbit meat, and I never liked rabbit meat.

Finally, we got to the narrows of Old Factory River—from there, we could see the red roofs of the Hudson's Bay store, the church steeple and many tepees and white, white tents. I looked back towards the rear of our canoe and looked at my father, who was smiling, probably relieved that we had arrived without problems. When we reached the beach, the Indians were all down to welcome us. Though we did not know them all that well, they were familiar from having seen them year in and year out—at least, I have because of having been born there. But my parents had known them much longer, as their parents had been around there since the late 1800s. They knew who was related to who, and who married who, who had a newborn child, and who it was named after. Whenever there was an Indian wedding, Inuit have always been invited to help celebrate, and they in turn did the same.

Every Indian had an Inuit name, not because Inuit have a habit of name-calling, but to identify the individuals among ourselves. However, the names varied according to whatever the Indians did or how they were treated. Some names described their personalities or public actions. There was a man whom we called Ijurtartuk—one with the sudden urge to laugh. He had a most beautiful laugh—he was one of those people who laughed so merrily that it was like it gushed out of him suddenly. Then there was Anauligak—person who is beaten all the time. When this woman was a teenager, she was supposedly beaten by her father every time she had been away from home, in order to keep her in line. And there was a man named Qaniliaaluk—big mouth. A trout is also called that. No doubt we, too, were given individual names by the Indians. My father was called Thomas Symma, only the Indians pronounced it Simone as they could not say Inuit words. They meant that my father was a son of Symma. And I was called Thomas Simone utanish—Thomas Symma's daughter. I had a cousin who was called Pichogee—Gum Crazy; he was always chewing gum.

Though Inuit and Indian adults got along and respected each other, and small children did not see any difference, teenagers always picked on each other. If an adult was not around to correct them, they tried to imitate each other's language. As I remember, this was started by a Belcher Islander, who had never heard Indian language. To him, Indians sounded like, "Ochee machee nio nee," and then he would add a meaning in his own language which did not really make sense. But to him it did. He would say something like this, "Taisumani kumassilaukagama"—it was that long time ago I discovered lice. To defend themselves, Indian teenagers always replied, "Alala kami mamarqsautiaaluit"—alala seal boots and lots of sugar. But I have never known of any other discrimination among Inuit and Indians other than teenagers, but they always grew out of them. The reason for this was that Inuit and Indians needed each other for celebrating weddings and feasts. Indians needed sealskin boots every fall before they went to their inland camps.

As the years progressed, Grandmother began to have regular customers for her boots, and as the years went by, she began to know the Indians that appreciated her work and paid her well. She knew the ones that kept saying, "When the beaver man [Indian agent from the South] comes, I will pay you." Every summer, the beaver man would come, but no pay for Grandmother. As the years went by, she made boots only for the well-paying individuals. The ones that appreciated her always made a special trip across the river to pay her. Others would wait until Sundays—when we crossed the river to attend the Sunday church services, they would make an effort to meet her after and pay her. But the ones that did not pay simply ignored her. She knew when the avoiding was being done on purpose, and she would simply say, "He will need boots next year and will have to face me then." So some were forced to pay that way, but Grandmother never went to demand her pay. I knew a family that owed her money for over five years. When Grandfather died, the family came to express their condolences and paid her in full. She tried to discourage them since it was so long ago, but the Indian family would not have it that way.

Grandmother took the money and bought a whole outfit for her arnaliaq—the child she was building. She bought a pair of high rubber boots for my father, summer jackets for Brother and me, some yardage of canvas to make a tent for Father's hunting needs. The only thing she bought for herself was a package of gum, and then she ended up sharing it out. When I think of it today, it does not seem fair, especially when she earned the money. Until the day she died, her index finger and her thumb were slightly flat from pulling the needle and sinew thread so many times in her past, and her teeth were worn down flat from chewing the skins to soften them.

COMMON TO NATIVES, BUT NOT TO DOCTORS

We settled again for the summer. Schoolchildren arrived back. Berry picking and netting fish began. Boats arrived, and the yearly distinguished visitors were welcomed.

My brother and I began to be attached to our father—at least, he seemed to want us around more than he'd had the chance to. Every month during summer, he would take us to the Hudson's Bay Company store to spend the family allowance. He bought us an outfit or socks or rubber boots for the summer. He never bought us anything that was sweet, or if he did, he would hang on to it and give us one candy a month. Sometimes, we forgot all about the candy because he gave us only one when he happened to come across them while looking for something else. He was not a stingy man, but to him, too much candy was too much luxury for his children. If we had a lot of gum and candy, it was usually Grandmother who splurged for us.

It was one of those trips when we were accompanying Father, and we started out early in the morning. Father said that he was going to try and beat the crowds to the store. It did not necessarily mean that there were a lot of crowds in a big line-up, like in the supermarkets in the South. In those days, people in small communities knew everybody and everything that went on, and when they got together at the Hudson's Bay store, they discussed matters in their own time, and never minded who was waiting to be served. That's what my father meant by beating the crowd—it was to beat them before they got too involved in discussions.

Father had some special friends among the Indian men. If he met them before he met the store clerk, he could end up playing checkers with them for hours. It happened that very day we were with him. My brother and I were too shy to stand around the players and watch along with the others, so we played hide-and-seek at the beach near one of the Hudson's Bay Company warehouses. It was fun to have such freedom away from chores, until we got very hungry. We started to look constantly towards the shore to see if Father was coming. It got later and later. Finally, he came, only to check that we were alright and to give us some dried fish to eat, no doubt from one of his Indian friends. He said that we could go and visit some Indians we knew, but not to stay too long. We did not, as we were too shy. Father never came back until very late, toward the colder late afternoon. I did not have much in the way of a warm coat, as it was warm when we left home. I became cold and chilly but tried to keep moving to stay warm. As the afternoon progressed, it became windy. The checkers players began to pass by on their way home, and Father finally came. The three of us went down to our canoe, boarded and headed back home across the river. I felt very cold! I looked at Father in the rear of the canoe. His face, which looked so old now, was concentrating on our route, trying not to hit a rock, as the water was very shallow, especially when the tide was out.

That same evening, all I wanted to do was to play with my doll, and I did something that I had never done before: I was the last one in bed. Grandmother kept urging me to go to bed, but she eventually fell asleep until I dropped something and woke her up. "Are you having the last time of your life?" she asked, for that is a belief when someone stays up late without reason, especially when it involves playing. Father had been visiting our aunt's tent, and he came home late. He looked very surprised when he saw me still up and asked me, "Itikilimaviit?"—Is your anus constricting? For we think that is what happens to a person's anus when they are sleepwalking. I just smiled, but inside of me was an urge to laugh because I had never heard Father use those kind of expressions. It sounded so odd for him to say that, when women usually used that expression most. But indeed, my anus was not constricting. I should have been very tired, especially since I had been out in the air all that day, but I felt wide awake and finally forced myself to bed. Then I lay awake just thinking about playing.

The next morning, I felt very nauseated, but could not vomit. My whole body felt weak. I did not tell anyone how I felt, because I knew I would be put to bed. It was a beautiful sunny day, the sun beaming down on our white, white tent. I could hear Grandmother outside near the door, scraping sealskin with a steel scraper against the wooden sealskin rester. I could smell the fresh shavings of the skin that my brother and I usually ate. We eat them like qallunaat eat potato chips, only their taste is like that of unsalted bacon. Somehow she knew that I was awake: "Mini, come out and look at the world." There I sat, counting my stockings, as Grandmother called it, over my toe, my ankle, my leg and my knee. I found it an effort to dress. Another reason why I did not want to tell how sick I felt was because there was a movie that was going to be shown at the mission house, the first one of the summer, and that always stirred the whole community up.

Grandmother came in and noticed how listless I was, and even Father asked if I was sick. I said no. I sat on the wooden box near our stove, which was still going after breakfast had been cooked. The stove is hardly lit during summer—only when the time comes to cook a big meal. During summer, we made a fire outside so we will not waste valuable wood on the stove for such a short time. The fire outside only used twigs that we gathered from around the tent area or down the beach, or sometimes broken dried-up tree branches. That way, it took only a few minutes to warm the food in the sunny warm days of summer. I sat on the box thinking that I should move around so it would not be noticed that I was sick.

I got up to join Grandmother with the oats she had made for me. Just as I picked up a spoon, my hand felt hot and stiff like it was full of needles pricking me. The pain climbed up my arm and when it reached my neck I became dizzy, and I suppose I fell, as I do not remember anything else.

When I came to, all my relatives were crying—they sounded so far away, and yet when I fully came to, they were all around my bed. One of my aunts was putting a wet cloth over my forehead, pressing and rubbing. The sun was no longer coming in, but our whole tent was covered with extra canvas so that the sun would not hurt my eyes and as a sign to the community that there was a sick person in that tent. The missionary priest had been called and apparently he gave me a shot of needle.

I have tried to explain this attack several times to different doctors, but they do not know what it is—either they don't know, or it would be bad for me to know, I do not know which. But Inuit call it "qisurtuk." I cannot translate it in one word, but it is an attack that can occur any time and it is believed that most people who get it grow out of it. Old people believe that it is caused by heavy responsibilities which weigh on a young mind, a mind that cannot yet cope in an organized fashion. My aunt knew how to treat it because she had a son who used to have it when very young. Sometimes it strikes girls and women who become chilled just before their menstrual cycle. It is also believed that anyone who does not grow out of it gradually grows smaller in size. As the attack occurs, one uses all one's inner strength to fight it, and having used one's inner strength can make one grow smaller. At least, that is the belief among my people. There was an Indian woman who had these attacks and who never grew out of it. Indians call this "ocheepitoko"—the pulling sensation. Sometimes this woman had it once a year, sometimes twice and sometimes she would miss a couple of years. She gradually grew smaller and looked weak and not very alert. Everyone noticed with sympathy, knowing what she went through every time she has an attack. She stood out, as Indian women tend to be tall and lanky before they have the middle-age spread.

My aunt began to say that I had passed the worst stage of it but that I would be weak for some time and that maybe one of my legs and feet would look like it was pulling upwards, which it did. This grows out too if it is treated the way it should be, the patient forced to walk with it until it comes back to normal. The double tent-canvas that had been thrown over our tent was now lifted, which means that there was no sickness in the tent. But I still had to stay in bed. Whatever kind of attack it was, it is common to my people. I hope I have grown out of it, as I have not had it for the last twenty-four years.

SHE HAD COLD HANDS, BUT THE LEAST PAINFUL

Again the first ship arrived and the usual excitement went on. I had no idea that I would have to leave on that first ship to go to Fort George. My father had been told by the missionary that I should have a proper medical checkup. That very evening, my father carried me on his back to board me on the ship. After he got me comfortable on his back, we went out of the tent. My eyes hurt from the brightness of the sun and the day. I looked at the world, and it was just like the day I got sick, the sun beaming down, the air so still, and I could see seagulls diving up and down. Below them were fish nets. Whoever the nets belonged to would have half seagull-eaten fish and big holes to be mended on their nets. My heart went out to whoever it was. The fish nets were another way that my people survived, and it was another way that some destructive intruder destroyed their equipment. At that moment, a heavy loneliness swept through my body. It seemed I could never stay long enough on this familiar ground, on the land that is so much a part of me. There is always something to make me leave it. I wanted to speak to the ears of my father, who was carrying me on his back, and tell him that I did not feel sick, that I was well enough to stay home. Then again, I thought that he too had to listen to the authorities who act so much more knowledgeable.

We reached my father's canoe, and he got the motor going, and off we went to the ship that was anchored half a mile away. I looked to the horizon; it was calm and there were many seagulls flying around. We passed our berry-picking place and I hoped to be back when they were ripe, and to help pick them with the women, when again they got permission to use their husbands' canoes. I put this in the back of my mind and became aware of my surroundings. We reached the ship and Father slowed down his motor. We got to the side of the ship. Father helped me up on the deck, and one of the crew showed him the cabin I was to occupy. He brought me down to it, and there again, I got the usual lecture that I had heard so often at my departures. Father went back up on the deck. I did not bother to follow him because I knew I would have tears. The sound of his motor faded away. I felt cut off from everything familiar. We left within a few minutes. I lay down and began to feel the motion of the ship. My stomach went with the motion, and I felt sick all the way. Some time later, one of the crew came down and offered me a meal, laying it near me. I was hungry, but I could not put anything in my mouth. I left it there untouched. I decided that the only way that I wouldn't feel so miserable was to go to sleep, but sleep would not come, and I lay there reliving my departing scene. It seemed I had done this so often that I should be used to it, but each departure got harder and harder.

Though I did not bother to go up on deck because I felt so shy, I could feel the weather was beautiful. At least we met no disasters on the way. Much later, the same man who brought me lunch came down again to feed me, but I still did not feel like eating. I never got to sleep but just lay there, thinking, thinking, thinking. I found the trip so long, even though the same route had been short in the past when I took it with the other schoolchildren. I began to get anxious to arrive at Fort George. My whole body felt like getting off the ship and never getting on it again. I decided right there that I would never take the trip again, no matter how important it was. Ironically, it was to be my last trip along that route.

Finally, we arrived. I came up on deck. It was still calm, and the sun was still high, staying longer each day. One of the crew helped me into a canoe, and we landed at the Catholic mission's anchoring beach. The same crewman carried me to the school, the school I had attended in the past. I could tell that it was the summer holiday, as the surroundings of the whole school were empty. Nothing was moving, not one sound of humans, but all kinds of sound were coming from the trees along the road, such as birds chirping. We came to the kitchen door of the school and entered. The first person we saw was a nun, the cook for the school, the same one who had been there a year ago. She was still the same, so French in manner and speech. It was good to see her. "Mini, êtes vous malade? Pauvre, ma fille." I just nodded my head. I was feeling weak and dizzy.

She escorted me to the second floor where the dispensary was located. She opened the door and gently, but loudly, called out, "Bonjour?" Another nun came out of one of the rooms, so brisk, a new one that I had never met. She had replaced the old one. The cook conversed with her. I understood everything she was telling her, that she knew me, that I had been to the school a year before. Then she left and the nurse sat me down on a chair. She disappeared into one of the rooms and not long after I could hear the bathtub running. She came back and asked me in what language I wanted her to speak to me, Cree or French. I just shrugged my shoulders, not caring if she spoke to me or not. All I knew was that I had to get to know her. She just gave me a smile, an understanding smile that these nuns all seemed to have in common.

She helped me up toward where the running water was coming from. She asked me to take a bath and closed the door behind her. She had everything laid out: soap, brush, towel, and a white gown. I was so glad to get out of the room—it was so small, and I felt cooped up. I went back out in the hall, not saying a word. I guess she could hear me, as she called out from one of the rooms, and I searched for her. There she was—she had the bed ready and asked me to get in it. She wanted to know if I wanted to eat, and I said yes. She seemed encouraged by my reaction and went downstairs to the kitchen.

I lay down, my body relaxed and the motion of the ship still with me. I looked out the window beside my bed. Everything was still, and loneliness swept over me once more. I tried not to think. Then I heard her open the door from the stairs, and she was speaking to someone. They both came into my room. She had a tray of food, and the person she was talking to was the Father who accompanied us when we went home with my father not long ago. He too was still the same, humorous and teasing. "Hello, hello," he said. "Hello, Father," I replied, feeling shy that he should see me in bed. "So, you decided to come back early to go to school, eh?" he asked, still teasing. I just felt shy and looked away from him. Then he got serious and asked me what was wrong. Of course, I said that I did not know, not knowing where to begin. Then he became tender-faced and said that I would have lots of company later. They both left, and I could hear him asking the nun many questions on the way out. I ate as much as I could, as the motion of the ship was still with me.

The nurse came back and began to examine me, asking me many questions pertaining to my health. She weighed me. A year ago, the other nurse had weighed me on these same scales and I had weighed then one hundred and thirty pounds, which was heavy for my height. I had always been chubby and my face round like the moon. Now I was looking at the same scales—they registered only seventy-nine pounds. I had been very sick! I got lots of company as Father had promised. Each of the nuns, brothers and the two fathers took turns visiting me every day. I got to know the nurse; she was gentle and so patient. Her quiet manner made me feel secure and made me know that I was in good care. What impressed me most about this nun was her cold hands. Grandmother always believed that people with cold hands were the least painful in caring for the sick. So I told myself that I was in good hands. Indeed I was. She was not only the least painful but a very good mother. I did not have one moment of idleness under her care. She would bring me labels for medicine bottles and ask me to label them in Fort George Indian dialect. She spoke and wrote in Moosonee dialect because she came from Albany, the Indian community near Moosonee, Ontario. The days spent under her care were never lonely, and somehow, she helped to erase the memory of my departing scene from home.

One day, she gave me the news that a doctor was coming in by plane from Moose Factory and that he would come to examine me. I explained to him about my attack. He looked at my foot, which was a bit twisted, moved it to see if I had pain, but I did not. They both looked mystified, but there was no explanation whatsoever for my situation. He never came back. After that, the nurse urged me to take walks and go outside every day and to come down for meals in the kitchen, as it was not worth it for me to eat in the children's dining room all by myself. Each day, I went out for a walk, had meals, did something for the nurse in the hospital, either dusting medicine bottles or sweeping the dispensary. If there was nothing to do, she would let me have my own idle time.

ONE COULD TELL
THAT THEY WERE WARRIORS

One day, I asked if I was going home soon. The nurse must have expected to hear that question one day, as she explained without hesitation, "Mini, school will soon start, you should go back to school and learn as much as you can. You have so much to give your people—you should take every advantage of learning. It won't be long before your people will need many things. People like you should start." I sure did not understand what she meant by it all, but I did not argue with her. I could see that it was useless to want to make my point any stronger. As far as I was concerned, I was trapped. I could never get home on my own. I think she knew how I was feeling because the next day, one of the Fathers came up and talked to me further about staying on and going home next summer. I was in their hands, so I said nothing. I put all thoughts of home in the back of my mind. The subject never came up again. I never went home that summer even though I was well and had started to put on weight again. As it was planned, I stayed and joined the schoolchildren when September came.

Some children were old attendees and some were new. No one was picked on, not even I. But somehow, the girls seemed to have split into two groups. The new students had flown in from Pointe-Bleue, Quebec. They were Montagnais Indians, entirely different Indian children who had their own language and spoke fluent French. My cousin, the former instigator, tried to form us James Bay attendees as her group to pick on the Pointe-Bleue girls. It did not work, and she was astounded that she failed to get the group going. It was a very interesting situation. The old attendees knew the instigator and knew her well. When she tried anything that involved ostracism, the Pointe-Bleue girls just would not take it. They retaliated and told our supervisor as loudly as they could about every little thing that happened if they did not like the way they were being treated. When they were blamed, they spoke for themselves and brought the truth out. I began to see the instigator being sent to bed early and to chapel for punishment. Dear, she looked so small and defeated. Somehow, I could not help but feel sorry for her. Somehow, it's painful to see someone who has been so aggressive get demeaned. It does not look like them—the way you have been used to seeing them all your life. I guess her time had to come sometime, and it was now. But she never gave up just the same.

One of the Pointe-Bleue girls and I became close friends. We did everything together: tag, hopscotch and played ball. If there was a game organized by our supervisors, she and I always ended up on the same team. Sometimes, we shared a chore. Pointe-Bleue children also brought in a new game which they called "sept pusheres"—seven pushes. We pushed the ball against the wall in different ways, seven times in a row, without making a mistake. If one did make a mistake, one had to start all over again. We used different positions with our bodies: two hands, left hand, right hand, left foot, right foot and without moving from one spot, we gave each other the distances we were supposed to stand, going around without dropping the ball. While we did this, we threw the ball to the wall and made it bounce once and caught it. Then we bounced it to the wall, let it fall to the ground and caught it, twice. Then we bounced it to the wall, let it fall and bounce back to the wall, and then we caught it, three times. Then we bounced it to the wall with the palm of our hand without stopping, four times. Then we bounced it to the wall, let the ball fall and bounced it on the ground once, five times. Then we bounced it to the wall, let it fall, bounced it once with the palm of our hands, bounced it back to the wall and caught it, six times. Finally, we bounced the ball on the ground, aimed the ball at the wall at an angle, let it bounce and caught it before it fell, seven times. We tried to beat each other at this and tried to finish before the other player with all the required positions. The first one who got through them all won.

When my Pointe-Bleue friend and I played, I would look at the statue of the Virgin Mary and then look at my friend. I would feel sad and happy all at the same time. I would laugh loud and yell at her and say, "You are it!" and run like mad until I was out of breath: She always caught me. For some reason, she was reluctant to use English and Cree language, so we communicated with some of her language, some Cree, some English, some French and then we waved our arms around for emphasis. We always managed to understand each other.

Seeing our growing friendship, the instigator began to spread a rumour among the girls that the Pointe-Bleue girl's brother, who was also at the school, was my boyfriend. At that age having a boyfriend is rather embarrassing to some girls, and that's what she was trying to make me feel, so I would be the laughingstock of the girls. She would laugh—so ugly—trying to get the others to do the same. I took it all in, while my friend defended me, loud and clear, telling the instigator what she thought of her: it was ugly! Every trick the instigator tried to separate me from my friends failed. Then she would try the other way around, but they fought, retaliated, stuck up for themselves and for others. One sure could tell that they had been warriors at one time!

GROWING PAINS

During that year, I did not seem to have much interest in what I was learning. It seemed everything was repetition and not at all challenging. I felt mixed up. My mind suddenly became aware of me. Who am I? What am I doing here? What will become of me? When will I need all this that I am learning? Everything that I did seemed to be so childish, and yet grown-up duties that I saw and did seemed to be too much. According to my customs and cultural upbringing, I was now a woman. But the routines I was expected to follow were not so womanly to me. In my culture, at that age, I was supposed to be married, having learned the skills and endured the duties I have acquired. But here in school, I was neither a woman nor a child. I was treated like a child and sometimes like a woman. Of course, the surroundings did not help, which were entirely different from the surroundings that my mind would fit in. I was certainly at the makkuttuk—the soft age, a teenager's growing pains. But as always, I survived that school year and went home after all the activities that marked the end of the school year.

MIGHTY, FANTASTIC AND MYSTERIOUS

Once more, my parents kept me back from school that following year. We summered at Old Factory and saw, heard, and did the usual summer activities. The following winter, my father did not move back to Cape Hope with all the others. Instead, Grandmother, Brother and I stayed with Father at Old Factory. We were given the new warehouse that had just been built that summer to live in—it was the only house available, other than the Frères store manager's and Catholic priest's house. It was part of my father's payment, as he was again working in the store for the winter. Again, there was no one around but the same people who were around during the winter we had stayed on the other side of Old Factory, when Father had worked for HBC. All of the other Indians had left for their wintering places to hunt beaver. The Indian man who used to work in the Frères store had moved to the other side with his sister. His aging body could no longer take the responsibility.

Once more I was denied the familiar lands that I loved so much. I was lonely, and had only my brother to play and work with. As usual, we did not agree on everything. We did our usual chores and were not allowed to visit unless Grandmother did so. I do not know why the Frères store owners could not handle the store themselves, especially during winter when there were hardly any customers around until December, when the first winter trading was possible. Furthermore, I could not understand because the whole family was there, even their four children. Their three sons were big pompous show-offs who did not do any work, let alone cut wood, which my father also had to do for them. I guess they were rather spoiled, always having had servants.

Our routine was much the same as the winter we had spent on the other side when both Father and Grandfather had worked for the Hudson's Bay Company. But something very strange arrived that winter. It was in the evening, and at that time of year, it was quite dark. My father was outside our doorway, shoveling snow, as it had snowed a lot the previous night, and our doorway was completely buried. Father had to shovel all the snow into the porch to get out that morning and then shovel it back out when he got out and managed to make a crawling hole, just enough to get himself out and off to work. Grandmother, Brother and I had to shovel some more out so the snow wouldn't keep falling into the porch. There was so much snow that winter that the roof of the house we were living in was level with the height of the snow. When we went out, my brother and I could walk on the roof and look down our chimney. Grandmother would hear our footsteps crunching the snow and come out to tell us to get off the roof, or we would come through it. We did not hear her if she called from the inside, and there she would be, just like a whirl of wind blew her out and blew her in again, talking as fast as she could. No matter how many times she told us not to, we went right back at it, while our chores waited.

Cutting wood or getting pails of water were our responsibilities, and also to keep the water hole down on the ice open so it wouldn't freeze solid.

That evening, when Father finished working, he did not come in to have his meal right away like he always did. Instead, he began to shovel the window area, which was completely buried under the snow. It was dark, but he could see enough of what he was doing as the cold-looking moon was darting in and out of the clouds. We could hear him shoveling near the window. We were very aware of him, as we were waiting for him before having our meal. We waited and waited. We could hear when he slowed down and when he stopped, but he did not come in for some time. We were hungry and wanted to eat. Grandmother just did her chores, showing no impatience like my brother and I were doing. We became very aware that he was not shoveling. Finally, after a long silence had passed, he started banging on the window, which he had just unburied.

I looked up, and he was motioning for me to come over. I could see his face, which he brought close to the window—he was bending down to see if he could see any of us. He was saying something quite important. He was not excited—Father has never shown any excitement all the years that I have known him. I could hear his voice but could not understand one word. He could see that I did not understand, so he finally just pointed towards the mouth of Old Factory River. I looked, but all I could see was a pile of snow obstructing my view. I ran out as quick as I could and crawled up the snowbank to stand on top with my father. I looked where he pointed, and there it was—a great big flashlight moving towards us. All I could picture was the train that I was once in so long ago. My mind asked, how could it get here, there is no rail like I had seen in Moosonee. The light got bigger and bigger. It was dark, and we could not see the body, just the light flashing with the motion of riding up and down on the uneven ice and snow. By this time, Grandmother and Brother were out watching too.

I asked Father, "Sunaalunginna?" What mighty, fantastic, mysterious, frightening thing is that over there? His answer: "Qamutiaaluk"— mighty, fantastic, mysterious, frightening sled. We also use the word to describe train, car, and trucks other than nunakuruut—land vehicles. Also, the word qamutiaaluk implies vehicle with machine or motor. The moving light turned towards the Hudson's Bay Company side of Old

Factory and disappeared behind the island. We ran back in, feeling cold and chilly, as we had been standing outside without our parkas. Father was dressed in his working clothes, and of course, he was calm and not showing any fear or excitement. My brother and I were so excited, and could not stop talking or asking questions, more or less to ourselves. We were not getting any answers, so we just decided on our own what it was. Maybe it was a war plane that could not fly? Maybe a train that travelled on snow and ice? Maybe a war truck, like we had heard about so long ago from Grandfather? Maybe it was Jamaniaaluit—Germans?

ONLY BEAVER PELT COLLECTORS

That evening, my brother and I scared ourselves to bed with our imaginations after we ate a tin of overcooked beans and bannock that Grandmother had warmed up before my father came home from work. That was another reason why we did not enjoy our stay at the post. We did not have good meals. My father had no time to hunt, and he would bring home beans, tinned bologna and cans of bacon. To me, these were not food because they did not satisfy my hunger. If we got any fresh food, it was fish that Grandmother caught through the ice, about a mile down the mouth of the river.

Even this was rare because Grandmother, too, had a job to do for the store owners. She had to make dog food for their dogs, which were tied down near the beach in front of their house. Every other night, Grandmother would make an outdoor fire and cook oats mixed with the leftovers gathered by the store owners, which Grandmother had to go and pick up before she started. On top of that, she had to feed our dogs. This was the only time that I would really hear her complain about her situation, not because she had to feed the dogs, but because she felt denied her own wintering place in Cape Hope among the Inuit women. She was torn between a desire to move around with the other Inuit and to stay with Father, who was now our household leader since Grandfather had died. She would leave the house and announce that she had to go out to feed the useless toy dogs. She called the store owner's dogs "useless toy dogs" because that's what they were. Those people did not hunt—they did not need to, as they were used to the food from the store. She felt that she was expected to give up all her traditional ways just so these useless dogs would be fed. That was the only time she complained, but no doubt she too felt lonely for the other Inuit women and her traditional way of moving around during winter.

Brother and I fell asleep, full of wonders and worries about the big light. The next morning was like any other: chores, and Grandmother trying to make our meaningless existence meaningful. Brother and I never forgot about the big light that we had seen the previous night and kept looking for it all morning. After Father came home for lunch, we saw it across the frozen river, but with no lights on. It was a snowmobile. It looked so small compared to what I had pictured in my mind. I was disappointed! Though it fascinated me—how does it move without dogs?—I wondered who would travel with something like that. It came closer, but Brother and I were not allowed to go near, as Grandmother said that it was qallunaraaluit—big, important, avaricious. So we stood outside of the house and watched, trying to find out who was on it. The snowmobile stopped in front of the store. There were two qallunaak men and one woman. Brother and I recognized one man, as we had seen him every summer when he came to collect beaver pelts from the Indians.

NOBODY TOLD ME THAT
I HAD TO GROW STRANGE

Our lives went on in the same routine day in and day out: get up, eat, cut wood, get pails of water, do chores inside, play and occupy fingers, and fight with Brother. But at this time, I began to notice that something awful was happening to me. I had never noticed it in other women, at least I never thought to look for it in other women. I had never been told that I would grow into a different shape than the one I had gotten used to seeing. I began to worry and wondered what was happening to me. My chest seemed to grow. I was growing hairs where I thought I should have no hair. I began to have cramps in my stomach for no reason. I would lie in bed and listen to Father's and Grandmother's snores at night and wonder, "What is happening to me?" I would decide that I would be the only one who will look strange! That I will be the only one who will have hairs in odd places. I would get scared and cry silently. I would dream about the priest in Fort George, standing in the doorway with his big, black beard, laughing his head off at me, and wake up so unhappy. I did not tell anyone. If Grandmother noticed or knew, she did not say anything about it.

I felt so unhappy that I did my chores with no interest. I was so occupied with what was happening with me that nothing else mattered. Whenever I spoke, my words seemed to be sharp, especially to my brother. He seemed to be the only one who noticed that I was unhappy. When he and I were alone at our wood-cutting place or down at the water hole, he would try and find out what was wrong with me. "Sullutuaalussalirpit?" What is the matter with you? Obviously, he was very much bothered by the unpleasantness I was creating by not seeming to care about my chores. Did he accept this strange way of growing better than I did? Or did boys and men just naturally accept growing strange? Did they grow strange at all? No one was there to tell me all about it, so it became something else I had to accept it as one of the things I had to go through.

CERTAINLY IT WAS A TIME OF JOY

December arrived, and Grandmother began to tell Brother and me to start looking towards the mouth of the river to see if the traders were coming. That gave me an exciting lift and made me forget about myself. It was exciting to see all our relatives again and to have playmates for a while. Christmas was coming too—the time when all Inuit went to the missionaries to receive gifts for the children. The missionaries had been doing this for years. Every child had to bring a little handmade fabric bag with his or her name sewn on it before they left for their wintering place, and we would pick them up around this time of year. The bags would be bulging with candy, gum, chocolate and a small toy.

Every day since our grandmother reminded us, we would look for the traders. By this time, my brother and I were a little bit more trained in how to look at the horizon, and we could recognize what we were looking for. Without fail, we looked towards the mouth of the river. Then, one evening, Father came in and announced that the qimussiit—dog teams— could be heard. We all went out to listen, and sure enough, in the still of the night, we could hear the breathing of the dogs mixed with the swish of feet and the crunching sound of the hard snow, and every now and then, a man urging the dogs to go faster. What a beautiful sound that was to my ears. Then we could see their dark movements, and Father began to call the dogs, "aho aho aho," until they all stopped right in front of the house.

All the women and children came in all at once. I should say, they all came sliding into the porch, because our door was like a hole in a den. Everybody was talking, handshaking, nose caressing, relations being strengthened, inquiring, Brother and I being noticed. There was so much excitement that evening. Every woman had a bundle of seal meat for Grandmother, all the special parts of the seal that these women knew she liked best from having lived beside her for years and years. Even her arnaliaq—bring-her-to-be-a-woman—brought her some braided seal intestines, which she had prepared herself. The excitement died down after a big meal of boiled seal meat and solid-frozen meat, followed by fresh bannock and hot tea. That, too, was much welcomed: the meat that warmed anybody up on the inside and brought the natural sweat to the skin. Men began to talk, each one taking a turn, and describing what kind of hunt they had had during the fall, how many tracks of fox were seen, how many each had caught so far, and what kind of trading they were planning on doing tomorrow. Bit by bit, the children were falling asleep, and the women began to make out a place to sleep for each family. By the time everybody was under their covers, the floor could not be seen; everybody was in bed. It certainly was a time of joy to be all together again.

TO BECOME A WOMAN IS EVEN STRANGER

With all the snoring going on on our floor, Brother and I were still not asleep. We took the opportunity to stay up as long as we could while no one noticed in all the excitement. He and I were still goofing around on our bed. Grandmother finally came to straighten out our bed, which she called "piluijartuq"—taking off the loose furs of caribou. The word originated from the time Inuit used to have caribou skins for mattresses, even though now, our mattresses were made of cloth and stuffed with eider-down feathers. In any event, this is what she did after she had made sure that everything was in order and that the stove was off. This is one chore she did without fail, to make sure the fire was out in case there should be a wind in the middle of the night that might blow the sparks inwards from the chimney and set fire to the house. She was not taking any chances, as the house was not hers, and she felt responsible if there should be any damage. This is not because she had been warned about it, but it is another one of our traditions—not to damage someone else's property, not to visit in an empty house, even if we should enter when there is nobody in, not to take to keep, if borrowing, any item or equipment, but to bring it back, not to pick up something that was left behind by its owner.

Earlier, in the middle of the excitement, I had noticed that I passed water every time I did something a little strenuous. It puzzled me, so I went to Grandmother and asked her why I did that. She had looked at me rather pained and sympathetic and ordered me to say no more, because I had asked her loudly in front of all these people. I did not think anyone had heard me—at least, no one turned around. Then I forgot all about it and I guess she did, too.

I sat on a chair while Grandmother fixed our bed. There was a qallunaat oil lamp on the table, which was near our bed. There was not a sound, only a few people dozing off. I felt itchy on my leg, on the inside of my thigh, so I decided to investigate. I pulled my dress up, and turned the legs of my bloomers inside out. I was so occupied trying to see what was on my skin that I failed to notice my bloomers. All of a sudden, my brother burst out laughing with all his innocent might, words coming out of his mouth: "Ha, ha, ha! My sister has excrement in her bloomers! Ha, ha, ha!" I pulled down my dress so fast, not because I believed what he said, but because I realized he had been watching me. I sat there stunned. Grandmother said, "Nauk?" Let's see? So I showed her while Brother curled up with laughter, no doubt pleased that he had found something else to pick on me about. I became curious and looked more intensely. Sure, it did look like dung, "but I didn't, didn't do it, I didn't do it" was all that went through my mind. The more I looked, the more I saw something. There was something there, dark, dry and flaking. Grandmother examined me more closely and ordered me to bed.

At this point, Father forced his drowsy voice and said, "Sualussalip-pitik?" What noisy, careless, irresponsible thing are you two doing? And he turned towards the wall and went back to sleep. A few heads looked up and turned our way. Grandmother dimmed the lamp. She did not turn it right off, as there were a couple of mothers with babies, and they might need the light to nurse them in the middle of the night. I lay awake and wondered what was happening to me, and began to cry silently. I could feel Grandmother was not asleep, as she was right next to me. When Brother fell asleep, she reached gently down under our bed, and pulled out the wooden box where we kept our clean clothing. She took out my bloomers and a pair of thick pants which she usually wore under her dress when we travelled in the winter. She ordered me to put them on and asked me to go to sleep.

The next morning, there was hustle and bustle all around, but more calmly than the previous night. When I fully awoke, I remembered my situation and, covering my whole head under the covers, began to cry. I pretended to be asleep when anyone came near. All my concerned aunts and my father kept coming over to ask if I was sick. I did not answer. I had enough questions of my own to think about. Suddenly, I could hear my outspoken aunt asking, why isn't Mini up and out looking at the world? Nobody answered. Of course, she got more curious. Nobody has ever been able to hide anything from her. She had to know in her own concerned way. As no one was answering, she became louder and louder. I uncovered my head and began to watch her as she walked back and forth in the middle of the floor. Grandmother finally said to her, "Let's go outside," and out they went. In a few minutes, they came back in, and with tears in her eyes, my aunt came over to me and gave me the deepest love sounds she had ever expressed to me. She kept saying, "Miningai, Miningai"—dear Mini, dear Mini, over and over. I replied, "Ee, ee"—yes, yes, puzzled at her. I wondered more than ever what was happening to me. Nothing else happened for a few minutes. Everybody seemed to think deep in their own thoughts. So then, I began to think again about my own situation.

Nobody was telling me anything, and I had no idea how to question them about it. So I went back under my covers and sobbed silently. Suddenly, I could hear my father giving me love sounds, so deep and concerned that I stopped sobbing. I opened my eyes, not uncovering my head. I could feel that my eyes were swelling. I must have cried for a long time. Father was giving the deepest love sounds that I had ever heard and urged me to stay in bed all I want. Has something happened to me that is known to everybody? Have I reached some kind of point of life that I should go through? Nobody told me anything, but their much-concerned and sympathetic treatment told me that something had happened to me that was nothing new to them.

During the day, everybody was getting ready to go trading. Grandmother had planned to go with the women to the other side, to the Hudson's Bay store and also to Frères on our side of the river, not to mention visiting the missionaries and some Indian families that were around the post. But Grandmother did not go—her and I were the only ones who stayed behind. Even Brother was taken by one of our aunts, and Father went to work. When Grandmother and I were alone, she began to talk to me. Mini, this is not play—it is serious. You have entered into womanhood. This will happen to you now every month. You have to tell me when it happens so I can fix something for you to wear. It will come to you every month, unless, of course, a man has touched you, then it will stop. Every woman has it. I understood everything she said and felt relieved; in fact, I felt proud, lifted, and it was a novelty to me. I kept telling myself that I was now a woman, not a little girl anymore, and I began to watch the other women and noticed their chests. They looked like me, I assured myself.

I was much relieved, though still one thing bothered me—about a man touching me. I asked myself if this meant any man. Did it mean I would no longer caress my father with my nose? Did it mean that I would no longer sit on the laps of my uncles? What about my brother? Did he count as a man or just a boy, and what about all my other boy cousins that I played tag and went sliding with? They were all men—could I not let them touch me anymore? And why will I not bleed, as my Grandmother put it, if a man touches me? I did not dare ask these questions, so I left them there in my mind, bothering me. What bothered me most was, how can I bleed automatically and stop bleeding automatically without doing anything? Usually, one does something when bleeding from a cut. It certainly was strange to grow up into womanhood!

ONE DRAINS BLOOD TO GROW UP

Grandmother reached down again under our bed and pulled out our clean clothes box and handed me another pair of clean bloomers. She reached further under our bed and pulled out a burlap sack full of moss, which is used to diaper babies. I felt I had grown both ways—to womanhood and back to baby days. It seemed Grandmother was well prepared for this event. Now, when I thought of it, I had seen her taking pieces of wood out of this moss last summer, and I had thought it was for my new baby cousins. She showed me how to fix a piece of rag and wrap this moss inside and how to fit it onto myself. She told never to leave it around, especially outside where dogs can get at it—that I should not allow the dogs to eat my blood or I would encourage them to crave for human blood. She told me that I should always put them in the fire discreetly, like a woman should, as she put it. Her last advice was that I should never discuss it with my little girlfriends, that they would laugh at me if I did. I was now a woman, and it was my very own affair. I felt elated and so grown-up—I felt proud that I was categorized as a woman.

The traders all came back and there was bustle all over again. I, too, joined in the excitement, but I felt very aware of my situation. I sat near Grandmother, who was dishing out seal meat onto a big dish, with plates laid around it for each family. I was supposed to be learning how to serve food on individual plates, but instead, I sat looking at every woman, thinking, "Imagine, every one of them has to put up with this uncomfortable diaper every month, and yet they do not complain. How patient they are. How can they control themselves not to talk about it when it is such a novelty? None of them show discomfort when they walk...." Grandmother woke me out of my thoughts by asking me to bring Father's plate to him. Then she called the others to get theirs to their own families—from there, their own mothers shared the food out among her own family. Grandmother let me have some tea. It was an adult treat, and usually, I practically had to beg for some. Now that I was free to have all I wanted, I did not really like it. I asked for my usual gravy, and Grandmother said, "Help yourself." She began to treat me like an adult. My body felt drained of all its blood.

ADULTS GET DISAPPOINTED TOO

The traders left to return to Cape Hope Island or to wherever they were wintering. Our family went back to our routine, but something was added to my little sewing box. Father made me a box of my own to store my own clothing in, instead of having them in with Grandmother's and Brother's things. I felt so proud, and every day I opened the box and arranged the contents over and over. Grandmother never complained about it, and she just let me go on, as long as my duties were done. Father sometimes sat on his bed, and I would realize that he was watching me. He would have on his face an approving smile and give me a love sound. It seemed that overnight, I was allowed to do things in my own way. Sometimes I enjoyed the sudden change of attitude, and sometimes I felt mixed-up. I was not reminded over and over that my duties came first. I could play before or after. I could drink tea if I wanted, I could help myself instead of being given something that I did not want. I felt that I was suddenly released from everything that at one time I had thought was such a heavy duty.

I received my usual bag of candies from the missionaries for Christmas. I looked at my bag; it seemed childish, as the adults did not receive them. Every year, my brother and I fought over our bags, comparing who got what and the different colours of the candies, and we did not dare share them between us. Now I was giving some of my candy to him, which he gladly took. I did not feel like hiding them under my pillow in case he took some out behind my back. I just left the bag there on the table. I did not feel like fighting over them. It was funny: Brother did not touch them either, now that they were all out in the open.

The New Year months January, February and March arrived, and my novelty did not come. I began to ask Grandmother, "I thought you said that I would get it every month?" "Not for a while. Sometimes it will not come, until it paces right for you," she said. Well, that I did not understand, but her attitude told me not to talk about it any further, so I let it be. We were quiet. But somehow, Grandmother could always see right through me and said, "You don't suddenly will everything to happen for you, just because you are an adult now. Disappointments also come to adults—it is up to you how you take them."

BAD TIMES ARE SOMETIMES GOOD LUCK

One day, Father came home from work early, acting very mad. His right cheek, under his eye, was bleeding. All he said was, "They do not know how to play or how to lose like adults." He was very mad. We were all dumbfounded, as we had never seen him like that before.

He was moving around very fast and ordered Grandmother to pack. He began to pack too. We did not dare ask him anything. We packed and packed. Finally, he slowed down and spoke: "We do not have to stay here. They do not deserve my services—it is not worth it to have the children lonely for the sake of people like that. We will leave first thing tomorrow morning and join the Cape Hope Islanders." We did not ask any questions, not when he was so mad. I looked at my brother. His eyes were dancing, trying to hide a happy smile. Even Grandmother's movements were joyous. I guess that was the best news we had heard since Christmas. Father ordered us to go to bed early and rise early in the morning, so that we might leave before dawn and reach Cape Hope before dark. We did so, gladly.

Next morning, Grandmother was warming the food when we awoke, and Father was already dressed. Brother and I forced ourselves to get up and act as normal as we could. We ate and brought all our belongings to the sled, which Father was then hitching, and we helped him to harness the dogs. The dogs looked stunned,as they had hardly worked all winter, except for one or two which Brother and I played dog-travelling with once in a while. We left the post. I looked back as we passed out of the mouth of the Old Factory River. I could see that no one was up—the whole island looked still and cold. I looked around me, to the horizon. Everything was snowy. The sun was barely up, but I could tell it was going to be a beautiful day.

Our dogs were slow, and some kept looking back towards our sled, pressing Father to command them. One could tell they had not been worked. They seemed to be glad when Father urged them on. Slowly, the sun got higher and beamed down, making the snow glisten with little dots in rainbow colours. Halfway to Cape Hope, we stopped for hot tea and frozen bannock. The snow under our feet was crisp and crunchy. The dogs never bothered to fool around like they usually did—they were tired, and all took a nap.

After tea, Father and Brother combed the traces. That is the word we use—"combed"—we use when men untangle the traces, which get tangled when dogs go from one place to another at the beginning of travel (though they eventually stay in one place while pulling the sled). No one had to bring out the whip, as not one dog got up during the combing. Usually one of them will try to run away at this time. A dog running from the team can cause all the others to run away too. That could be dangerous for travellers, if they are left by the dogs when they are nowhere near home, far from the settlements. It has happened to inexperienced travellers. Men have walked all the way home, leaving their belongings, when this happened to them. It has happened, too, to experienced travellers who were just a little careless. People have to be ready at all times to run after a dog that is running away, to make sure that the others do not follow. The sled has to be lashed up at all times before men begin to comb the traces.

While Father and Brother were busy untangling the traces, Grand-mother and I were sitting on the sled, whispering (so we wouldn't excite the dogs) about nothing in particular. She was picking up snow and washing her hands, melting it slowly in her palms. Grey-looking dirt was dripping off her hands on the white snow at her feet. She then looked at me and said, "Don't ever make bannock before you wash your hands." She had a sick look on her face. Somehow, that episode stuck in my mind, because I could tell Grandmother was trying to prevent me from asking what had happened at the Frères store the previous night, and I was dying to know.

When we were all set after tea and untangling, Father urged the dogs to go. Some were willing to run, and some were doped with sleep, but finally all fell into an even pace. It was high noon now, and the land-marks began to look familiar. There was the area where Father had gone camping with the other couples when Mother got very sick. There was the little island where we picked seagull eggs every spring. There was the big point that had a tree keeling over in the shape of a human being. It used to be called by the Cape Hope Islanders "nalunaikkutak"—unmis-takable mark. But apparently, when I was very small, and first noticed it, I had yelled at the top of my lungs to Grandmother, "Anana, inna inurujartuq."—Mother, that over there looks like a human being. Ever since then, it was called that, even though it was baby talk. If I had been talking adult language, I would have said "inujartuq." But adults accept a five-year-old's description of what they see in their own way. That mark had borne that name ever since. Just beyond that was Cape Hope Island. What a pretty sight!

We arrived before dark. Everybody came down to meet us. Father looked so relieved. All the men were around him, shaking hands. News was being exchanged. Grandmother, Brother and I were brought to our aunt and fed with good, warming food. All the men helped Father to unharness the dogs, to bring in our gear, and put away his equipment. It was so good to be there among familiar people. We did not bother to settle into our house, as we had just arrived in time for the move to the goose hunt at Charlton Island. We stayed with our aunt, crowded but nice and warm with people we knew well to talk to.

The next day, while Grandmother and Father, along with some helpers, went to our house to gather some equipment that Father left there last summer, my brother and I went around visiting all day. We got fed with seal meat and ptarmigan, followed by bannock and hot gravy in each household we went to. In each house, I was offered tea—obviously everyone knew that I was now grown to womanhood. Anyone who offered did so with pride and joy. Though I was happy again to be among friendly faces, I still had not forgotten about Father's sudden departure from Old Factory. It was not like him to leave his responsibilities. In the past, he had preached to Brother and me to look after our responsibilities well and to the bitter end. I had never known Father to talk about his problems, his worries, or his joys to Grandmother. If he wanted to discuss his personal feelings, it was with one of my aunts. In a couple of days, our aunt told us what had happened at Frères store.

Apparently, Father had been playing checkers with the younger sons of the owner, and Father had kept winning the game. The younger boy did not take it as a game—he got mad—and started a fistfight with Father. Father did not take it and fought back, which made the boy madder. He went at Father and pushed him right against a wall, catching his eyelid on a nail where a calendar hung. No wonder he came home so mad, puffing like an old walrus. People could not understand why some parents would allow a young boy to fight an adult. That was unheard of. Everybody was glad that Father had left. They, the Frères, did not deserve his services—that was the agreement in our camp. That was the news, and it was forgotten after that. So, it was bad times for the Frères, but good luck for Brother and me to be among the people we knew so well.

INNOCENT WOMAN

After a couple of days, when everybody was ready for the trip, we left in the early morning for Charlton Island. It was March month, and the ice and snow were glistening and shimmering in the sun. Children were now warned not to look at the snow too long, or else they will get snow blindness. Every family went. We made a couple of stops for tea, to relieve ourselves, and to rest the dogs, and we arrived safely at Charlton. We camped at the usual place that my people have been to year in and year out since the late 1800s, when Grandfather Weetaltuk first found these hunting and camping areas. It was now 1951. Men stalked basking seals while women worked on the skins. Every person who could walk a long distance tried to visit Grandfather Symma's grave, but no one could find it. There was so much snow that year that we could not even find the mark Father had made on a nearby tree. We all gave up visiting and waited until the snow had melted down a bit. Our lives went on. Men hunted seals; women sewed and tended skins. Children hunted ptarmigan and rabbits and gathered spruce gum. They chased wiskitchans and got their mitts stolen by them. Mothers kept busy sewing more pairs for their children who were careless with their mitts.

Each day, the sun was hotter, and the snow was melting fast. Anyone who felt a duty to visit Symma's grave went. Grandmother, Brother and I visited. We could see the mark on the tree, which by now was seeping sap. Some other visitors had already dug the snow to make sure the cross was standing upright. No matter who they were or how close they had been to her, Grandmother always felt it a duty to visit graves. She would take me with her if anyone had died while I was away at school. From her, I know whose grave is where. They are scattered on little islands, deep in the woods, and some in the valleys. Some have no crosses and some do; none bear the names of the dead, but I know who they are, what they were like and how I was related to them. Each year, she visited Symma's grave, and she accepted his death a little more, with less pain. By this time, too, he had a namesake, my aunt's newborn son. Grandmother called the baby "aipa"—partner, mate or husband. Symma's soul was no longer everywhere, but rested in peace in its grave. She now had someone to talk to, the way she used to talk to Symma.

Towards the April month, we all moved southeast of Charlton to the goose hunt. At this time, I suddenly remembered about my novelty. It had not come at all. I thought back, trying to figure out what man had touched me. Father had caressed me with his nose many times, I had gone sliding with my boy cousins, and all my uncles caressed my nose when we arrived at Cape Hope. Yes, I assured myself, I have certainly been touched by many men. Yes, they have all stopped my novelty from coming again. I was indeed an innocent woman!

BROTHER WAS GROWING TOO

We did our usual goose hunting and returned to Cape Hope to wait for the spring season to turn into summer. It was the most beautiful spring we had ever had. There was hardly any rain and the sun just shone, shone, shone. It was as if nature was saying, "Had a lot of snow this winter, now I must hurry to melt it away." The ice, along with our sled tracks, melted without any help from the winds. People were getting ready to move to Old Factory. This year, we decided that everybody would go, as a way to see each other off, as Weetaltuk never stayed at the post. He went back after trading for a couple of days. The ones that stayed netted fish, hunted ducks and welcomed the school children and ships. Father navigated as usual.

Brother and I fought, but sometimes I ignored him when I remembered that I was growing up. That summer, Father gave him permission to use his motor and the canoe if he needed it. Brother was very careful and did not dare waste gas or motor oil. The only time he used it was to check the nets or to go and meet the ships down at the mouth of Old Factory River. He never had anyone to give a ride to back to the settlement, as all the other more important men, like the Frères store owner, the Priest—anyone who had more importance in the community—rode in with other men. But he always came back with news—that it was the boat of so-and-so's, that the person we have seen before has arrived, that there were new crews that he had never seen before—and always, he had an orange or apple that the crew had given him. He would share the two fruits out in many little pieces among our little cousins. By the time I got my share, it would be half of a segment of an orange. He would look at me when Grandmother finished sharing them out and say, "At least you got to taste!" and laugh his head off.

One evening, Brother had gone out to check the nets. He took some time to come back. It was getting dark. Grandmother and I waited, and every now and then, we would look for him from our doorway to see if we could spot his canoe. We kept listening for his motor, as every motor had a different sound, and we always knew who was coming by their sound, even if we did not see them near. We did not hear him coming, nor did we see his movement down where we anchored our canoes. Grandmother decided that maybe we did not catch any fish in our nets, so maybe Brother was visiting instead of coming right home as he often did, just so Grandmother would not be disappointed with his empty hands. Brother had always been very close to our grandmother. He had never hurt her feelings or disobeyed her wishes. He always seemed to know how to cope and take care of her in our crises. If he knew ahead of time that there would be some sadness, disappointment or bad news, he always tried to prevent them before Grandmother knew. Sometimes he was successful; other times, Grandmother found out before he could do anything. The worst thing that could happen, what made Grandmother most unhappy, was the ruining of Father's equipment. When that happened, Grandmother would have to do some painful explaining for it. It was she who was blamed for what we ruined, as she was the one who was responsible for seeing that Brother and I followed Father's rules while he was away.

That evening, Brother came in, acting as though nothing had happened. In fact, he looked so pleased. His pleased look made me suspicious and very curious. He kept on smiling while he was eating, probably trying to find words to explain his lateness. Neither Grandmother nor I questioned him, for we believe that if a person is questioned or forced to explain themselves, they will only lie. They could turn into a person who has a lying personality, always explaining things away with lies until there is so much guilt inside them. When a person lives in guilt, they lie to cover the truth, because of the experience of being questioned. It is like the qallunaat saying, "Ask me no questions and I will tell you no lies." Only we fear that we might cause permanent damage to people. I sat there, dying from curiosity and dying to ask him a few questions. Grandmother had warned me before he came home that I should not do so, that I should act normal. That was very hard to do. As usual, Grandmother could see right through me. I was itching to get at Brother. But she always knew what to do. She was sewing a pair of kamiit for an Indian. She asked me to fix the sinew thread, so she could just thread them to her needle when she wanted one. Brother kept on eating, Grandmother sewed, and, just as she planned it, I was now busy with something else. That made me forget my urge to ask questions. Bedtime came, and we all went out to relieve ourselves and then climbed into our eiderdown blankets.

Grandmother was already sewing when I awoke the next morning, and Brother was nowhere around. I got dressed and went out to look at the world. Seagulls were flying above the nets making guttural sounds, birds were singing, and the river in front of our settlement was shimmering, shining from the sun above. It was calm, so deep, deep blue. I went back in and fed myself with the oats that Grandmother had left on our stove. I asked her where Brother was, and she said that he had gone down to check our canoe, to see that it was safe in case something had happened during the night.

Grandmother finished the kamiit. I could see that she was tired from sitting so long. She yawned and stretched herself and made a comment about these kamiit being finished, at least. How many more she had to make, that I did not know—that was not for her to tell me, as it was her own adult affair. All I knew was that I had to chew a lot of skins and think about red berries, so the skins would get soaked faster. She asked me to put on the fire outside and make tea; she was going to visit for a while and went out. She was not going far, just next door to my aunt's, probably to empty the thoughts that she had been gathering over the last two days while sewing and fixing skins, and also to catch up on what had been happening next door.

I made the fire and filled the kettle of water to make tea. Brother came back and the first thing he asked was: "Why is our tupik—tent—so empty? Where is our anana?" "Anana" is what we called our grandmother—"mother". There was no special reason why we called her that; at least, there was no ritual when it happened. I asked Grandmother about it once—why we did not call her Grandmother. She said that we wanted to be the same as the other children who called their mothers "anana," and today we still call her "anana." It seemed so natural, as she had been our only mother. I told Brother where she was, and he sat down near the fire where I was watching and waiting for the kettle to boil. He began to talk and sort of asked me, "Would you tell anyone why I was late coming home last night?" I could feel that he did not really trust me. I had forgotten about that, and here he was reviving my curiosity. I did not look at him but just pretended to fix the fire. I was thinking: shall I ask him or just give him the trust that I will not tell? I could easily use whatever he was about to tell me to retaliate the next time he picked on me. I gave him the trust.

He began, "When I came back from the nets, I was late because I had to take the whole motor apart. I dropped it in the water when I was trying to take it off the canoe to put it back in the shed." Some men had little sheds down near the dock area to keep their motors safe from the rain, or in case little children played with them behind their mothers' backs. He went on: "After I fished it out, I took every screw, bolt and little wire, and dried every piece with my shirt, and put it back together." I could not believe my ears. All I could think was, I wonder if it works. Father would find out, and would he and Grandmother get it! I asked him, "Does it work?" "Yes, it works. I tried it after, did you not hear the motor over and over last night?" No, I had not heard it, nor had Grandmother. Probably it was a good thing that we had not heard it, because we could tell the sound of a motor running on land; we have heard them often when men were fixing their motors—it is the most awful noise. Sometimes, though, nature seemed to muffle noises, no matter how calm it was. I guess it had been one of those evenings, as Grandmother would have investigated if we had heard it. I asked Brother, "How did you know how to take it apart and put it back together again?" He said, "I have watched Father, I have seen the insides of motors many times, and I memorized every piece, where it goes, as I took it out. Please, don't tell Grandmother—she might tell Father."

I felt nallinik—love, sympathy, sorry for him. Momentarily, I put myself in his mind and thought how he felt. I felt fear for him in case the motor did not work in the future. I agreed that I would not tell, ever. I looked at him as he got up to enter our tent. Poor little Brother—he is growing and can take a motor apart and put it back together like a man. It is true that he always watched Father when he was fixing something or working on any equipment, like motors or watches. I gave him the trust and to this day, neither Father nor Grandmother knows it ever happened. It has been a longtime secret between the two of us. The motor did work all that summer, and Father had it for a few more years until he decided to get one with a higher horsepower. Then he gave it to Brother when Brother began to go hunting on his own.

After that, our relationship began to change. We gave each other more secrets and talked about our father and grandmother. But we never talked about their good sides, only what we thought to be their bad sides. We no longer fought over our duties, but talked about our only two close relatives, how much work they wanted us to do, how we always had to control ourselves for them, how they always wanted us to look after our responsibilities well. We were growing physically but not so well mentally. But I noticed that Brother was growing, too.

NOVELTY CREATES SMELLS

The school ships arrived again, and I went back to Fort George. At the school, some changes had been made. There was a new hospital that had been added to the school. The nurse with the cool hands was still there. The girls got a new supervisor who spoke perfect Cree. There was a new cook and one new brother. There were more servants, more new Pointe-Bleue children and more Indian children from the area surrounding Fort George. The instigator was not there.

Before the school year started, the priest who was the head of the school asked me to come to his office. He told me that I would have to repeat grade eight, because the grades did not go beyond that at Fort George, that to continue I would have to go away somewhere else. He gave me an alternative: that I should do it and if I did not like it, I would go to work around or by Christmas time. He asked me if my father would object to that. Father had no idea what was happening, least of all that I was going to work instead of learning. He had no idea about qallunaat grades at school. The priest said that he could write and ask him about it. But Father would not receive the letter before Christmas—he had gone to where they wait for freeze-up. He would not get the letter until they went trading in December. So I told the priest that I thought he would not object, though I was not even sure myself. To me, it sounded more challenging to go to work than to repeat what I had already learned. A Fort George Indian girl was in the same situation as I was. She and I were good friends. She too was given the alternative.

Before school started, we all took a bath in a tub behind a curtain in the girls' playroom. There was no running water in the school, other than in the hospital. The supervisor, with help from the older girls, had to bring in the water that has warmed up in the kitchen. While each girl was in the tub, the supervisor came in to make sure they were washing right. My turn came, and the nun came in. She could see that I was washing right but pretended to help me. I could tell that she had things to say because she was not washing me properly. After sizing me up, she began to ask, "Did you menstruate yet?" I did not know what she meant by menstruate, and I told her so. She began again, "Did you bleed down there yet?" Yes. "When was the last time?" My first and last time was in December. "Oh, mon Dieu! Did any man or boy touch you?" Yes, yes, many times. "Oh, mon Dieu! Where?" Here and here, and I pointed to my back, my legs, wherever I remembered that Father, uncles or boy cousins had touched me. "And you have not bled since?" No. "Oh, mon Dieu!"

I answered her questions very matter-of-factly, full of innocence. How could I know that she had other things in mind, things that were not known to me? She ordered me to keep washing and ran out very excited. I could hear all the girls through the curtain getting a bit noisier, because she had run in the direction of the hospital. Some fooled around while some watched to see if she was coming back. Finally, I could hear one of the girls announce discreetly that Sister was coming. This is what we were expected to call the nuns. She came back in, more calmly, and ordered me to dress. When all the girls had bathed, it was suppertime, and we all lined up to walk quietly to the dining room. The rules were the same as they had always been, and the children still had to conform to them.

The next day, first thing in the morning after breakfast, our supervisor took me to the hospital and brought me into the examining room. I had not been in this new section. She asked me to sit and wait for the nurse, the same nurse that had impressed me with her cool hands. By now, I had heard, she was not just a nurse, but a nun-doctor. The supervisor left to go back to the girls' room, and I was waiting in the dispensary. It seemed that I had done this a long time ago in Moosonee. But I was not as afraid as I was then, and I kept my mind busy looking at all the pretty bottles behind the glass doors of the cupboards. I wondered if this nun doctor knew what was in those pretty bottles. I sat there thinking, she must have fantastic knowledge. I did not know why I had to be seen by her. I wondered if I was sick without knowing or feeling it myself. I convinced myself that she will probably know just by looking at me with her fantastic mind. What will she do to me? Will she use all this equipment that looks too fantastic for anyone to use on simple me? Will I be in pain? I shivered. Finally, I could hear the swish of her long, white gown coming to the dispensary. I had not seen her since I had arrived. She was the same—tender-voiced, gentle and with cool, cool hands, such a kindly face, and a smile that warmed you up. I must have looked scared, as she assured me not to be afraid. She spoke to me as she was examining me all over, some Cree, some English, and some French.

Then she began to ask, "Have you ever been touched by a man?" Yes. "Mini, I do not mean touched with a finger, or with your body against any man. What I mean by touch is when you and a man have intercourse." I was bewildered, and she could probably see that, and so she went on: "You see, Mini, intercourse is when a man puts his penis into your vagina." I was more bewildered. "You see, Mini, when that happens, a woman can get pregnant." More bewildered. "You see, Mini, when a woman gets pregnant, it means that she will have a baby growing in her stomach."

How was I to know that she was telling me the truth? Throughout all my growing years, I had been told by Grandmother that all my little cousins arrived by dog team, that someone found them while they were away cutting wood, that everybody decided who to give them to. Some had allu—a seal hole—on the floor where these cousins had come out to be taken by their mothers. Grandmother proved it so, pointing out that the hole in our floor in Cape Hope was such a one. It was a hole where a knuckle of the tree had been cut along with the board. My brother and I had loosened it to play, pretending that it was a seal hole. Grandmother had always made us cover the hole for her own reasons—the wind blew in through it, or mice might get into the house—but she told us that we should not play with it because that is where Brother and I came out to go to our mother and father. If another baby should come in through that hole, nobody would be ready to keep it, that we would be responsible if a baby came when nobody was ready to have one, that she was too old now, and that Brother and I were too young, that Father did not have a woman who could be a mother to one, and that all the other people who could have one already had one. She never told us anything about sex or intercourse, even though we had been well-prepared with what she considered essential for marriage, as far as duties were concerned.

The words "husband" and "wife" were never allowed to be discussed among children. If a child was heard to describe so-and-so as a husband or wife, that child was considered to be knowing too much, and all the other little children were asked to avoid the child who had been heard using those words. The ones who did not use such words described married couples as the "father of the wife" and the wife was the "mother of the husband." I believed in this for years and described married couples that way when I wanted to say something about the mate of a husband or wife. I know now that it was the boys who were taught when they reached an age—the time to know about sex—not the girls. The girls would learn from their angilissiat when the time came. I had not reached that stage. I was utterly confused and did not know who to believe.

The nun went on, "You see, Mini, you do not do this until you are married." Do people do things other than attend to their duties when they are married? I understood her words, but not what she meant. "Did you have nice holidays at home?" Yes. "Mini, have you been sick in the mornings?" No. "Do you want to eat more than you usually do?" I did not know, and I had not noticed. "Does your chest itch?" No. "You have not had intercourse with a man, have you?" No, I do not know, and I do not understand. Poor nun, how she must have felt at that moment! When I think back on that episode, I realize that she was probably caught by many things in her mind, as much as I was. Knowing nuns, she was afraid to give too much information about sex when she was not sure how much I knew. Little did she know that she gave me more information than I had received from anyone. At least she made me wonder what goes on with married couples. Somehow, she had to find out if I had been touched by a man and was pregnant. She examined me, the usual way doctors examine pregnant women, then ordered me to get up and dress. "You are fine," she said, "there is nothing wrong with you. You will bleed again, you have to. All girls do at a certain age, and you are at that age." Well, that Grandmother had told me about. But why had it not come back? Nobody knew, least of all I.

I went back to the girls' room, and our supervisor asked me if the doctor had explained or told me anything. I said yes, without much interest, because I did not really understand. It was so vague, yet it sounded so natural, mysterious, and a bit frightening. (I swear on the solid ground I walk on today that my daughter will know everything.) The supervisor ran over to the hospital, and all the girls went wild and noisy. She came back, looking very relieved.

After that, she asked all the girls who were ten years old and over to come and see her in her bedroom before we went to bed. There were five of us girls who were over ten. We went to her room. She asked, "How many of you have had woman's bleeding?" All five hands went up. The supervisor had flannelette grey sheets that she said she would use to show us how to make diapers for ourselves. She did this the next day. We cut them out into squares and we were given twelve each. The edges had to be hemmed. The supervisor told us, "When you need to put one of these on, go to the toilet and pin them on your underwear. When you have to change, wash them and hang them in the bathroom."

The new bathroom had just been finished, added to the girls' dormitory. Our initials were sewn on our flannels. We were asked to keep them under our mattresses when they were clean, but never when they were dirty. If anyone was caught doing that, she would be punished. The supervisor continued, "If you put them under your mattress, they will make the dormitory smell, and that would not be nice for Sister Superior, who has to pass through our dormitory every day to go to our classroom." Not to mention the Priest, who came up every morning to lecture us on the catechism. She told us that we should wash the flannels as best we can, and that they will be sent to the laundry every month. That's why they had to be initialled, so it would be clear which ones belonged to whom.

I didn't know that this novelty would create a smell.

THE SICK GAVE ME STRENGTH

School began. I was very bored. The thought of work was challenging and attractive to my eyes, especially when I saw that the servants received different treatment from the others. They had work to do. They could go to the store once a week. They could go for walks when they had finished work. They sat at the back of the chapel. They were much more involved with other things, while the school children went to bed early and conformed to the rules. They wore the clothing they wanted, not what was passed on to them to wear for a month. Some of them changed everyday. Most of the time, I wondered if I would be put to work. Will it be in the kitchen? Laundry? Father-house? Or the new hospital? At this time, the rules that schoolchildren would work had been phased out because there were more servants.

The end of November came, and at this time, our school pictures were always taken. They would be framed and hung in the girls' and boys' rooms. The same pictures were always sent home to the local priest's house to be hung in his living room, where the parents would see them when they came to visit. After mine was taken, I was told that another would have to be taken, but this time, I was given something to wear against my skin and across my chest. It was completely flat and shaped like what Inuit mothers use on their babies across their stomachs to prevent hernia. I called it my harness. The nun explained to me that I did not look nice with my chest showing too much, and that I had to wear this to flatten it. It was painful, and it hurt me all over my chest. My breathing was very uncomfortable, but I sat and posed as I was directed. Once again, we were shown our pictures, but my chest was still too obvious to the nuns and priests. It seemed schoolgirls should not have chests growing normally. Believe me, the nuns were as old-fashioned as my grandmother. My picture was given to me instead of being hung, and I sent it to my father.

The next day, the priest asked me and the Indian girl who was also repeating grade eight to see him in his office. By this time, she and I were good friends. He began by saying, "The kitchen and the hospital need extra help, and I think you two are a bit grown to be with the children. You will be paid five dollars a month. The Sister will make arrangements for you to move in with the servants." That was that. My friend was put to work in the kitchen, and I was sent to help at the hospital. There were four of us servants in one room, with four beds and one side table. The rest of the room was just big enough to open our door and to take two steps to get to our bed. I lay on my bed that evening and thought how odd it was that I was in this room again. It was the same room I was put in the time I did not get sick when Fort George was hit with an epidemic of flu. It seemed so long ago.

As there were more schoolchildren that year, there were more servants. All of them had something to do. Three were in the kitchen, one at the Father-house plus the laundry, and one seemed to be all over the place. I suppose she was there to give a hand wherever the work was lagging behind. I saw her in the kitchen, playing piano during services, helping the supervisors for girls and boys. Somehow, she was kind of special to everybody. She acted like it, too, always very smart when she opened her mouth. Even the sisters seemed be in awe of her. I heard so many stories about why she was there. Some said that she was given a special trip to see the school. Some said that her future brother-in-law, who was a brother there, asked her to come help out. Some said that she was there to be used to convert some children to being Catholics. Her room was at the hospital, as there were no other spare rooms available.

My friend was the extra helper in the kitchen, in the laundry and at the Father-house. The day I began to work at the hospital, the nun doctor showed me around. The building itself was long with a corridor in the middle and rooms on both sides. There were eleven patient rooms, one kitchen, the doctor's room, linen room, X-ray room and adjoining film developing room, an office for the doctor, dispensary, and operating room. There was an entrance in the kitchen, an entrance at the end of the building, and an entrance on the side, where outpatients came in. The other end of the building was joined to the school and had big wide doors that opened both ways.

There were four patients in the hospital when I started to work. One was a retarded, half-blind Indian girl from Great Whale River. She had been there for a long time, as I had seen her since I first came to the school. She was bedridden before the nun doctor came, but now she was walking. She walked up the stairs to the chapel, and she walked by herself to the bathroom. She knew all the hymns and prayers by heart, having heard them over and over, as the dispensary was right next door to the chapel. She understood when she was spoken to but could not converse. During her years in bed, she had put on so much weight that she had more trouble in lifting herself up than in walking. That much I knew about her. I could see there was no way she could ever go home, not in her condition, if her parents were hunters who had to commute back and forth to hunt beaver. My heart went out to her, especially when I had to see her every day and would not be able to stand thinking how much she must be in pain. I called her "the clever one" in her language. It amazed me that she always knew who it was who came into her room, that her gestures showed her understanding when she was spoken to.

Another patient was a baby, a year and a half old, also retarded. I was not sure if she was really retarded, but I could see that her whole body had no strength, and her head constantly swayed around and around from the neck. The nun had started to put her in a baby walker with wheels, until she could push herself around. Every morning, one of us would put her "on wheels," and let her out into the corridor. We had to make sure that she did not disappear into the other rooms, but she had the whole corridor to move around in. She was from Fort George, and her parents came to see her every time they came back from the bush. My heart went out to her, too.

There was also a two-year-old boy. Though nothing seemed to be wrong with him, something was wrong with him internally. I got to know him too—he was very mischievous and got into all sorts of distresses. We had to watch him extra carefully—in fact, he made things happen at the hospital. Sometimes he made the nun and I so mad; other times we couldn't help but laugh at the things he did.

The fourth patient was an Indian man. I was used to seeing this man at the school ever since I had come back to Fort George. He was the janitor at the school. For as long as I could remember, everybody made fun of him, yet no matter how much ridicule he was confronted with, he never answered, never fought back, never retaliated and just kept on with his work. I could see that he had a lot on his mind. People in the community said that he was not married because he was not wanted by anyone as a son-in-law, least of all by any woman. Some said that he did things that were not normal, and all the adults in the community had managed to scare their children with him. Sometimes I used to hear the Fort George children say that he was crazy, and that was how he was known in their community. If he was seen coming to the school when he was still janitor, all the children used to run, calling behind him, "crazy man!" I would run too, hesitantly, because I always remembered Grandmother saying, "People who have a lot in their mind usually go crazy." We certainly gave him a lot to think about with our attitudes, not to mention what he probably went through when he returned to his community. I left Fort George without ever finding out what was wrong with him medically. Now, he was here, in this hospital, confined and chained to his bed. The chain was just long enough for him to reach the toilet and to allow him to get up and around his bed.

The nun showed me what I had to do every day and what routine to follow to get the work done. I had to rise at 7:00 a.m., attend the chapel service with everybody else, have breakfast, then leave like all the other servants who had work to do. For a week, the nun stayed with me to show me what had to be done, and eventually I had to be on my own, learning to use my own discretion. I would go back to the hospital after I ate, fetch the tray that was on wheels, and bring it to the school part of the building. Then I would fill the dishes on the tray with food, whatever was being served that day. I'd wheel the tray back to the hospital into the kitchen, add medicine and vitamins for whoever was on those pills, and bring them to the patients. I would bring the tray to my clever one, and to the little boy, who knew how to eat on his own. The nun and I took turns feeding the baby.

She did not let me bring the man's tray to him for about a week. She brought it to him herself, or some days she would bring me with. She always knocked on his door first, before she opened it. Some days he would be sitting on his bed, some days he would be dancing, sweat dripping down his face. Some days, he just smiled. Some days, he said something like "good, good." The nun would watch both of us, probably studying how we were reacting. She watched me the most—I guess trying to find out if I was scared, and I was. My heart would pump, pump. I would try to hide my fear—after all, I knew him once when he was free out in the world. Grandmother's wisdoms would flash in my mind, what she knew about crazy people. She used to say that they had the knack of knowing how people felt about them. I would gather all my strength and act a little more brave. When we got out of the room, the nun would pat my shoulders. I took it as an affectionate gesture, not as praise, as I did not know that she was studying me too. The day she decided to let me take the man's tray by myself, she made me a nurse's cap. She felt it would help the man see that there was some authority. He tended to grab our arms, and he would try to terrorize us if we did not wear our uniforms. But if we went into his room wearing our white uniforms, he was passive and obedient.

I put on the cap, and she spoke: "You know, Mini, you should think seriously about nursing—you have all the capabilities. You are patient, you are pleasant. But there is one thing you have to have, which you could learn to have with training, and that is mental strength, to be able to cope with pain without fainting. Can you see what could happen to a patient while you were busy fainting?" I could not help but smile at her, as I have been trained by my people to have a sense of humour when fear is at hand. So, I said, "The patient would probably die while I was on the verge of collapse." That she took seriously, and said, "You see, Mini, you have the right attitude—all the more that you should be a nurse."

She was feeding the baby, standing with her back to me while talking, opening up my mind, putting there wishes and hopes that I might be as knowledgeable as her. I stood there for some time, leaning against the counter by the kitchen sink. I looked at her and wondered if she was serious. Did she mean that an Inuk can become a nurse, too? I thought only qallunaat could do that. How would I go about wanting to be a nurse? Where would I have to go to learn such things? The questions bothered me, but the idea sounded challenging. I sized her up. She was always so helpful and so willing to share her knowledge and easy to talk to. I began to ask her the questions I had in mind. She explained, "You see, Mini, if you are serious, arrangements could be made for you to go to Ottawa with the Sisters. The Sisters have a big hospital there." Now? "No, it would have to be next summer." Where would I stay? "They have places for girls like you. But you do not have to wait till then, you could begin here, right here, in this hospital. We have all the equipment and you have the grades that are necessary to learn. If you start here, you could continue down there. Sometimes we don't have much to do here, and when you have some spare time, you could read the anatomy books. You think about it, and let me know. There are many things you could learn to help patients, not just nursing. There are X-ray technicians, office workers, secretaries, and many more. Why don't we talk about it later on and I will see what you like to do."

Our daily jobs were never dull—there was always something to be done. When the patients finished breakfast, I made and changed their beds, cleaned the bathrooms, dusted and swept the whole hospital. As she promised, she taught me anatomy names—some sounded like Inuit words and were easy to memorize, others I had to go over and over. No matter how busy she was, she would have me repeat the anatomy names when we were alone together. Some day, she would take me into the X-ray room and show me how to use and develop films, how to handle them in the darkroom, how to mind the timer so the films wouldn't be ruined. I liked the X-raying most because the machine fascinated me, and the more it fascinated me, the more I got curious about it. One day, she asked me to X-ray a six-year-old boy from the school. He was from Pointe-Bleue, and he only spoke French. He was not feeling well in his stomach. I lined up the machine, put in the film, asked the boy to stand against it and take a deep breath. I clicked the button at the end of the wire. I asked the boy to wait and went into the darkroom to process the film. The nun was in her office, and I told her that I was finished. She came and looked at the film. When she put it against the light, all I could think was, is that how we look? The shapes of the bones were the same as the pictures in the anatomy book. How did the person who wrote the book know all this? I did not ask; I just listened to her and began to trust her more.

Then I had to sterilize all the equipment in the operating room. I had to wear rubber gloves to handle them. I did not like that, my imagination would go wild with all those sharp instruments. Would I have to use these on human bodies? I would shiver and get on with the work. I hated that room. I was so glad to get out of there.

It had been a couple of weeks since she brought me to the man's room. Now she was asking me to bring his tray to him on my own. His door was always locked. I knocked, unlocked it, and opened the door. I had a good look at him for the first time since the times when the school children used to run away from him. He looked so much older, and the expression on his face was vague looking. My heart was jumping very fast as I placed his tray on his bedside table. His window was wired from top to bottom. He talked the whole time with incomprehensible muttering and pointed everywhere just like he was seeing things. The nun had been with me for the first time, speaking very gently, telling me that I should be gentle with him, that as long as I was gentle, he would not harm or attack me. I was never to show my fear—he will feel it, and that will make his nerves react. I tried to be calm, but it was very hard for me, trying not to show my fears. Every meal time, I dreaded it and wondered, will he know that I am afraid this time? I would force myself to be as calm as I could be, but sometimes I could not control it. When I felt that way, I would unlock his door very sharply and place his tray inside as fast as I could. Nothing ever happened.

Then she began to take me into his room to help her make his bed. I was alright as long as she was there. One day, I had to make it on my own. My whole body felt my heart thumping. I forced myself to be calm, trying not to hurry, in case my speed made him react. Most of all, I wanted to make his bed right, to put him in comfort. I had to make the bed the way the nun showed me how. It was not like making an ordinary bed. His bed had to be changed almost twice a day, as he slopped all over it with his food. There were drip stains and spill marks. Very often, because I was so afraid of him, I would be tempted just to leave his bed, but I would be aware that the nun would know right away. Most of all, I did not want to cheat her with the work—she had been so patient and willing to teach me. So I would do what I had to do.

All the time I was there, my fear of him never diminished. I forced myself the whole time until I began to have nightmares about him. I would wake up at night still hearing his laugh, the chains on his feet clanging as he was dancing until I came to reality in the darkness. All the lights were turned off when the children were asleep. He used the tap dance with rhythm and scream at the top of his voice, "hey haw" over and over. Some days, the nun had to go and stop him. Just seeing her used to make him stop—she didn't have to speak. Some days, she would let him go on, and when she opened his door, he would be covered with sweat running down his face.

Every day, our routines were the same. The month of February arrived. Indians began to come to the hospital with heavy colds, complaining of pains in their chests. There was flu again. In just a few weeks, every bed in the hospital was occupied. There was more work. I had to be with the nun constantly. I could not even take my daily walk outdoors, except to bring the laundry to the laundry house. Some nights, we would be up so late, trying to keep up with the work. There were more temperatures to be taken, read, and recorded. More bedpans to be washed. More beds to be made. There were small emergencies happening.

One particular woman was very sick with the flu, had pneumonia on top of that, and was pregnant. She was so sick that she had to be given oxygen. The nun and I took turns watching her at night, and we ourselves got less and less sleep. She got worse and worse. There were no airplanes coming to Fort George, and no way she could be sent out to another hospital. I could see the nun doing her best to help her in every way she knew. Though I did not have much knowledge of medicine, even I could tell that she was beyond help by human capabilities. Some days, she did not know us. We asked one of her relatives to come and stay with her, but he could not stay every day as he had children to mind. On top of all her discomforts, she ended up having a miscarriage.

The nun had asked me to watch the bedpan and not to flush it down the toilet if I noticed anything. She wanted to examine it to make sure. She tried to describe to me what it would look like, saying I should flush it down if it was just a blood clot. I could not tell, no matter how I tried. Everything that I saw in the bedpan looked like something to me. I did not flush it down but brought the pan to the nun each time. If she was in the dining room having her meal, I just waited and left the pan in the bathroom. Finally, she noticed it and brought it to the dispensary. She took it out with a clamping device and put it in a little paper box, explaining to me that her religion did not allow her to discard it, no matter how

179

small it was, because it was considered murder of a human. I accepted her explanation only because I was so amazed at her sincere obedience to her religion. We left it sitting on the counter in the dispensary and went on with our work.

It had been a very trying day for me. My feet were aching for not having had a chance to sit for a while. I felt so tired, but we must keep going. I never complained and neither did the nun. I could see that her whole heart was in her job, and she did it so expertly. That same evening, the very sick woman died. It was very late in the evening, and all the other patients were asleep, not to mention everybody in the school. The nun spoke: "Here is where you have to control your nerves, and have confidence in yourself. Of all the things you have to do to be a nurse, this is the most difficult part for your mind, but you have to get over it and be strong. You will wash the dead body now, and I will show you where to begin and where to end." As I began to wash, my imagination went wild. Creeps were moving all over my body as I lifted her arms and legs to wash them. It was such an odd feeling, moving parts of her body and she was not responding as she had before. She was not moving like she had to make it easier for me to reach other parts of her body. I have kissed many dead bodies before they were buried, as my tradition demands it, but I had never handled a dead body.

I finished washing and put a clean gown on the body. I could hear every little noise, and my heart jumped faster each time. I could hear the nun cleaning the oxygen tent in another room. I went to her and told her that I was finished. She looked at me, searching into me, and I did not dare show how I was feeling, though I felt like collapsing in her lap. I could feel that she was testing me when she again asked me to go back to the room where the dead body lay, to go into the closet and bundle the woman's clothing so that the relatives could take them back first thing in the morning. Creeps that I had thought were over came back again. I began to bundle up the clothing on a chair next to the white-sheet-covered body. I tried to convince myself that dead bodies do not revive like in the stories I had heard from other children, that this dead woman was too nice and patient and had too kind a face to do such a thing. My mind was hurrying while my body tried to stay calm.

I was so glad when I finished bundling the clothing and put it on a bench at the outpatients' entrance. I went back to the nun, who had also just finished. She looked tired, her rosy cheeks were pale, but she did not complain. She squeezed my shoulder with a gesture of appreciation and said with a shivering voice, "You are tired. Tomorrow, you can sleep as long as you want. I will tell the supervisor that you can miss chapel." I left and went up the stairs quietly through the boys' stairway to the third floor. It was so dark, as all the lights had been turned off. I went through the classroom, which was opposite the boys' bedroom. I could hear their sleep sounds as I passed by. I went through another door and entered into my room. All my roommates were sound asleep. I lay down and felt so tired—so tired that I could not think anymore and fell asleep with my clothes on.

I got up at noon, in time to have lunch, and went back to the hospital. The dead body had been removed, the relatives having taken it back to the Anglican side to be buried. That same afternoon, the nun and I went to bury the little paper box which had been sitting on the counter. She did the rituals as her religion demanded.

Some patients began to go home until we had just the four patients again. Our work returned to normal. The mischievous boy was kept tied in his room with a baby harness and loosened every day for a couple of hours to run around. He would let loose all over the place and run up and down the hall. We could hear him going everywhere. One day we heard him crying, coughing, and making vomiting sounds. The nun and I ran out to the hall so fast and we both looked down in the direction of his room. He came out of the room running and almost collapsing, swaying like a little drunkard. We both ran to him. He smelled like the Lysol that we used to clean the toilets. There was a bottle of this in every bathroom. The nun lifted him and brought him into the kitchen, and pushed her hands into his mouth. She had no time to do anything else. He began to vomit, and she kept forcing down some water and got him to vomit more. There were some spots of blood in his vomit. I checked his room while she worked on him. I could see that the harness string that had been tied to the legs of the bed had snapped. In the bathroom, there was Lysol all over the floor, and the strong smell of lye hung in the air. I do not think he drank too much, as the bottle was too heavy for him to hold to his mouth very long. Most of it had spilt down the front of him and on the floor. I cleaned up the room. I could hear the nun talking to him in French. She lectured him never to do that again, and we made sure by having a cleaning cart to wheel around into the rooms when it was cleaning time. As for the nun and me, it was something extra on our hands, to check on him constantly, especially when he seemed too quiet. Though I felt weak each time these little catastrophes happened, somehow the sick gave me mental strength.

WHAT I NEEDED
WAS PHYSICAL STRENGTH

I was so tired that I was not feeding myself well, and in the mornings, it was hard for me to get up. If I had not felt responsible to the nun and to my duties, I could have slept for a year. She looked tired too, but she did not complain. I did not complain either, but she always knew how I was. She put me on vitamins—that perked my appetite, but my body wanted sleep. When the patients were many, she wanted me to wear a mask whenever I had to be near them. I hated the mask: my face would sweat, and I would feel like I was suffocating. I could not stand it. Whenever I was the in X-ray developing room, the feeling of suffocation would come, and I would pant. Today, I am still like that, especially in small elevators and rooms with no windows. When I knew the nun was not around, I would not bother to wear the mask, but only wore it when she was near. I was not getting over my fatigue, even though our routines were back to normal. The spring was coming, summer would soon be here, and I would go home. I felt elated to think that I would have a good rest at home where things were familiar. Yes, Grandmother would take away my tiredness once I got home. I would be able to sleep all I wanted. I would hear birds singing all around our tent. When I went out and looked at the world, I would see seagulls hovering over our fish nets. Yes, everything wouldn't be so alien once I got home again.

The spring came. Home was everybody's favourite subject. During this time, the nun decided to take an X-ray of me. She examined it but said nothing. In the evening, when our work was over, she showed me the X-ray, comparing it to the film that she had taken at the beginning of the year. There was a small spot on my left-side lung. She said it was vague, and she would have to send the X-ray to Moosonee Hospital to make sure. She sent the film on the first plane that spring. I think she had known all the time that something was wrong. She put me in one of the hospital beds. She was so gentle when she told me—that maybe it was nothing, that I should not exert myself anymore until we heard. I went to bed. She let every girl from the school come to see me. All the nuns, priests, and brothers came to visit, a different one every day. The first few days in bed were so welcome that it did not really bother me. All I wanted to do was sleep and sleep. I woke only for meals and wash times.

My want of sleep began to diminish, and I began to get restless in bed. I wanted to get up and around on my feet, and most of all, to go outside and smell the nice air. The nun came in every day to bring my food tray, to change my bed, and to make sure I got washed. She always had something to say to cheer me up. I guess she could see my anxieties. She began to keep my hands busy—once again, I began to write out labels for medicine bottles. It seemed I had done this before, so long ago.

The summer came. I could see from my window that all the snow that had come up to the windows was gone. The edges of the trees were looking green. Though I could not see the sun, it was beaming down on the boys' playground, showing perfectly the diamond-shaped baseball field. I could tell it was still mushy and wet. I could tell when it was recess, as I could see the boys playing on the playground. I could tell when class hours were over, because again I could see the boys. I could tell when it was suppertime for them, when again the playground was empty. They came out again before bedtime. Some were running, some were just sitting. Again, suddenly, the ground would be empty and the darkness of the evening would be upon the ground and I would look no more out the window.

The nun would come in to check everything in my room. She would say, "Well, Mini, dormez bien." And she would turn the light off. I would lay in the darkness, thinking home, home, home, and wake the next morning still in bed under white, white covers with the smell of the hospital hanging in the air. The nun always opened my door on her way to the chapel. Every door was opened in the building. There was not a noise from anywhere, but I could hear the chapel service. I could tell what part of the service they were on from the hymns they sang, which I had heard over and over, year in and year out. I could tell when the service was over. The hall would echo with feet coming down the stairs, but not a verbal sound. I would hear the dishes being handled and finally the children saying their grace. Then the nun would come with my breakfast tray and the day would begin all over again.

I did not feel so tired anymore, and I did not feel sick at all. Then the news came that the airplane was coming from Moosonee. It came and stayed overnight. The nun got the news that I would have to go to Moosonee Hospital or to Moose Factory—she gave me a choice. She said that I had to go to have the proper tests. All I could think was that I would be passing Old Factory—home, and my parents. Early next morning, all of the nuns, priests, and brothers came to say good-bye. Two of the nuns walked down to where the plane was anchored in the water. I had not walked for a long time, and I became tired in that short distance, which I used to walk in only a few minutes to get to the Hudson's Bay store—about a quarter of a mile. I kept falling behind the two nuns, yet they were walking at the same speed that I had been used to only a year ago, when I used to walk with them. They, too, were going back to Moosonee, as they were due to be replaced by others.

We boarded the little plane which sat in the water, anchored to a little wooden pier. The pilot was different, but the plane was the same little one that I had gone home on to Old Factory, long ago. The plane took off, splashing water behind it. The engine was so noisy to my ears. There were just the three of us and the pilot. We sat on little seats against the walls of the plane, no seat belts, and we felt every little turn the plane made. It also carried cargo and mail. We were indeed pioneers, in the early flying days at Hudson and James Bays.

We landed at Moose Factory. I had chosen to go to Moosonee Hospital, as I felt that I knew the nuns there. Also, I had heard so many stories about the new hospital in Moose Factory—that they did not allow you to speak your own language, that the doctors pushed wires into your mouth and nose, that you had to be examined naked inside out, that they gathered your sputum and your urine in bottles. They never said what these were used for, but it sounded awful and scary to me. And I was not ready to be known inside out.

I stood around the two nuns while the plane was unloaded. Then we discovered, after waiting for so long, that the plane was not taking us across to Moosonee. The nuns would have to make arrangements for us to be taken across by canoe. We stood there wondering what to do—the nuns had no place to go on this side, as their familiar grounds were on the other side at Moosonee. And me, I had no intention of walking up to the hospital with strange people in it. But we happened to notice someone going over to Moosonee, and the nuns asked him if he could take us. He was very helpful. We took the same route that Grandfather Symma had used in taking me to the school when I was only five years old.

That trip flashed through my mind as I wondered what would happen to me now. We arrived at Moosonee and walked up to the convent, the same building my grandfather Symma had taken me to with my impetigo-covered face so long ago. At the door, the nuns were bubbling with recognition of each other. I stood beside them, feeling very lonely. One of the nurses came down and brought me to a room with two beds in it. She spoke to me in French, with her arms pointing at everything. I could see that she was not sure if I understood her or not. I did what she told me to do. I took a bath, changed to a gown, and bundled my clothing. I looked out the window—the sky looked grey and lonely to me. I climbed into bed and cried silently. I thought about my parents, how I had flown over Old Factory that very day.

I had nothing to do—all I did was wash and have meals. Hardly anybody came into my room, and my door was always kept closed. I did not get examined. I did not get any medicine. I began to wonder what was wrong with me, and I would assure myself that I did not feel sick at all. The nuns were strange and cold here, not like the ones I was used to at Fort George, so warm and helpful.

It was now July. A whole month had passed since I had come here. My room was close to the front door, and I could hear the door being knocked on whenever anyone came. One evening, there was a knock at the door. I heard the swish of a long gown and the door opening. I could hear the nun speaking in Cree, and a few minutes, later my father came into my room. What could I do? I cried and cried. I was so glad to see him. He had heard that I was in the hospital and had taken the navigating job again so that he could visit me. I wanted to tell him so much, but I had no words. I sat there on the bed while he gave me love sounds and advice: "Don't feel sad, don't disobey, don't think about home, you will only feel and make yourself worse. Just listen to the doctors, and you will get better faster." He came once more and the next day left to return to Old Factory. I felt a little better, knowing that everybody was alright at home.

An Indian cleaning woman started to talk to me while she worked in my room. I began to look forward to seeing her everyday. She began to ask what was wrong with me, and I did not know. Then she told me that a doctor from Moose Factory came over every month, that the nuns were maybe just waiting for him. I felt a little relieved, and I waited. My door was always closed and all I could hear was the nuns talking at certain hours of the day. Then one day, I heard a man greeting one of the nuns at the door. It was the doctor. Hopes and fears began to mix in my mind. Maybe I would go home after he had seen me, or maybe there was something drastically wrong with me, maybe he would put wires down my throat. The doctor entered my room. I was neither glad nor scared to see him. He greeted me in English and told the nun that he did not need her. She left and left the door ajar. The doctor sat on my bed. His first question was, "Why didn't you come to Moose Factory Hospital?" I said I didn't know. "Did the nuns tell you not to come over there?" No. He told me that he could not find out what was wrong with me unless I came over to Moose Factory, that all the necessary equipment was over there, and that if I went, I would have roommates, other Inuit people. He asked me if I would like that, and I said yes. He never examined me, didn't even take my pulse. It seems he had come only to convince me to move to Moose Factory, and he left just as suddenly as he arrived.

In a few days, I was transferred over and put in a room with four empty beds in it. I was confined to bed, though I had to get up to wash and use the toilet. I could hear and see other Inuit and Indians when they walked down the hall. Some came in and stood for a few minutes at the foot of my bed. I did not know any of them. They were from other communities, and none from Old Factory River or Cape Hope. Everyday I got examined by different doctors and asked the same questions. No, I had never been seriously ill, other than those attacks. Some came twice to get me to repeat the story of my attacks. I could not understand why such a common thing like that was so strange to the doctors. They were all mystified, and one of them admitted to never having heard of it. For days, the same doctors kept coming back to ask me over and over about it, and I would describe it over and over until I got so sick of it. I was X-rayed again, my sputum and urine were gathered. Though I got examined all over my body, I was not examined inside. I kept expecting it, that all kinds of tubes would be put inside me. It never happened. I stayed in bed with no medicine, though everybody else was getting some. But I was getting the sleep which I so craved only a few weeks before at Fort George. I felt that I needed even more physical strength than ever before—it was bad enough that woodpeckers were picking my brain.

WE WERE SHIPPED LIKE CARGO

In a few days, some of the patients who were up and around came into my room. They told me that there was an airplane leaving for Inuit nunanganut—Inuit Land. It did not mean anything to me, as I had enough to think about. The next day, we could hear the plane leaving. That same evening, the plane came back. Anyone who was allowed to be up ran to the windows and stuck their head out. Even the window of the room I was in was packed with heads—rear ends and bare feet were all I could see from my bed. They were all trying to see if they could spot passengers, as the plane always flew over the hospital very low and landed on the river in front.

They announced that they could see Inuit-looking people as it flew by. There was silence—I could not hear the noisy engine of the plane anymore. Everybody was stretching their necks out trying to see, and finally they could see people coming up the bank to the hospital. Everybody wondered and hoped that it was not their husbands or their children. They all became silent, waiting for the next news. It was as though we were waiting for the thunder to peal. Anyone who was allowed up was standing at their door waiting to see who was coming through the big entrance down the hall. They knew that they had to come to this ward, as they were women. I felt nothing in me, though I felt all their anxieties.

Suddenly, the silence was broken. I could hear a voice that was familiar, talking at the top of her lungs, announcing that she, too, had come to play in bed, followed by her familiar laugh. Yet the tone of her voice was so sad. I knew and would know that voice anywhere—it was my outspoken aunt. A group of women came into my room, already bathed, and in white gowns. They made a full stop when they saw me, even an Indian woman who was with them just stood there. In a few moments, the three empty beds were filled. Nobody spoke, and I began to cry. They sat on their beds, and all three began to soothe me, and they told me that they did not want to see any more tears as they had seen that enough when they were leaving home. My outspoken aunt kept telling me not to cry anymore, over and over.

This was the woman who was to be my future mother-in-law. She told me the news from home, a bit here and there, that my parents had heard that I went far away, meaning South. "And here you are," she said, "it just shows that you cannot believe one word qallunaat say." She questioned, commented, teased, advised, and humoured anyone who came into the room. We never knew what she was going to say next. She made us laugh. She got us to see the funny side of our situation, sometimes more or less convincing herself. Then she would become sad and think out loud, wondering how her children were, her husband, were they eating right? Did they have kamiit for the coming winter? "This is not how I hope to bring responsibility to my irqsi," she would say. She was talking about her adopted daughter, who was the real daughter of the other aunt with us in the room. The real mother never interfered, because that is our custom in the Inuit way of adoption.

Now that I had seen the inside of a hospital and had nursed patients at Fort George, I was given a chance to view hospital life from the other side. Our days would start with breakfast, with washing and brushing our teeth. The ones that were up and able to go to the bathroom washed there. The others who were confined to their beds had to roll over to each side of the bed to allow the nurses to make them. I was in that situation. Every week, we had different faces catering to us. The doctors and nurses were all imported from the South. The ward I was in became very fond of one particular nurse, and so did I. She had such a gentle face and nature. She tended to us without ever appearing impatient—her heart was in her work. She handed us our basins without throwing them at us. She had a way to human hearts, and we responded accordingly to her. When she was on duty, we behaved for her—her pleasantness kept us pleasant.

When she was off duty, we were just the opposite. We wore long faces like the ones that were on duty. We sneaked around behind their backs. We ran to the windows to look out. They treated us like children, so we acted like children. The other nurse treated us like human beings, so we acted like human beings.

The weekly arrival of the train in Moosonee was exciting and saddening at the hospital. Patients looked forward to it because other patients would arrive back from the Hamilton Sanitarium on their way home. But it was also saddening, because someone would leave. Nobody was ever prepared mentally when they were leaving. The doctors would bring with them a translator and tell the patient that he or she had to go south to Hamilton. No preparation, no warning, no choice, and no reason given why they had to go so far away to be cured. One afternoon, we boarded the train to Hamilton.

There were seven of us—two aunts, two men from Fort George, an Indian husband and wife from Great Whale River, and myself. My outspoken aunt never stopped talking, at times with humour, at times with sadness. Often she spoke to herself, saying, "My little family is just getting further and further away. Will I ever see them again? I wonder how long I have to be away. I am not sure I will get home again—most people that have gone away... I must not think about it if I want to get better." The rest of us kept quiet. We knew in our hearts that she spoke for all of us. She brought our feelings out into the open. All the way to Hamilton, I translated for them when our escort wanted to say something.

We arrived at Hamilton early in the evening and were met by the head nurse. We were put into an ambulance and driven up the "mountain" where the hospital was. For the next few days, all I did was translate for all kinds of nurses and doctors, back and forth between the rooms. The other four women were put next door; in my room were all qallunaat. I did not see the men we travelled with since we were separated at the door. It seemed I never got to bed, just translated every day. I was beginning to think that there was nothing wrong with me. But I went through the whole examination again, like I did in Moose Factory, and was getting used to it by now. Every time a different doctor came, I wondered what would happen to me—maybe I would be told what was wrong with me at last. I translated for all the Inuit and Indians that I had arrived with. All were told what was wrong with them, what kind of medicine they would be on, and how long they could expect to be there. Me? I waited.

My qallunaat roommates began to urge me to ask when I was going to get needles like everybody else, to find out what was really wrong with me. It is your body, they would say, and you have a right to know. The cultural beliefs that I was raised with and their urgings began to get mixed in my mind. My culture told me not to ask, that in this situation I might cause the people who were taking care of me to alter their behaviour completely, that I should accept what was happening and not force the hands that I was in to take a different course. I waited, while my roommates urged. I figured that the doctors would tell me when they were ready. I was X-rayed again, blood samples were taken, and the questions asked all over again. Did I have such a complicated sickness that they did not know what to do with me? Finally, I was told that I had a spot on my left lung. I had known that at Fort George. It was not serious, but it was enough to put me to bed.

I began to get needles. The first needle I got gave me all kinds of lumps on my skin, all over my body. My body felt numb and my ears were ringing. I sat up on my bed and showed my arm to the qallunaaq beside my bed. Her eyes almost popped out and she rang the bell. The nurse came, and I was given another needle to get rid of the first one that I got. I was allergic to the medicine! I was given something else. Though I did not produce any more lumps, my body always felt numb after each needle. Every week, I dreaded them. Some nurses did not hurt, but others gave needles that sent pain all the way down my leg. We began to know which ones were not painful and which ones were. We called the days on which we were given needles "shot days." On shot days, we would wonder which nurse was coming. If it was one that we knew who pained, we all said, "oh, no!"

I asked one day if I could be up and around more, since I had to be up all the time to translate in the different rooms. The answer was no, I could not, as I might cause my lung to get worse. I could not understand that—why I would get worse if I walked a little more when I had to walk and strain my brain when I translated. Yes, we were shipped like cargo and meant to be like cargo.

WE KEPT OUR HOMES
AT THE BACKS OF OUR MINDS

A couple of months after our arrival, we were all moved to another building. We were put in one big room. There were eight of us, my two aunts,
five qallunaat women, and myself. We all got to know each other. The
qallunaat women were always visited by their relatives, and these, too, we
got to know. They always brought fruit, which was always shared with us.
Our only visitors were Red Cross people, and they were always in a hurry.
They dropped off cigarettes and were gone as fast as they came in. I did
not smoke, so I gave the packages to my aunts, or sometimes they just
gathered in my drawer.

Time passed by, and the month of December arrived. Everybody was
talking about Christmas, while my aunts talked about the cold weather
at home, wondering how their families were and how they were coping
with their clothes for the winter. Some nurse would come in and tease my
outspoken aunt about the cold weather outside, and she would laugh and
say no, her face running with sweat. She would try to explain how much
colder it was at her home. Arms in gestures of explaining would wave in
every direction, and eventually, I would rescue them by translating. Some
nurses could not believe what we told them about our winter weather.
They could not believe that we could survive in such temperatures. They
could not imagine that we had ways of keeping warm.

A week before Christmas, I got two visitors, a man and his wife. I
had never seen them before. It was such a surprise to me that I cannot
remember their names to this day. I know that they had kindly faces.
They brought me a Christmas stocking, about three feet tall, all made of
wire. It was stuffed with all kinds of fruit, candy, and a pair of pyjamas. I
did not know what to do or say. They spoke to me, but no words came out
of my mouth. I was just so stunned. My mind was racing with thoughts.
Who are these people? Why do they want to give me something like this?
Was I in a position to be in charity because I was in bed? The big wire sock
sat at the foot of my bed. I kept looking at it. Everybody wanted me to
open it up. The couple stood there, while I felt awkward. They finally left,
and all my roommates began to speak at once, some urging me to open it,
some wondering who they were, some wondering why me? I wondered
if they had made a mistake. I looked at the card that was tied to the sock,

but it was no mistake. My name was written on it with all the Christmas wishes from the couple. I shared out the contents to all my roommates, and gradually the sock emptied. I could not store the sock anywhere to keep. It was taken out and probably put in the garbage. I kept looking out for the couple, and so did my roommates. They never came back.

Christmas came and went. I was knitting a lot, while my aunts were kept busy making Inuit dolls and parkas. Sometimes I stuffed the dolls for one of my aunts. Most of the time, I was bored and wondered what I could really do. Teachers came around, each trying to find out who would like to take up something. But permission had to be granted by the doctors if a patient wanted to take on an extra project. I got my permission, so I took grade nine and ten in math, spelling and history. Now I was busy, so ready to please my teacher who came around every week to see my work and to bring me homework for another week. All of us were doing something—one was taking art lessons, one was knitting, one who was from Yugoslavia took English. Two still had no permission to do projects, while my aunts made dolls and parkas.

The winter of 1952 passed by. To me, it seemed that it had never come. I did not see much snow out the windows. Then summer came, and it was so hot! One of my aunts would suddenly throw down a parka she was sewing at the foot of her bed and say, "Whoever heard of making parkas in the summer?" She was so hot, and her face was constantly sweating. Even the fan on the ceiling did not do much good. In the midst of my complaints about the heat, my shots were stopped, and I began to be put outside to walk on the lawn, as were my aunts. All three of us got excited, as it was a sign that we would be going home soon. My outspoken aunt had picked up a lot of English by now. We would sit in front of our room on the lawn, waving to our roommates who were not allowed out yet. My outspoken aunt kissed the grass and looked toward our room, talking to the ones inside, telling them that it was so nice. She was turning around and around, her arms stretching out. We could hear our roommates laughing with deep understanding. I sat there on the grass looking at her and thought: how has she managed to be cooped-up indoors this long without going insane, when she grew up all outdoors? I was glad to be out, but even more so for her. What she was doing on the lawn, she was doing for all of us. From then on, at bedtime, she would think out loud and say, "I am going outside tomorrow," with such an elated voice. The lights would go off and silence came. She would be the first one to say something in the morning, bubbling all through breakfast. No doubt she, too, had thoughts about home at the back of her mind.

NIGHTINGALE KEPT CALLING ME

One day, I was called to the doctor's office. All I could think was, I am going home! I felt excited. There was no other reason why the doctor would want to see me. I couldn't have gotten worse, as I am still going outside. I went down to the office where I usually translated for the doctors. Heads were popping out of the rooms as I passed by them. One qallunaaq man whistled with his fingers between his lips. I felt insulted, as we whistle only to birds when we try to lure them while hunting. I ignored him and went on to the office.

I entered, and the doctor was sitting there at his desk. He offered me a chair and asked me how I was. He began, "You could help so much here. There will be more patients coming from where you come from. We could arrange for you to take up nursing, you could live at the nurses' residence, and if you don't like it, you could always go home." Just like that! "Thank you," he said, and I left, back to my room.

I sat on my bed thinking, thinking, and thinking. On my way to the office, I had been so excited. Now I was all mixed up. My roommates were asking what was new. There was a nurse in the room making beds, and she explained it to them all. Apparently, she already knew the course of my future. In the midst of my thoughts, I heard her say, "Yes, she is certainly needed by her people here." I thought no more. I knew that there were not many Inuit who spoke English at that time. I could not stand the idea of them coming here, given this and that without understanding. I thought, too, that people have a way to make one feel guilty when they want and need you. I would feel guilty if I left all these Inuit and Indians. My home had done without me this long and did not need me—they were only waiting for me to get married. I was not prepared for that yet.

So I moved into the nurses' residence in a couple of days. Here was something I had to get used to all over again. I had my own room. All together I was on my own: there was nobody there to get me up, to bring my breakfast, to turn out the lights or to tell me when to take a bath. Though the surroundings were the same, as were the faces, the change was tiring. I could tell that I had not used my body for a long time. I would get so tired by the end of the day. I was put to work on shifts in the children's ward. There, I got my instructions from the head nurse. Once a week, I spent time with another nurse, reading anatomy books. She would get me to memorize all of the body names. Each week, she gave me a chapter to work on.

Every day I walked to three different places: the residence, the dining room, and the children's ward. My legs became used to the distances, and soon, I could get to each of them in no time. Without warning, my supervisor at the children's ward would get a phone call, someone needing me to translate in another building. I would be in the middle of my lessons and I would drop everything and go. Sometimes this would happen on my days off. I got one day off one week and two days off the next week. I would spend them doing my own laundry, or I just slept and slept. One day while I was off, I decided to go downtown, which I had heard so much about. I took the bus. I was sorry that I went, because going downhill from the mountain scared me so much. I sat there in the bus, looking at the driver, and wondered if he knew what he was doing. I looked at the other passengers—they looked so relaxed, so I tried to be, too. Downtown was noisy, smelly, and there were so many people. I never did anything. I just walked around the same street I got off on. I was too scared that I might get lost, and I didn't want to lose the bus route in case I couldn't find it again. That was my day in town, and then I went back up the mountain. The air was better, and there were not so many people.

I didn't know which was getting better, my routine or myself. Whichever one it was, I was enjoying my adventure, though my home was always at the back of my mind. I kept telling myself that I could go home at any time. My two aunts had gone back by then. I would think about them, how close they were to the sea. Here at the hospital on the mountain, all I saw were trees, tall buildings, cars, and many lights at night. Yes, I had to get used to them too. I had no special friend, no one I could talk to about many things. As far as I was concerned, I was there only temporarily and did not try to make friends. The nurses and doctors spoke to me only when they needed a translator. Otherwise, I was different and strange to them. The people I worked with were polite, that was all. They didn't stand around with me to discuss little personal experiences, like they did among themselves.

I saw and I heard. I never made my feelings or frustrations known. Though I was enjoying this adventure and found my classes challenging, there was something missing, drastically. Humanity was not there—that which I had been brought up into ever since I was born. I missed it, but I also learned how to ignore it when it wasn't there. I put it aside and kept on with my duties. I kept telling myself that I would know and feel it again once I got home.

We were now preparing to be part of an exchange with another hospital, called Henderson Hospital. A few of us were to commute back and forth. I felt that I must be getting somewhere, and I looked forward to the change. But being "Florence Nightingale" always called me somewhere else. The phone that sat on the desk of the supervisor of the children's ward rang. My supervisor answered. She hung up and came to me. She said that the head nurse wanted me to go back to the nurses' residence and rest up because Inuit patients were arriving from Baffin Island at Mount Hope airport that very evening.

My mind reeled. First of all, I was glad to be off in the middle of my duties. I went to the nurses' residence and rested on my bed. I could not sleep. I thought about my grandfather, who used to talk about the Baffin Island Inuit so long ago. I began to wonder if I would understand them. Whatever, I thought, at least I am here to help them. I had my rest and went to the dining room to have my supper. The head nurse and her assistant met me there, and all three of us went to the airport. They didn't know how many were coming—all they knew was that this plane was a special flight, straight from Baffin Island. Three ambulances followed behind us. The three of us were allowed to go out to the runway. We stood there as the plane was landing.

The sun was out and it was hot, but thank goodness, it was windy, which made it cool for the Inuit. They arrived all dressed in parkas and sealskin kamiit—boots. Some women carried their babies on their backs in heavy carrying-parkas. The plane door opened. The passengers began to come down the stairs while the three of us watched at a short distance. There seemed to be no end of them. I heard the head nurse wondering where we were going to put them all for the night. We went towards them. I felt mixed-up, mainly because in my culture, we have no such thing as introductions between strangers, but I felt it was impolite not to introduce the two nurses. I let it be. I just smiled at all those people.

The two nurses started towards the airport, and everyone followed. I was hearing many things being said. The Inuit were wondering if I was Inuk. Some were saying, "Thank goodness, there is Inuk here," and others said, "No, she can't be Inuk—she is all dressed in white like the other two." Someone was already complaining about the heat, and someone else was wondering if they had reached their destination. The two nurses were wondering if they could get everyone into the ambulances, and they were worrying about the need for extra help once we got back to the hospital, because it was evening and most of the nurses were off duty by this time. The night shift had begun.

We came back and drove straight to the main admittance building. The elevator took a few trips up and down to the second floor. For a couple of hours, the new patients took turns to bathe. Each time a new bath started, I was told by the nurses to go into the bathroom and hurry the person up. Each time I felt awful, frustrated, mad and sorry for these people. I know they were thinking, wondering, worrying and feeling very strange. And then I had to be the mediator and worry them even more. I knew too, that the nurses wanted them to settle down before the midnight shift started.

The ward the Inuit were put into did not have enough beds. We had to get some more from another ward. We crammed the beds together in a couple of rooms, especially for the ones with babies. Some slept with the children they had brought. I did not like that, because then some of them thought that they would always be together. I knew that they would be separated by the next day, and they would be so disappointed. I tried to explain to some of them about this, hoping they would spread the word around. But I did not know if they understood me, because they had a different dialect. They said "no" and "yes" with their noses and eyebrows, which means in my dialect "you are unwanted." At first I didn't notice that they were answering. I felt completely useless and wondered why they didn't speak to me. Finally one woman said "no" verbally with her nose wrinkling. I got the idea. I was so relieved! I realized that they too had facial expression, just like the James Bay people. I thought about my grandfather Symma, who used to say that these Inuit further north spoke very differently, and I assured myself that they must be the ones.

I had another problem. The nurses, doctors, X-ray technicians, blood compilers and dieticians had no idea about different dialects. They all thought that if you are Inuk, you understand every Inuk. I never tried to explain about that: nobody had time to listen anyway, they were always in a hurry. In such a short time, they wanted me to convey so much. On my own, I found a way, thanks to the flexibility of my language. I would try every kind of word that I knew, and somehow along the way, one word or another of mine would be understood. And if I did not understand some of the unfamiliar words, I would ask the Baffin Island people what they meant. They too tried to use other words to help me understand.

I was always so glad that we got through without too many complications. I was so glad that I had been taught by my people how to memorize—the practice that has been used by my people from generation to generation, either for remembering stories, events, objects or travel routes. My supervisor would be so mad that I did not have note-papers. When we were learning all those Latin names for anatomy, she would be so amazed that I knew them by heart. She would say that I was careless just because I did not make notes. She did not see that I compiled everything in my head. I never tried to explain to her how I knew the answers, and she never bothered to ask. I just used the way I was taught to learn by my people. On top of memorizing these Latin words, I had to start memorizing the new words I was hearing from the Inuit patients so that I wouldn't have any problems understanding them in the future. I began to get to know the patients, and I was always so glad to see them. When I had been off-duty, they would all want to know where I had been.

The ward went back to normal routines after everybody was put where they should be according to their sickness, age and sex. It was so sad to see the Inuit get separated when they had thought that they would be always together. The children had to go to the children's wards. I went back to shifts at the children's ward. But, I was never really free, to the point where I never looked forward anymore to being off duty. I had to be everywhere, in different buildings, to translate. After a while, that too settled down when the patients did not have to be examined extensively anymore. If I did not learn anything from all these heart-breaking human miseries, I sure learned that a "Florence Nightingale" knew what was needed to ease physical suffering.

HOME WAS JUST MEANT TO BE A MEMORY

Two years went by, and I received a letter from my father saying that I had a duty to come home. That my aunt had told him that I was not needed where I was. That there were a lot of nurses. Whatever else she told him, he wanted me home right away. She knew him well—that his beliefs were for his children to learn all they can. Telling him that there were plenty of nurses here was one way to get me home so that I could marry her son.

I went to my head nurse and told her that my father wanted me home. She wanted to know if there were any problems at home, or if it was an emergency. Or did I want to go home that badly? I said yes. I could not be bothered to explain to her that in my culture, there were certain things arranged from the time we were born. I don't think she would have understood. All she saw was that I was needed here too. She took a deep breath and said, "You have one year before you finish nursing—that is not long before you are certified." I just sat there, not answering, even though my head was saying stay and finish, and my heart was saying go home and stop being lonely. I was not answering at all. I longed for home. She spoke again, "A year is not a loss—you can go home and come back and finish. I will make all the arrangements." I left to pack.

A couple days before I left, the head nurse told me that I had to go to the radio station, that someone wanted help with Inuit language. I went over to where they had radio programs broadcasted for patients, and I met the man who handled the radio station. He wanted me to tape some things to remind Inuit patients how to look after themselves while here in the hospital. That was my last helping hand to my people in the hospital. A few years later, while I was working in Frobisher Bay, I ran into a man who said to me, "I know you from the radio broadcast in Hamilton." He had arrived in Hamilton way after I had gone. He had heard about me, and former patients had pointed me out to him while I was in Frobisher.

But what a creepy feeling, to meet someone who I had given service to without knowing that I did it.

While I was at the radio station, I also met another man, a Frenchman. I could tell by his accent, as I was used to hearing it. When I said a few words to him in French, he looked so surprised, and his eyes almost popped out. He asked me where I had learned to speak French. I wanted to say that it was a long story, but I just said, "From the nuns." We sat for a while. His biggest dream was to learn Inuit language. We made arrangements to meet at the radio station once a week. I did not tell him that I was going home in a few days, but we did manage to have lessons. He too was in a hurry all the time. He wanted to learn so many words in such a short time. I could not explain to him that my language has so many depths. I taught him only simple words, the way I was taught to teach children. Ten years later, I met the same man. By now, he had learned more Inuit words from Baffin Islanders. He still had his notebook with the words that I had taught him. He had progressed and told me that I taught him baby talk. He was now working with Baffin Island language, and Baffin Inuit used to say that James Bay Inuit talk baby language. We, in turn, say that about them. However, he became my friend—at least, his face stuck in my mind out of the many qallunaat people that I have known.

I began to pack for my trip home. My mind wanted to stay, but my heart was singing with joy. The head nurse advised me not to pack all my things but to leave some of them behind—I could always send for them if I did not come back. She drove me down to the train station early in the morning. I sat in the car, not saying anything, while she talked and talked, reminding me that I had much to give to my people. Though I could hear her clearly, her meanings were not sinking in. All I could picture was my home and my parents. She gave me a hug and said goodbye. I boarded the train and sat close to the window. The train began to move. I watched the many strange things that we were passing. I sang in my heart, neither seeing nor hearing the other passengers.

Then suddenly, it hit me that I was completely alone, on my own on a strange travel route. I had no one to speak to. I had to start thinking. I had to start remembering what the head nurse had said about changing trains, where to eat, who to ask for assistance. I began to find the trip long, and anxieties grew that I might take the wrong train while changing. I began to look around me. People were in every seat, looking so relaxed. Then I heard the conductor shout the name of the next stop, and I wondered if he would shout about the next change. He did—I could have jumped up and given him a hug, but I didn't. Instead I told myself that he was doing his duty well. The train changed at North Bay. I did not have to wait long, thank goodness for that. I sat again near a window. While the train was still loading, I felt hungry and decided to go to the dining car. As I made my way through the train, every head was turning to stare at me. I stared back at some of them, and they didn't stare anymore. Grandmother's voice came to my mind—she used to say that if I wanted to stare, I should at least stare with a pleasant smile. They didn't smile back—they just looked away, like they didn't see anything. Grandmother would have said that it was hypocrisy to look away when you had been staring, especially if the one you had been staring at saw you.

While I was gone, a man had sat down next to my seat. He got up to give me room to seat myself. He began to ask me what part of the Arctic I came from. It was amazing to meet a qallunaaq who knew right away what my nationality was. This got me interested in him. He had been a Hudson's Bay Company clerk for many years on Baffin Island, and he spoke my language very well. He was on his way to Moosonee and Moose Factory, travelling for Northern Affairs. Though I felt very shy, I was so glad to talk to him. The next day, toward the evening, we arrived at Moosonee. He automatically looked after me with such protection—I felt for once that somebody was with me who understood Inuit minds, who knew that I was in a strange land.

We went over to Moose Factory, and I stayed at the nurses' residence and ate at the hospital where the Hamilton head nurse had made arrangements for me. I found out that a plane was not leaving for Old Factory, where my parents were, for another two days. For two days, I visited the patients. They were all new faces, though some of them had heard of me. I ran into the man I had travelled with in the train, and we went for a walk. I showed him where I had gone to school. The building was no more, but a new one was standing not far from the old location, and it still bore the name Bishop Horden Memorial School. We went down to where the Indian village had been—now, it was all houses, no more teepees. I showed him the church that all the schoolchildren used to go to in long line-ups every Sunday, so long ago, when I was only five years old. Though I did not tell him, I remembered, too, the time my grandfather and father had arrived at Moose Factory to get me out of school. I looked at the river bank where I had boarded the little plane one Sunday morning. I could recall the pillowcase bag that was full of toys, which I had dropped in the water just as I was climbing up the steps. That was one thing that hadn't changed; the loading pier was still there. It looked so small now that I was a little older.

The next day, I was boarding at the same little pier, into the plane, with two suitcases. I was the only passenger, but the plane was full with mail and parcels. We skimmed along the water, and the noise got louder and louder to my ears. It seems that I had gone through this before, not so long ago and yet so long ago, at Fort George. My heart began to be excited as the plane climbed higher and higher. It was such a beautiful day, not a cloud in the sky. Below us, the water was blue, blue. I spent the flight just looking out the window. The two pilots turned around once in a while to find out if I was alright. All I could see was their heads—the rest of their bodies were obstructed by bags of mail. One of them asked me if I was happy. I wanted to babble and babble to tell him how I was feeling, but all I said was yes. "It won't be long now," he said.

I kept looking out the window, until finally, I could recognize the landmarks. They looked small from the plane, but they were all familiar. We were circling the Old Factory River. I could see houses, tents, and people moving around. I scanned over the area where Inuit people have always tented. There was only one tent up. I could see a motor canoe racing towards the little plane's landing spot. We touched the water, and the plane crawled slowly to its anchoring site. The engine stopped, and the motor canoe was slowing toward us. It got closer and closer. I didn't recognize the man behind the motor. The pilot opened the door just as the man anchored to the plane. I got out and stood on the landing floats. I balanced myself to have better footing and looked at the man again. It was my little brother—he had grown so much! He had a very shy smile. We just looked at each other for a few seconds. The pilot asked me if I knew the man, and I said yes. I guess he felt responsible to deliver me to the right people. I wanted to hug my brother and lumps were in my throat. I was fighting my tears.

As we approached the Inuit dock area, I could see that swarms of people had gathered. I felt shy. Among all those Indians, my grandmother stood out the most. She came walking down to get hold of the bow of the canoe. Oh, it was good to hear the sound of the canoe rubbing against the rocks. I jumped out of the canoe and gave Grandmother a hug. I wanted to hold her there for a long time, but I was aware of the audience at her back. Though we had performed feasts with all these Indians for many years and knew their idiosyncrasies, I still felt shy to show them my true feelings. As I climbed up to the bank, each of them came over to shake my hand; all said something to help the happy event. Grandmother and I walked up to our tent while Brother put away the canoe. As we walked the path that the Inuit have walked for many years, I became aware of nature around me. Bees were buzzing, butterflies flying, birds singing, and mosquitoes trying to bite. I looked to the horizon and the scene looked the same, though the trees had grown taller. The seagulls that used to hover over the fish nets were still there, diving up and down. It was a clear, beautiful day. We entered the two tents that stood facing each other. Grandmother lived on one side and Father on the other. Oh, it was so good to be in the tent again and to feel the fresh air all around.

Though I was now used to thinking and deciding on my own, I still felt awkward to ask questions about the thing I wanted to hear about. According to my culture, I was still not privileged to do so. Grandmother began to tell me the news: first, Father had been to Moose Factory Hospital with a broken finger. He came back and then left again to navigate the same boat he had been handling for many years. Just Grandmother and Brother were there at Old Factory—they had come waiting and hoping for my arrival. The rest of the Inuit were all at Cape Hope. Brother had grown so much, both physically and mentally. He was as shy as I was. We didn't tease each other anymore. He showed me his sleeping area. He now had his own covers, and his own separate spot. He was proud of that because it was a sign of growing up. Though we still had the big sleeping platform area, we now each had our own covers. We had fresh-netted fish for supper, and all three of us went to bed early.

Grandmother had not changed her ways: after serving me breakfast in bed for a couple of days, she began to tell me to go out and look at the world. Brother and I got into our routine chores. Somehow, they were not the same anymore, as we were not fighting. I did not miss the fighting—everything seemed to be done much faster. We had a lot of idle time. But Grandmother always found something for us to do. The arrival of the ships was still an event, but it was not the same because all the other Inuit were not there to enjoy it. The RCMP ship arrived, and as always we were asked to produce the discs which had our numbers. They asked who had given birth and who had died, and then they left.

A few weeks went by. Though I could tell that Grandmother was happy to have me home again, she acted strange a lot of the time. It was as though she was nervous about something. I could feel that she wanted to discuss some matter with me, but she never really came out with it, whatever it was. I tried not to be bothered by the feeling and enjoyed every minute of my time. As I slowly began to get into our cultural routine again, other things were happening too. One morning when we awoke, the weather was terrible, and the sea was raging. Grandmother said that there must be a ship nearby, coming to Old Factory. Her belief was that the crew of the ship was shaving their beards and that the sea did not like the hairs—it caused the sea to itch and made it rage.

During this rage and wind mixed with rain, I went out to look at the world. I stood for a second, and there in the raging sea I saw a canoe with two people in it, paddling with the motor turned off. Their canoe was appearing and disappearing in and out of the waves. I ran back into our tent and told Grandmother. She looked through a hole that a spark from the stove had made in the tent. She watched for a while and said that there must be bad news from Cape Hope Island. She began to talk, more to herself: "Maybe our Weetaltuk has died, maybe there has been a very bad accident." She could tell by the way the two men were arriving, with their motor cut off, as that is a sign which we use to prepare the people on land for bad news.

They docked their canoe beside ours in front of our tent. They came in, very sad. It was Weetaltuk's youngest son, Pili, and my angilissiak. Grandfather Weetaltuk had died. He had not been sick, nor did he ever say that he was sick, but he was found dead in his bed. I sat there thinking that I had never got to see him again, and I began to remember all the things we had gone through with him. He had been our long-time, faithful leader since the 1800s. He always got us through hard times and easy times—we never went hungry, as he always had a capacity for knowing where the animals would be in certain seasons. I wondered what would happen now to the Cape Hope Islanders. Would they choose another leader or just drift apart? Or would the government come and move them to another settlement? (The government wasted no time and moved them to Great Whale River. There the group was no more. Such a proud people just mingled in with the other crowds who had already begun to rely on an alien culture for survival.)

I had no tears even though my heart was heavy. I did not accept his death right away. I wanted to think about it. I kept telling myself that strong and towering men don't die and leave their duties. If I had been to his death rituals and participated in his funeral, I would have accepted it more easily. Even though I know that the Cape Hope Inuit are no longer there, I still think that Weetaltuk lives on in that place. But I would have liked to see his grave so that I could finally believe and accept it.

I became aware of our company who were having hot tea and fresh fish. They were talking to Grandmother and asking where my father was. Pili, who is my sanarik—my builder—commented on how I had grown into a woman. He looked proud, as he had had a lot to do with the shaping of my mind. He strengthened the relation by saying "arnalian-gai"—dear whom-I-shape-into-woman. I replied "ee"—yes. I felt shy for it to be noticed that I had grown. My angilissiak, who was sipping his tea, smiled and looked shy too. He was the one who had been waiting for me to grow up, according to the arrangements made the day I was born. He was my future husband. I began to wonder why these two particular men, who had had a lot to do with my birth, had been sent to notify us. No doubt it was a trip with a double purpose—both of them had been sent to get me to marry my angilissiak. Grandmother never discussed it, and neither did the two men try to, at least when I was around. They probably felt awkward, especially since my father was not there. He would have consented right there and then.

I felt nothing. I did not feel bad about going with them or not. As far as I was concerned, I was in the hands of the people who knew the course of my future. I could not fight my elders, but nothing was said. I looked at my brother, and for the first time since I arrived, he had a teasing look on his face. He did not have to speak. I could see what he was thinking:

"Hoo-hoo, my sister is going to be married off." He thought it was funny because both of us knew nothing of what marriage was all about. We were both scared, intrigued, and had accepted the fact that that was what people eventually did when they had grown. But nothing happened or was said.

The two men left after a couple of days' trading and after notifying the qallunaat authorities of the death. The three of us stayed put and waited for Father. Grandmother's nerves seemed to be on edge. I could tell she had a lot on her mind. She had been this way since I arrived, but I did not dare ask her anything. In a few days, we heard that the big Hudson's Bay ship was arriving. I guessed they were the ones who were shaving their beards, who made the sea rage. In the evening, while Brother was out checking our nets, Grandmother spoke, so nervously and so fast: "Mini, you will never survive with that man. He is too lazy, he will bring nothing from his hunting trips. I have taught you well, not for a lazy man. You will go away and go back to school when the ship arrives." My mind was confused and feelings were jumbled up, full of question marks. She must be right, she is my elder, I have no way to answer her. But surely she is not serious to send me away. What about my father? He is not even here, I haven't seen him yet, where will I go? As always, she could see the questions in my mind. "You will stay with your cousin Nellie who is at Moose Factory." I did not know the cousin she was talking about. Nellie was originally from Fort George, and at one time it was thought she might be my future step mother, but I had never met her.

She was married now to a boy who had emigrated from Belcher Islands to Cape Hope. He was the boy who had arrived with a bow and arrows, and I had wanted so much to have my own bow and arrows that Grandfather Symma eventually made them for me. Now, she was married to him after they met at the Moose Factory hospital. They both stayed on, trying to find jobs. I had heard a lot about her at the time when everybody was looking for a wife for my father who had stayed single for so long after my mother died. I also met her parents in Fort George. They were very successful people, with six girls and one boy in the family. I hardly knew her, even though she was in some way related to Grandmother. And him, I only knew as a rabble-rouser in our community.

I could see that Grandmother had no choice, and I sure did not either. I looked at Grandmother. I had always thought that she would be the one who would force me to marry and strongly follow the traditions, but it was not so. It must have been my father who was in full agreement with the marriage arrangements. Grandmother was anxious for me to leave before he got back. In some ways, it did not surprise me that Grandmother did not want this prearranged marriage to go through. I had always felt that it was phoney, probably for the sake of peace and survival amongst our group. She had always stressed how lazy my future husband was. She never allowed me to have mating dances in front of him. She never allowed me to run out and help him when he was getting ready to travel. She did not allow me to pull his umiit—thick whiskers that grow in the faces of men (they are not ordinary hairs). Young girls and women are supposed to pull them out as a sign of love and care, to practise how to put a man at ease, as they itch when these hairs are growing. (I tried to explain about these hairs once to a qallunaaq, but he had never heard about them. All he knew and had words for was whiskers and long beards. The ones I am talking about are not whiskers or beards—that's why they have such an individual name in my language. Old men often sit and handle their chins, pulling these hairs. Both men and women get them on their heads as they get older. They make the scalp itch and so they have to be pulled out. They don't pain when they are pulled, like the ordinary grey hairs do.) Anyways, I never was given permission or encouraged to do this to him, while all the other girls were going through the rituals preparing for marriage.

I came back to my thoughts about Moose Factory. It seemed I had just come from there. I came to grips with myself and planned to go back to Hamilton and finish nursing. Then it hit me that I had no money for either transportation or food, let alone for accommodation. I did not have a penny. I could not tell Grandmother about my private worries—she would not understand. She thought that everybody was like the Cape Hope Islanders, who helped you out when you were in need of help. I worried about it, thinking, who do I really know in Moose? Nobody came to mind, except the immigrant and his wife. Grandmother was determined for me to leave and encouraged me to pack.

The ship arrived from Fort George on its way back to Moose Factory. The three of us walked down to our docking area, and there I said goodbye to Grandmother. Brother took me over to the ship. I felt too shy to ask right out if I could have a ride. The captain looked so enormous, standing there on the deck. He wanted to know if I was going to Moose or to Cape Hope, and said that they were not stopping at Cape. I figured this was their last trek for the summer season—it was now the end of August, and all the ships would be beginning to anchor for the year. I told him that I was going to Moose. He helped me up and told me to go inside if I got cold. I just stood there, not moving, and watched Brother turning back. We had not said a word to each other and spoke only with our gestures of sadness. In the ship were two qallunaak crew members and three Moosonee Indians, and one woman who had a child with her. Though I knew that she was a Fort George Indian, I never found out why she was taking the trip. All I felt was sadness and a sense of loss. I kept thinking about my father, that I had not even seen him, when he was the one who had written such an urgent letter, telling me that I had a duty to come home. It was in the middle of the morning, and the ship was moving slowly out the Old Factory River fjord. I stood on the same spot and looked at the scene that I have seen so often as we travelled back and forth for many years. I felt so lonely as we were passing by all the familiar scenes—they seemed to say, look at me a little longer, you will remember me well.

I mentally photographed every spot, with the Inuit place names going through my mind. The real landmarks began to appear, the Inurujartuq and beyond that, Cape Hope Island. We came around the little island that we had picked blackberries from every summer for many years. I could see the settlement of Cape Hope. I still did not believe that Grandfather had died, and I pictured him inside his house, which stood out so big as we were passing. I could see someone waving. The island began to get smaller and smaller, while my legs got numb from standing for so long. I had not moved at all. Others had gone into the ship. It was getting dark and so cold, as the fall weather had begun. We passed our spring campsite, Charlton Island, and finally Moosonee. We did not land, but slept on the ship as it was too late at night. I lay on the bunk hearing the water swishing against the ship. I could hear the Indian crew putting a canoe into the water—no doubt they were anxious to get home.

I awoke the next morning, my mind determined to get across to the Moose Factory side. One of the qallunaat crew fed me eggs and bacon. I did not even know his name, but I would never forget his face.

He was kind and seemed to understand that I was at a loss. After my breakfast, one of the Indian crew came back to the ship. He loaded his canoe with some parcels and took me to the land. Just as we landed, we saw someone going over to Moose. I caught a ride with him. He was an Indian originally from Fort George, and he knew my father well. He was living at Moose, married to a Moosonee girl and working at the hospital. I asked him where so-and-so, my cousin, was living, and he pointed to an area at the edge of the trees, not far from the riverbank. I gave him a thankful smile and walked up.

As I reached the sandy bank, I stopped. I looked to the right—there was the hospital and a row of houses just behind it. I looked to the left, where the man had pointed, and there were trees and a path. I followed the path, and as I got closer to the trees, I could see smoke. Shocks have a way of coming in groups. I found my cousin living in a small tent with nothing on her floor, just earth. I was used to tents that had wooden floors. She was sitting among blankets, sewing, and a small baby was sound asleep beside her. I told her who I was. She welcomed me happily. I could tell she was very lonely. Her husband was working now at the hospital. They were the only Inuit at Moose Factory, other than the ones in the hospital. The rest were all Indians and qallunaat. All the others who were employed by the hospital had room and board, and men with families had apartments.

Many things went through my mind: I cannot stay here and make her suffer more, her parents would have been shocked if they could have seen her living like this. I knew she had been born and raised in a solid house. We spoke shyly to each other. She looked so tired and underfed. She did her washing by hand and hung it on trees. I had to sit, think, and plan a way to get out of there so she wouldn't have an extra worry with me. Her husband came home and broke my thoughts. I shook his hand and was glad to see him, and that was all. I had known him for many years in our community. He still acted like a rabble-rouser, his manners with no care. I had known him to have a bad temper. Though he grew up with very traditional Inuit ways, he behaved like he was not Inuk, and had beautiful, roving hazel eyes to go with his nature. He, too, welcomed me to his little abode. I cautioned myself to be very careful of how I behaved or what I said in front of him. I never knew what might trigger his temper, and I hoped to leave them with at least a feeling of being distant friends.

I did not feel that way about her. She was gentle, kind, and understanding—the kind of woman all Inuit men dream about and want to keep safe and secure. She had nothing like that. Already, that very evening, he was mad at her because his tea was not ready. She said nothing and went on to make the tea, more or less humouring him. He dropped his anger when he remembered my presence. We all went to bed with what few spare blankets they had. I had to use their little extras. I was cold all night but fell asleep with a last thought that I must find a job or go back to school. The husband was leaving for work when I awoke. The baby was crying, and my cousin came running in. She had been outside to build another fire to make hot tea and oats. She put the baby on her back with a shawl. I got up and dressed, went out, and looked at the world. At least the sky promised a nice day. I joined her at the fire, and both of us ate the oats. I told her about my plans and left shortly for the hospital and school.

I went to the school first and stood for a long time in a hall near an office. The principal finally came down the stairs. He asked me what I wanted, and I told him. It seemed that I could not go back to school there—the grades did not go beyond the eighth. He told me that I would have to go away to Sault Ste. Marie or else get a job. I left the school and walked back towards my cousin's tent, thinking about what I could do next. As I walked, the fresh air was giving me hunger pains. I felt very hungry and thought about the nice fresh fish that Grandmother had fed me just a few days ago.

When I arrived back at the tent, my cousin was washing diapers by hand, her baby on her back. I offered to take the baby while she finished. Later, we sat outside and discussed my prospects. I did not want her to know that I felt hopeless, but she knew and could see. I could stay with her as long as I wanted, she said, though she felt that I did not deserve such a home to wake up to every day. I tried to reassure her not to worry about me. She kept saying that she would welcome me more if she had a proper home. I gave her an understanding smile. Then she began to tell me about her marriage—how hard it was, that she had never thought she would experience such cruelty. She had a fear in her voice—she was amazed that anyone could have such a bad temper, sometimes over absolutely nothing. "However," she said, "I put myself here—the mistake is my own. I should have listened to my father and married your father." That statement jolted me—she knew all the time who I was. She went on: "I was bothered by the difference in our ages and so married a young man who needs to be brought up a little more. I had nothing against your father but his age. Now that I have met you, I am sorry—your father must have a great deal of sense to have a daughter with a nature like yours. I know that I should not think like this, to allow another man to enter my mind, but I have to say it. Maybe I will never have another chance to apologize, at least to his daughter." Then she gave a little laugh and pointed to the tent, saying, "Look at me, I look old enough now from all this worry to be your mother."

I never made a comment. I just sat there giving her actions of understanding. She became quiet, and with a completely different air, she said that their house was being built down at the village. "If I had my way, I would stay in this tent while he moved." She was making light of her situation, just what an Inuk would do, even though she had fear in her voice. We realized how late it was getting, and she quickly got up and lit the fire to make tea. Yes, I could see that she was trained to keep peace, just as other Inuit women are shown by example how to humour their men. Grandmother used to have a saying: don't let him spill. She thought of a man's temperament as a cup full of water—if you handle him without spilling, he is fine, but should you spill, watch out for his impatience.

Her husband came home from work. Surprisingly, he was in a happy mood, much joy to his wife. He left again shortly after to go down to the village, saying that he was going to check on how the house was coming. We women sat again and talked some more. She said that she had not experienced this kind of peace for a long time, that perhaps I was controlling his temper because he was ashamed to show it to me, that perhaps I could live with them. I sat and thought. I decided to be very honest with her and told her that I planned to find a job and my own room, and to go home next summer when the ships were running again. She understood and did not blame me for how I felt. The air was getting chilly, and evening was coming on. We both entered the little tent, and she lit a candle. I felt cold and wanted to go to bed. I told her that I wanted to go to the hospital early in the morning, and I went to bed. She, too, got under the blankets not long after I did.

I was nicely falling asleep when her husband came back. He was noisy and loud with his mouth. In no time, the little tent was filled with the smell of liquor. He had been drinking. That is one thing that I had not experienced—drinking, or drunken people. But I had heard what it does to people. I was scared of people who drank because I did not know how to confront them when they were in that state. I was scared about drinking because I had heard that it made people lose their minds. I lay there, not moving, pretending to sleep. Obviously his wife was doing the same, because I did not hear her answer his slurred demands. Eventually he slowed down, and the intervals between his words started getting longer. Finally, he didn't say a word. I could not go to sleep for a while. I could feel the wife moving around. I raised my head and looked toward her. She was just about to blow the candle out when she turned her head and saw me. She put her finger to her lips, giving me the sign not to say anything. Her face had fear, but her eyes had a sneaky look. I nodded my head in assent. She blew out the candle, and I slowly made myself comfortable, falling asleep with the hospital in mind.

The next morning, I never heard the husband leave for work. Cousin was outside sitting near the fire, her baby on her lap. I dressed and went out. It was a beautiful day—the sky was blue and the birds were singing all around us. I could almost hear the silence of nature. Nothing moved—there was no wind at all. It was beautiful fall weather. After I looked at the world, I went over to the fire. Cousin had oats cooked. I had some and told her that I was going over to the hospital to see if I could find a job. That was the only place where I might find a job. (There was the Hudson's Bay Company, but they did not hire Natives.)

I went to see the administrator, who had no manners whatever and not one polite word. I could see that he felt very important with himself and was eager to impress the Natives with his high and mighty job. He hated his job because there was no one there who understood his importance. There was no one there to compete with him. He was not listening when I introduced myself, but I began, "I want an office job. I type forty words a minute and know how to file. I am also interested in nursing." I do not think he believed one word I said. He suddenly got up and went to the outer office. He came back and told me that the qallunaaq girl would give me a test in typing. I sat there while she prepared some papers. I was so determined to get a job that I lost all my nervousness.

Suddenly, the administrator appeared again. One of his secretaries had not come in—apparently she was having problems with her babysitter. His voice became loud and he pointed at me with mighty manners and asked the girl, "What the hell is she doing here? Phone Mrs. Qallunaaq So-and-So, and get her over here." He pointed to me. "Send her over to babysit." He was puffing, and his manner reminded me of a child who was not getting his own way. He disappeared into his office. I could tell the girl was feeling awkward—she had to listen to him, and yet she tried to be polite to me. I could tell that she understood more than him about the Native culture that was involved in her job. She called someone on the phone to come down to take me over to Mrs. Qallunaaq. This person appeared in no time, and I recognized her right away—it was one of the Moose Factory Indian girls that I went to school with so long ago. She recognized me too, and we left the hospital and walked towards the row of houses behind it. We entered into a porch, and she knocked on the door. She tried to tell me that this woman had a different babysitter almost every week. The door opened.

The woman who opened the door looked terribly in need herself. The whole house was a mess, toys all over the floor and dishes piled up in the sink. My former schoolmate left. The woman's orders were to keep the house clean and to make sure the children were clean and taken care of. Did I cook? At that time I had never cooked any food other than fish, seal, whale, geese and ducks. Make bread? I couldn't even remember how to dissolve yeast as I had learned in home economics at school. She never gave me a chance to answer any of her questions, as she was one of those women who talk without ever stopping to get an answer. I was amazed that she was willing to hire me and leave her young children in my hands when she didn't even wait for my answers. Obviously, she was desperate. She asked me to watch her children for the day, and she left to go back to work.

The front door closed. I took a deep sigh, and my mind told me to think things out. I have baby-sat since I was seven years old, for baby cousins and neighbours. But this job involved a lot of other things. All day these two little children would be in my hands. And she mentioned cooking and cleaning too! I suddenly felt a great responsibility fall on me. But I looked at it as a challenge and told myself that another job would come my way, that I wouldn't be there long. I was still standing where I was when the woman had been talking to me. I became aware of the two little children sitting on a worn-out couch. They were making strange with me. They had massive red hair and were fair skinned. They showed no dark colouring like their mother, who had black hair. I went over and sat on the couch next to them. I asked for their names and they told me. Both had English accents, just like their mother. I showed them that I was harmless and spoke to them at their level. Both got up and began to bring out their toys to show me. The more I was showed interest in their toys, the more came out, until the whole area was full of toys. I could see that they were beginning to relax with me. Neither had lost their baby fat and were so cuddly.

I fell in love with them. I gave the four-year-old a hug while he was talking away, and immediately the two-year-old came forward. I hugged her too. I could see that I was going to have my hands full with their competition to see who got the most attention. I decided right away that I would have to treat them equally. Then they asked for a drink and led me to the kitchen. They told me that the drink was in the fridge, and I served them. They became even more relaxed and started running around, going in and out of the back door. I let them go on as long as they were not in danger. The four-year-old asked if we could go to the hospital confectionery to see his father, who worked there. I said no, firmly. They were testing me to find out how much I was willing to let them have their own way. I reminded them of the toys on the floor—the way I have been taught in my culture to make children forget what they'd had in mind. Besides, I was not ready to meet the father. God knows what he was like!

The morning went by, and the mother came home for lunch. All four of us sat at the table and ate toast covered with beans, which she made. That was easy enough, I thought. The woman was more relaxed by this time and began to ask me where I had come from, that she had never seen me around before. She appeared patient and loving to her children, but I could tell that she had no time to express her affection all the time. She was a working woman. She was originally from England and had married during the last war. She explained to me how she had met her husband. I was not interested in her past life just then. All I wanted from her was understanding and patience until I got used to what she expected of me, and that she would let me go the next summer, so that I could go home. She understood my predicament right away and told me that I could move in with her family, with a room to myself, that very night. She would pay me twenty dollars a month and I could have days off if I wanted. She would slowly show me how to cook. I did not say anything, nor did I ask any questions. I figured that if she was willing to teach me slowly, I too would find out slowly how they would treat me. So I just gave her gestures of understanding. Then her lunch hour was over, and she had to go back to work. She called out to her children, "goodbye," and they both replied with behaviour that said loudly, "You are free to go, Mommy." She was aghast and asked me what I had done to them. She said that she had never been able to leave without them crying and pulling at her dress. She looked relieved and said, "They like you," then left for the hospital.

I called the two-year old in. I lifted her up and tickled her little round belly. I walked her to her bedroom. She knew right away what that meant. Her little face went sad, so I told her that she would go out and play again when she got up. I used a very firm voice. Then I gave her a big hug and laid her in her crib. She never fussed and made not a sound when I closed the bedroom door. I went out the back door and told the little boy that I had a secret to tell him. He was curious. I told him that I was going to wash the dishes and when I finished, I would come out to play ball with him. He excitedly agreed to this. I could not help hugging him, and I could see that he enjoyed every minute of it. I washed the dishes and joined him out in the backyard. Oh, it was a delight to see his chubby little legs run. He had such a cute laugh.

The afternoon passed by. In a couple of hours, I could hear the crib shaking in the bedroom. I ran and opened the door. The little girl was awake, so I picked her up and brought her outside. I held her on my lap until she fully awoke. She freed herself from my lap and went to a sandbox. I sat on the steps and watched them both. I thought about my new situation and assured myself that I would find another job more suited to my dreams. For the moment, I had to accept what came my way and do it well. I had to enjoy it and learn from it as much as I could—this is the way of thinking that I had been taught by my people.

While I was sitting on the steps, I looked to the horizon: the new school was right there, just behind the fence of the house where I was. Further down was the village. It was getting chilly, though the sun was still quite high. I ordered the children to come in and closed the back door. We played in the living room. I had nothing else to do—the woman did not give me any other instructions. I just waited and used the time to get more acquainted with the children. I could see that they had learned their own little ways of telling the time. They both began to stand around at the front window. Suddenly, they announced that their mommy was coming. They ran to the door and left it open.

The woman came onto the porch and greeted her children cheerfully. I could tell that she was glad her working day was over for the night. She greeted me very happily and asked if the children had been bad. To me, that was a strange question—in my culture, we expect children to be bad and good, and that parents will teach them the difference. I did not answer her, but only returned her cheerful smile. She went straight to the kitchen and called me there. She had decided to invite me for supper and to meet her husband. I thanked her and stood watching while she peeled potatoes. She reminded me again that I could move in and have my own room. She wondered if I would like to do so that evening after supper. I was not answering as I was thinking about the whole idea, wondering what I was getting into. I wondered if she would ever let me go once I decided to leave for something else in the future. I would like to leave in peace, with a feeling that I had made friends. She knew my situation well. She knew that there would be no ships or planes leaving for my home until next summer. She knew about the people I was staying with. She knew everything that went on outside her home—it was a small community. Everybody knew who was who, and who did what. I said that I would think about it and discuss it with the woman I was staying with. "Oh yes," she said, and made a comment that the woman who I was staying with was nice. "But him? He is a rabble-rouser and bad tempered," she said. I knew that too, but I did not say so.

The front door opened, and a towering, massive curly-red-haired man entered. He went straight to the children and lifted them both in his arms. He put them down and tickled their tummies. He looked so happy to see them, and the children were delighted. Both were trying to tell him when they'd done today. His eyes were going back and forth to each of them, giving them gestures of interest. Suddenly, the little boy asked if he knew Mini. "Mini who?" he asked, still funning. "Come to the kitchen and see her!" The boy was pulling him by the arm. He looked surprised when he saw me and asked his wife who I was while he kissed her on the cheek. "This is Mini, who is going to look after the children. Mini is staying for supper." Mini this and Mini that. She told him everything she knew about me, right down to my situation and that I might be moving in with them. He was quiet, standing there, one of his arms leaning on the fridge. He was looking at me and sizing me up. Finally, he asked me who my father was. He knew him and knew that he navigated ships in the summer. He kept looking. I felt awkward and very shy. Obviously, he knew nothing about the new babysitter. He never said another word and went into the bathroom to freshen up for supper.

The woman had it all ready, and all of us sat and ate. The children and I were quiet while they discussed their jobs and who they had seen today at the hospital. He was the manager at the confectionery. His father had been a settler from Scotland, and his mother was a native of Moose Factory. He looked like a Scottish whaler, with a deep sense of humanity and the humour of an Indian. The children left the table and played quietly in one of the bedrooms. I felt so shy and ate so slow. The husband was very outspoken and commented with humour that I ate like a mouse. I ate even slower and smiled, my eyes glued to my plate. She asked him not to tease, making me feel awkward. He suddenly got up and practically ran into the kitchen. She followed him. Something was wrong—though I felt very shy, I could feel his doubts. He did not hide anything, not even his words. He began to throw questions at her, loud and clear. "How long is she going to last? How old is she? Fifteen? Sixteen? Does she know how to care for small children? Look at her, she is so slow! She wouldn't move if a bomb fell. Christ! Why don't you quit working and bring up our children for a change? Our children are picking up all kinds of things from these week-to-week babysitters!" The woman did not say a word.

He spoke no more. She was calm and calming him at the same time, and then she said, "Okay, dear, I will work just for another year and pay off our bills. After that, I won't ever go back to work." She knew how to placate him, making him realize her reasons for working. He went into the living room and picked up a magazine. She came over to me and more or less apologized for the outburst. I just smiled at her to let her know that I understood, but my own feelings were anxious about whether to accept this job or not. I still had a feeling that I could find a job somewhere else. If the couple agreed among themselves to hire me, then I was willing to show them what I was capable of. The woman asked me to help her bring in the dishes to the kitchen. She asked me not to mind what her husband said, that he was not all that mean. Once I got to know him, he would be like a father to me. I could see that she was determined to hire me.

No doubt the man was listening from the living room, but the woman seemed cheerful again and this cheered me up too. I began to ask her if so-and-so that I went to school with was here at Moose Factory. The woman knew everybody, and a couple of the names I mentioned were of people related to her husband. He came into the kitchen and spoke, "Christ, you women sure know how to make a man feel small and guilty." He banged the counter with his fist right in front of me and said, "You are hired! Come at nine o'clock tomorrow morning with your belongings." The woman jumped for joy and hugged him and turned to me and said, "See, Mini, he is not so mean." I felt shy and awkward because I had never seen couples hugging so intimately. He gave her a loving pat on the rear and went back to the living room. The woman and I finished the dishes. I asked her if I could go now, and she gave me a cheerful "yes."

I left through the front door. The air was fresh, and the sun was just disappearing behind the trees. I suddenly felt very tired when I was walking back towards the little tent. It felt strangely good to be back. Although there was a lot of apprehension and anxiety in this place, at least the faces I was now looking at were not so strange. I told my cousin that I had found a job and that I would be moving tomorrow morning. She was glad for me and wanted to know where I was going and who I would be living with. She knew the couple, that the man was good, but the woman? She was a strange qallunaaq with stiff manners. I did not say anything, although I wondered if I would be happy there. My cousin looked at me and began to encourage me, reminding me that I would at least be busy now, that the next summer would come fast, and that if the woman fired me, I could come and stay with her when she and her husband moved to their house. I felt good knowing that I had somewhere to go if I got fired and thrown out on the street. I wanted to tell my cousin that I appreciated her kindness. Of course, nothing came out of my mouth. I always felt phoney and unnatural when I was supposed to express gratitude, even though I was deeply grateful. I just gave my cousin gestures of thankfulness and went to bed.

The next morning, I got up and arranged my two suitcases, which had hardly been unpacked since I had arrived. I went out and looked at the world—it was the same as the day before, just beautiful, I had oats for breakfast. I told my cousin that the woman wanted me there at eight-thirty this morning. I told her, too, that I would come to see her when I was free and said goodbye. As I left, I turned around to look at her. She was standing and watching, her hands wiping tears from her eyes. I knew that she was not crying for me, because I was not going very far. She was crying because I had been able to give her some peace and had controlled her husband's temper. She lived in constant fear.

I walked on. I arrived and knocked on the front door. The woman opened the door and was so cheerful, talking a mile a minute. I just said "yes" and "no," trying to hide my apprehension about what I was getting into. They had moved everything around. They put the two-year-old in their bedroom, the boy into the dining room, and I was put into the children's former bedroom. The dining table was in part of the living room. The woman had the bed all made in my room and the closet emptied. I had a bedside table and a chest of drawers. That was all there was in the room—the rest was bare. I put my two suitcases near the bed. She hurried on to get to work and left. The children were still in their pyjamas, toast crumble on their cheeks. Oh, they were so cute and bubbling, and I gave them my full attention. I thought: home was just meant to be a memory, and make one wherever you are as best you can!

HOUSEWORK IS A LONELY AFFAIR

A couple of months passed by. As she had promised, the woman showed me what to do every day. Every morning, before she left for work, she would tell me how to prepare the roast, the pork chops, the hamburger, beans, bread, or whatever. Eventually, I took over the meal plans and chores. Some I knew that I did well, and some I just could not, especially mashing potatoes. One day, the husband called me into the kitchen while I was setting the table. "Stand right there and watch," he said. He began to mash the potatoes, adding to them salt, butter and milk. I had been putting in only salt. "That is how you mash potatoes," he said, slamming the masher on the counter. The potatoes were tasty. That is how I have mashed potatoes ever since—even today. Each time I put down the masher, gently, I still hear the bang, loud in my memory. He was not angry or mean—he was just that kind of teacher. Though I learned a great deal about cooking from both of them, the mashing of potatoes is what I cherish from him, and from her, Yorkshire puddings.

That was the only complaint I heard from him. I did not receive any from her. She was just so glad that I was there while she was able to go out to work. She seemed lonely. She hardly had any company, even though men came to see him. Slowly, she began to tell me her worries, anxieties, and interests. She began to tell me who should be my friends and who should not. She wanted my friends to come anytime I wanted them. She told me about a woman down the street who gave piano lessons, that she would speak to her to ask if I could have lessons from her once a week. I had had piano lessons from the nuns in school, but I didn't tell her that. She had spoken to her and made arrangements for me to go in the evenings, once a week, for fifty cents an hour. I began my lessons. The teacher was the wife of one of the doctors at the hospital. She, too, had an English accent. I was her only Native student—the rest were all qallunaat children.

I arrived at the house, which was only four houses down from mine. I knocked on the door, and a woman in high heels opened it. She looked so out of place, all dressed up while everybody else was dressed in country clothes: slacks and sweaters. She knew who I was and sat me at the piano. She asked me if I had ever had lessons and I said, "Just a little." I wanted to see how she was going to teach me. As I expected, she taught altogether differently from what I was used to when I was with the nuns. She used the keys with ABC's, whereas I was used to Do Re Mi's.

I wanted to get to know her, to find out how she was going to treat me. I had met and come to know many qallunaat by then and had learned to be cautious with them. Some are nice and kind, but none want to see or understand my Native culture. Some don't want to know, some don't have time, some try but find it too deep to understand or accept. They all want to cover it up with their ways. They always want me to be different, a novelty, and they refuse to see that I am a plain human being with feelings, aches, hatred, the desire to cheat, lie, love, adore, understanding, kindness, humanity, pain, joy, happiness, gratitude, and all the other things that every other being was capable of having, doing, thinking and acting. They think that the Inuit were nothing but a bunch of smiley, happy people. They never stop to think that Inuit, too, are capable of killing and murdering, just as their society is full of. They want Inuit to dress and talk like them, and to forget their own ways. Yet they will never really accept the Inuit fully. They want us to remain as different from them as cold is from hot. But if I have learned anything from my twenty-one years of living in the South, it is that I, too, cannot accept qallunaat fully, and I always have to be cautious. We are as different from each other as hot and cold.

I took my piano lessons weekly. The teacher started me with a simple piece that I had already learned at Fort George. Most of the time, I played my pieces by heart, as the tunes began to come back to me. I had a hard time with her use of ABC's, because my mind was saying, "Do Re Mi." One evening, I arrived at the teacher's house and as usual took off my coat and sat myself at the piano. She came into the room directly from the kitchen. She never had greeted me, ever—just gave me the lesson and showed me the pages of the books I was to follow. She never used my name. This evening, she did not get on with the lesson, but spoke. "You Natives are so talented, you Natives should take advantage of your free education, you Natives should aim for higher things." You Natives should this and that. I just sat there taking it all in. She had never spoken so much to me before. I was not answering, though I was thinking that no one had ever shown us how to use our talents to their full capacity in our changing world. No one had ever told us that we received a free education, or shown us what their way of education might prepare us for. Nobody had told us what was high or low in this culture we were forced to learn.

She gave me a page to follow on the piano and disappeared into the kitchen. I sat a few seconds and thought. I felt frustrated. I felt that she should tell me how to use her way of education to full capacity, not blurting it out with her mouth twisting with the word "Natives." She forced it out like a dirty word. For the first time, I felt a hint of hate growing inside me—I did not have to take this stranger's attitudes in my land and home. I folded the page she had given me and, with all my heart, played a tune I once performed at a school concert. I played it right to the end, loudly and with my fingers shaking, which made the tune even better. I finished it like an expert piano player, as if I was going to get an encore, running my fingers from the low notes right down to the high notes. I rose, took my coat, and went out. I never went back again.

Once outside, I took my time to walk back to what was now my home. The air was cool, and a bit of snow was already on the ground. I entered the door, which was never locked. As usual, the woman greeted me so cheerfully and asked how I was doing. I said, "okay," as if nothing had happened. I drank a glass of milk and went to bed. The next day at lunch time, the woman told me that she had seen my teacher, that she said I was doing so well, that I should come back, that she would give me more advanced lessons. She also returned the fifty cents that I had left on the piano. I told the woman that I would see. She encouraged me to keep going, and said that I should take advantage of the opportunity. That the teacher was strange in many ways, but meant well. Did she really mean well, or did she just want the money to collect and save for her holidays in the South? I never tried to find out. I felt that if the Natives bothered her so much, I didn't have to make her put up with me. I had learned long ago that you don't hang around when you are not really wanted.

My daily chores went on, day in and day out. I got so that I could do them in no time, and the children didn't feel like such a handful anymore, as I had got to know their little ways and habits. But I felt very lonely. Nobody visited me: my old schoolmates did not want to come. They felt alright with the man of the house—some of them were related to him—but they felt strange with her. A few said that she was too stiff and cold. I did not find her that way, or maybe I was just used to her. Instead, I visited them, but all were doing something: some working, some married, and some going steady with boyfriends. They had no time for me, so I did not visit them anymore. My cousin had moved into her new house, and I went to visit her one evening. I was aghast and pained when I saw her condition. She had a black eye, and one side of her face was all colours, pink, blue, red and black. She seemed to be in pain in other parts of her body when she walked. I did not have to ask her what had happened. She began to cry and blurted out all her fears. She begged me to move in with her. Her husband had beaten her while he was drunk. She said that I was the only one who was able to control him and make him ashamed of his temper when I was around. I gave her gestures of sympathy and told her that I would speak to the woman I worked for. My cousin was also pregnant, her second child-to-be. I went back home, and everybody was in bed. I moved around quietly and went to bed too. Cousin's bruised face kept coming to my mind before I fell asleep.

The next day I spoke to the woman and told her that I wanted to move in with my cousin, that I would come every day at nine o'clock. She looked shocked and said that she would discuss it with her husband that evening. I did not expect them to discuss it right in front of me, but they did during supper time at the table. "Mini wants to move in"—she mentioned the bad-tempered one's name—"with so-and-so." He looked aghast and turned to me. "Do you know the people?" he asked. I nodded yes with my head. "Christ, he beats his wife—imagine what he would do to you. No! No way are you moving there. You are a stranger here in Moose—do you know what that means? You are in our hands, you are under our care. You may be working for us, but you are in our hands. We would feel responsible if harm should come to you."

As usual, he got up and stomped to the kitchen, as he always did when he was in a lecturing and caring mood. He came back to the table and continued, "You are welcome here—we have taken you in as part of our family. You are safe here, you eat well here, you have a private room. Do you know that this is the first time the children have had anyone they liked—and probably love even more than us parents? Over there, you won't even get decent sleep, you will be up all night while he's drinking, and Christ! He might even get you to drink. My wife and I have plans, and you are included in them." He told me enough to make me realize that I would be safe here until I got home next summer. I never looked at him while he spoke, just listened to his caring and responsible Indian nature, which he inherited from his mother. Otherwise, when I looked at him, all I saw was a towering whaler. "You go and tell that cousin of yours that you can't move in with her," he said. "If she keeps begging you, tell her that I will go and see her and tell her myself our reasons for not letting you go."

I went the next day and told my cousin that I did not want to move in. I never mentioned what the man had said. I did not have to, as she understood as usual, with her kind nature. But I still visited her once in a while. She always had a lot to say about her feelings and needed to get rid of her bottled-up emotions. I gave her no advice, nor did I make her any promises. I just sat there and let her pour out her fears and gave her gestures of sympathy. She had another baby girl and died a few years later. She was so young. Whatever killed her probably had much to do with her living conditions. The husband went back to his mother with the two little girls. The two girls went to the Fort George school that I had gone to. He has since married again. I have seen them since, and his second wife looks happy. He drinks but does not get drunk anymore. He has started a new family. I guess he is one of those people who learn slowly, and eventually grow up and become wise in later years.

Gradually, the woman had me doing the grocery shopping down at the Hudson's Bay to supplement the food her husband was receiving as an allowance from his job. She asked me to shop for the children's clothes. The children and I would walk down to the Bay, half a mile away, pulling a cart to bring back whatever I bought. Sometimes I felt that the children were my own. They cried to me, they expressed their fears and joys to me, they called for my help, they ran to me when they were in pain and asked me to kiss away their aches. I was in their parents' hands, but the house and the children were in mine.

I did not visit anymore, though sometimes I went out to a movie. I always found someone to sit with—an old schoolmate or someone I was just beginning to know. That was all. I did not have a special friend and eventually gave up trying to find one, as everyone was involved with their own little affairs. Eventually, I did not bother to take my days off, which were on Saturdays, outside the home. Most of the time, I spent them in my room, sewing or knitting something for one of the children. Sometimes, I mended some clothing or did ironing in my room. The couple always sat in the living room, discussing their private affairs. Sometimes they were invited out to a party, and I would stay in and babysit. Sometimes I went to bed with the children and would wake up to the radio blaring from the living room. The man liked to listen to the morning news which was coming from Timmins, Ontario. He would have the bathroom door open, shaving and listening at the same time. I would dress and start the breakfast for both of them. They would eat and leave at the same time.

The children would just be waking up, and the three of us would have breakfast together and discuss what we were going to do for the day. Of course, they always suggested something that was not allowed, like visiting Daddy at his work. My mind would get busy, planning and plotting how to make them forget the idea. I would suggest the next best thing, like playing ball. Though I loved the two children, my whole self craved for company whom I could talk to at my level. Physically, I was very busy, but mentally, I was very, very lonely. I learned that housework is a very lonely affair.

I STILL KNEW HOW TO BE HAPPY

Winter came, and sometimes I would go to hockey games. A team would come over from Moosonee and play with the hospital team. Christmas came and passed. Then spring was in the air. Thoughts of home preoccupied me. I began to take longer walks with the children. They enjoyed the fresh air as much as I did. Sometimes, we went down to the river and watched people coming and going in their canoes. All of them knew us and greeted us so kindly. The days were getting longer while the sun began giving life to nature and waking up the blackflies and mosquitos. Then that spectacular ice break came, and there was no more ice in the river. Little airplanes began to arrive.

One day, during one of my usual walks, I met up with the Moose Factory Indian Agent. He always said hello whenever I saw him, but today he stopped me and said, "Mini, have I got good news for you! You are wanted in Ottawa—you have a job there." Normally he did not have a serious nature, so I did not believe him. Who the heck knew me in Ottawa? I walked off and told him that he was teasing. He yelled back that he was serious. I kept on walking and gave him a teased-feeling little laugh. "Come and see me in my office sometime, when you get the time," he said. I did not answer him again and altogether forgot the whole episode.

I began to wonder how I should approach the couple about wanting to go home. I knew the ships would be running soon, but I kept putting it off, as I did not know how to go about it. In the meantime, the family and I started going out on picnics by motor canoe. Sometimes I ran the motor while they enjoyed the scenery. While we were out, I could not help but notice that the woman was a complete stranger to these surroundings. I could see that she knew nothing about picnicking. She didn't know how to make a fire, she didn't know how to explore the beaches, the woods or even the water. I could see that she had grown up in a city. Her husband was just the opposite—he enjoyed every minute of the outing. As for me, it was natural to be in the wilds of nature. I played with the children on the sand and taught them to make sand cakes and igloos. I taught them how to skim a flat stone on top of the water. I would gather firewood from along the beach, and the husband would make the fire while his wife sat there on a blanket, looking out of place. I wanted to show her how to enjoy the wilds like she had shown me how to enjoy cooking, but I felt shy about taking the initiative. We would hardly have gotten there and she would be begging her husband to go home. He would start playing with the children as soon as she mentioned "home," trying to make the best of what he enjoyed. But, she was patient and understood him. She probably had gone through this experience many times and knew how to cope.

And me? I did not show my thoughts and feelings. I did not express my natural happiness while we were on the true land. I did not take sides, even though I knew that they each had different tastes. I could be in the wilds of the land and in their man-made home, wherever they decided to go. I just made the best of everything. The woman's tone, when she spoke while we were out, would stay uninterested the whole time. Then her husband would announce that we were going home. Suddenly, she would become cheerful and would be bubbly all the way home. She would let out a big sigh when we entered the house and look so relieved. Her body would look so secure and relaxed then. All of us would be full of fresh air, and we felt tired. We would all make an effort get ourselves to bed.

Though I longed for my own people, I felt happy and accepted by the couple, especially by the children. Time went by, and the news was in the air that the ships were running. I still didn't know how to approach the couple. The longer I left it, the harder it became for me to tell them that I wanted to leave. They had no idea I wanted to leave—I had never mentioned the subject of home to them. They never asked me either; they acted as though I was there permanently. They never realized that I, too, could long for home. The woman made plans for all of us to have a summer holiday, and I said nothing. Who was I to shatter her dreams? The chores had become routine, and I automatically did them by reflex now.

One day, they came home early, both full of excitement. He spoke first, as he had a more excitable nature when it came to human feelings, saying, "Mini, have you got a surprise coming! You had better change!" I just had regular housework clothes on. I was very surprised to see him so excited, but I followed his orders anyway. The wife was ordering me not to wash the dishes that night. They wouldn't tell me what it was all about. I felt a little scared, because I thought they might be trying to fix me up with a boyfriend. They had mentioned several times that I should find one. I changed while they made supper. We ate, and they both did the dishes, all the while watching the clock which hung over the sink in the kitchen. They finished the dishes, and he said, "It won't be long now, Mini." I sat on the couch in the living room as if I was the company, not the maid. Both of them put the children to bed, but the children were screaming for me. "You leave Mini alone for tonight," the woman ordered both of them. "I want to kiss Mini goodnight!" was the reply. I went and let them give me a hug, and kissed them both on their chubby cheeks. Their mother kissed them and closed their bedroom door. The three of us sat back down in the living room.

Suddenly there was a knock at the front door. The man practically ran to answer it, and she got up, too. Two men came in: one was a tall Indian, and the other was short, tanned, and ugly as ever. It was my father! I jumped off the couch and went to him. He gave me a grown-up caress. I shook hands with his partner, and we all sat down. I wanted to say so much to my father. I wanted to tell him that I longed to go home. I hoped he would order me to go home in front of the couple. I was using so much energy thinking about how I should begin to tell him that I was happy, but that I wanted to go home. But nothing came out of my mouth, and I felt shy and awkward. He asked me how long I had been with the family, and I said, since I came. I was expecting him any minute to tell me to come home. I was expecting him any minute to talk to the couple, saying that he wanted me home. But every time he spoke, we both felt too awkward to speak our language in front of these people who did not understand us. That was something we did not do, unless it was an ugly situation. So, he began to talk to the man. The Indian sat there and listened. I had never heard the man speak his mother's tongue before, but there he sat conversing with my father in Cree. It was odd to hear him speaking Indian words, sitting there with his massive curly red hair and whaler-looking body. They talked about ships, Old Factory, and hunting.

The woman made coffee and served everyone. She looked uncomfortable, still very English in her ways after having been among her husband's Native people all these years. Having met middle-class English people myself, I think she probably felt yucky serving Natives. Somehow, I couldn't ignore her—it was as though I was seeing her for the first time. Now my wonderings were answered. I often wondered why all those relatives of his did not visit, not even his parents, who came to see their grandchildren only at Christmas. And they had not relaxed at all when they came. It was as though they did their duty and that was all. We once visited his parents—they had acted polite with her, but I could see that it was a cold relationship. She had wanted me to sit near her, which was a strange request. I guess she needed a little security at the time. The visit was straining—even I had felt it. It was not natural, the way children and grandchildren usually visit grandparents. We never went back to visit. I did not miss it, even though I could not help but wonder how grandparents could ignore such cute grandchildren. Whatever had happened among these in-laws in the past, I did not know, and I did not ask. I imagined that the parents had picked out a wife for him while he was away during the war in England. Instead, he had come home with one who was a stranger to his own people. Maybe that broke up the relationship. Maybe the parents had accepted and welcomed her but could not melt that cold middle-class English nature. Maybe she was shocked when she first came to the wilds of Canada. Maybe she was in a state of shock from the war. Who knows? It could have been anything. However, I saw her for the first time that evening, and somehow, I could not help but feel sorry for her. I got up to help her, and she did not urge me to sit anymore.

Father and his partner visited for a couple of hours more and then left to return to the ship at Moosonee. He said he would come back the next day. The three of us sat for a while. The man began to tease me. "How can such an ugly father produce such a pretty girl? Christ, I could not believe that he was your father when he was brought to the confectionery this afternoon! He sure knows a lot about ships," he went on. "What did he say to you in Eskimo?" I told him plainly. Then she spoke, first to him. "Do you always have to be so outspoken? You are insulting Mini!" She did not have to worry about that. I had always known that Father was not the best-looking, but he had a heart as big as all outdoors, kind and loving. She continued, "He must care an awful lot for you. How many fathers would come all the way from Old Factory to see their daughters? Do you think he will ask you to go home? Surely, you don't want to go home?" Of course, she did not wait for my answer, but she was thinking and so was her husband. Then he began, "Christ, you wouldn't go just like that, would you? You don't even have time to pack. We couldn't replace you in one day. It would take weeks for us to find someone else. I'll speak to him myself tomorrow." That was the end. We all went to bed before I had a chance to speak for myself. I lay in bed thinking and knew that it looked impossible for me to go home with Father. I knew that the man would manage to persuade my father, that Father was too soft-hearted, that he would give in. I prepared myself for whatever would happen and fell asleep.

The next day I felt so happy, knowing that I would see my father again. The weather was hot now. The blackflies and mosquitos were everywhere as I went out to look at the world from the back door. I had to start rubbing some kind of cream onto the children's faces, legs and arms so they wouldn't get bitten so much. I sang and had the radio on all day, which was rare for me to do. I was just so happy. My chores were nothing to me now, and I did them in no time. I was moving around like a madwoman in order to get them done. The hours went by, and the couple came home. They, too, felt my happiness. I guess I was glowing all over. I couldn't help but notice that I had not felt so elated in a long time. I still knew how to be happy.

FATHER, PLEASE TAKE ME HOME

The family and I had our supper and waited for my father. He arrived at the same time as the day before. He had gotten a ride over from someone who was coming home to this side of Moose Factory, so he had no ride back, and he was leaving early the next morning on the trip to Old Factory. He visited for a couple of hours and, as I expected, was persuaded to allow me to stay on. The man offered to take him back to the ship in his own boat and said that I could come with. We dressed warmly, as it is always colder on the water. It was a dark night, and the tide was out. In the boat, Father offered to run the motor for the man. I could see that he did not feel safe with the man, especially when the tide was out. It is tricky to travel at night at low tide. Father had much experience with this kind of travel, and he knew that the man did not. He had just gone out on short trips in deep water. But the man refused Father's offer, and then he wished he had not. We kept running into rocks, and then suddenly, the motor would stall. The man could not see beyond the bow of the boat. As Father had expected, the man did not know the correct travel route for when the tide is out. Father knew that the man did not depend on such travel: he was a wage earner, not a nomad like himself. So, Father finally started pointing with his arms, showing the man where to go.

When we reached the ship, the man held on to the side to keep the canoe anchored. Father didn't move out of the canoe, but faced me and spoke: "Be kind, be patient, and take care of your responsibilities well. If you are confronted with unpleasantness, do not respond the same way. If you will be good to people, they will be good to you, and most of all, do not be makkutuk"—a soft-headed teenager. It is at this stage, in my culture, when teens are considered noisy, prone to doing daring things, easily-led and impulsive. It is a stage that adults accept because everybody goes through it. Eventually, adults teach teens what they need to know so that they can get out of this stage and become adults. This is why teenagers were never marked down as "juveniles" until the qallunaat came. Inuit believe that all teens will eventually come out of this impulsive stage if they are treated as teenagers first. Their daring, noisy, impulsive and easily-led behaviour eventually come to be ignored by adults, as Inuit believe that if a person who is acting like a teenager isn't ignored, they become more challenging to deal with. They become even more daring, testing adults all the time. Although the teenager is not ignored on a human level, his or her behaviour is ignored, so that the teen will become a better citizen. It is like telling them quietly, but with firm actions, "We are not impressed anymore. The novelty has worn off. So grow up, show us your ability to be adults." Some teenagers are believed to come out of this stage faster than others. That is another reason why Inuit never really cared about age, how old one is, and how many years since a person was born. Some adults, Inuit or qallunaat, are called makkutuujartut—like teenagers, because they have makkutuk personalities.

Father need not have worried about this with me. It seems to me that I never had the chance to be a teenager, that I grew right from a baby to an adult. It seems to me that I was never allowed to express myself as a teenager would. It seems to me too that I was kept so busy, both physically and mentally, all the years I was growing up that I was prevented from ever being a teenager. Grandmother sure knew how not to let me spill water over. She kept my brother and I so busy with chores that we never got to enjoy the teenage life, it seems now. That is why whenever I saw teenagers acting silly, smart, impulsive and daring, I could never understand why they got such a kick out of what they were doing, because I was never allowed to do that. To me, it was a waste of time and not worthwhile, wasting many hours, because I was made to use my time doing chores. Whenever I saw a lot of teenagers standing around the Hudson's Bay stores, around Coke stands or anywhere else, I could never understand what they got out of hanging around so foolishly, because I was never allowed to be among my teenage peer group. Later, when I had a chance to be among them, away from home, the very thought of acting like them or even being with them used to make me feel uncomfortable, because I did not know about or understand their behaviour. Today, of course, when I see a group of teenagers, I know that they are going through one of the necessary stages of life, and I am so glad that they get to be teens for a while.

While Father was advising me, my only answers were yes, yes, and yes. I could see the man was getting tired of holding on to the ship. Father's last words were, "Just be patient, you will come home again soon." The man wanted to know if Father was finished, as he did not understand our language. I said yes, and he let go of the ship. While the man was trying to start the motor, Father yelled in the dead of night for me to watch the front of the canoe for rocks that we might run into. I tried, while my heart was heavy, tears bursting out of my eyes, and my mind

ONE BOOK ONE FREEPORT 2023
LIFE AMONG THE QALLUNAAT

Freeport Public Library FOUNDATION

One Book One Freeport

Freeport Public LIBRARY
More than books on a shelf.

Youth Storytime & Craft
We will be reading Kumak's River: A Tall Tale from the Far North by Michael Baniea and making our own Inukshuk paintings.
Saturday, February 4th 11:00am
Meeting Room A/B

Film Showings
"The Last Ice" [National Geographic documentary] preceded by a short film "The Owl Who Married a Goose."
Monday, February 6th
6:00pm – 7:30pm &
Wednesday, February 8th
1:30pm – 3:00pm
Boardroom

Book Discussions
February 7th 2pm – 3pm
February 14th 6pm - 7pm
Learning Lab

Adult/Teen Craft:
Soap Stone Carving - REGISTRATION REQUIRED
Soapstone Carving is a well-known aspect of Inuit culture. For decades, Inuit carvings have been prized the world over. Come try it yourself!
Monday, February 13th
6:30-7:45pm
Meeting Room A/B

Hoopla

Musical Guest: Pamyua
Brought to you by the Freeport Art Museum and Arts Midwest.
February 15th 2:30pm
Meeting Room A/B

saying, "Father, please take me home!" We had no problem until we came to the same area where we had hit rocks earlier. Thank goodness, nothing serious happened.

We arrived back at the dock, and I helped the man pull the canoe to the land. He put away the motor in a shed that he owned. I started walking back to the house while my mind still said, "Father, please take me home." The man caught up with me. I was so glad that it was dark—I did not want him to see my tears. He wanted to know all that my father had said. "Christ, I thought he would never stop talking. My arm was getting tired holding onto that ship! He's very understanding—you are a lucky girl to have a father like that." No doubt he was relieved that Father let me stay on. I made no comments whatsoever, and we reached the house, which was only about five minutes away from the dock.

His wife was in bed with her door open. "Pretty happy day, eh, Mini?" she said as I passed. I stopped for a second and gave her a smile, then went into my bedroom. I was tired from crying silently in the canoe, from the fresh night air, and from the strength I had used up, hoping Father would have been strong enough to say to the man that had to I go home. It was good to be in bed and to get rid of the excitement that lingered in my mind. I felt thankful to have had a chance to see Father again, and I fell asleep.

FATHER HAD HIS OWN REASONS

The next day, everything went back to its routine as if there had been no excitement during the previous couple of days. I forced myself to do my chores. The two children kept my energy running and my day interesting. They helped me to forget my father and my home, to put them at the back of my mind. But once in a while, I could not manage to pay full attention to the two of them. I would sit and think, trying to figure out what my father had planned to do before he came to see me. No doubt he had come to see what kind of life I was leading or growing into. Probably he had planned to take me home for good, so that his worries about my marriage would end. To him, and according to our customs, I should have been married and having my own children to strengthen our Inuit group, to contribute to our economy. All that is very important to Inuit fathers. Yet his loving heart and his capacity to see that his daughter was needed by others made him give up the thought of taking me home. And, as long as there was peace, he was going to be peaceful too.

As I sat there in this strange home, I kept feeling his thoughts, that he was definitely thinking about taking me home next time. He had a reason—a reason that every Inuk man had regarding his daughter, which was almost like a law because it was followed and obeyed, from our ancestors' way of doing things long ago. To him, and to our culture, and according to our systems of belief and our customs that we followed for many years, I was now eligible to marry, while my young body and mind were still able to take on the responsibility of caring for other human beings, that is, my future children. My father was worried about and felt responsible to our culture. He was worried that I might get too out of hand and taste other ways of life that were alien to him. He knew that according to our culture, I was eligible to marry at my age of eighteen—and that in fact, I was already overdue. He never once thought that there were many other men, maybe from different cultures, who I could easily marry. He was not aware of his children's changing world. He only had one man in mind for me: the one he had helped to choose at my birth, my angilissiak. And for me? I was too young to understand his worries, too young to understand what marriage meant, too young to even think of marriage at the time.

Years later, I found out why he did not fight to take me home. After Grandfather Weetaltuk's death, the James Bay group had no leader, no one who kept them together. They had tried to elect one of Weetaltuk's oldest sons as the leader, but he was not strong like his father and had been ailing. Both his youngest son and my father were too young, and neither was outspoken enough to be able to lead other adults. They would have been taken advantage of all the time had they tried. At this time, too, the qallunaat from the Department of Northern Affairs had already visited twice, asking the James Bay group to move to Great Whale River. Father felt at the time that nothing was right at home—there was no solid base. Everything was in upheaval. There was no security left among them, and Father did not want me to come home to that. As Father put it, "Our home was nalunartuq"—hard to understand, future unknown, solid security missing. It was as though my group had dispersed into nothing—the proud people were no more. Grandfather had taken it all with him when he died. So, Father did have reasons for not taking me home.

HARMONY IS NOT FOREVER

My father has never expressed regret or happiness about my marriage into another culture. As always, he gave me only advice. "Do what pleases him, and he will please you, too. Don't arouse him to something you will regret. You may not always know it, but you will be the foundation of your home—it will be up to you how that foundation stands. You are the woman, the mother, who is capable of thinking, planning, or even plotting which way the marriage will fix itself. If you show goodness to him, he will return it to you."

Somehow, I do not believe that advice—it does not work in the qallunaat culture. Father did not know that qallunaat men are not like Inuit men. I have tested his advice to see if it works. I have learned that some qallunaat men do not know how to appreciate goodness in their wives, do not know how to return goodness to them. I have learned that the nicer you are and the more willing to cater to them without complaint, the more they think they have a regular maid or even a slave. I am not saying that every qallunaat marriage is that way. I, too, have learned to argue, to fight, and to tell my qallunaaq husband loud and clear that while I am his maid in many ways, I, too, like to be served. To me, slavery has an entirely different meaning than working hard physically everyday. I would feel like a slave if my affections were not returned, when what I have done to improve my household and motherly duties was not noticed, when whatever I made was not complimented by my husband. To me, marriage is a very private venture among the many adventures of any society.

After my father's visit, the summer came into full bloom. I felt happier now that I had seen him. Though I had accepted my responsibilities well up until this point, I now began to accept them even better. I got to know the individual idiosyncrasies of the couple, just as much as I did with the ways of their children. They became concerned about my health, my loneliness, my feelings, and what kinds of friends I was making. I could tell that they were happy and appreciated my services. The more they showed it, the more I was willing to serve them better. The children were my reward, my company, and they made me feel that I was a worthy person. Though the couple decided what kinds of clothes the children wore, what kind of foods they ate, where and how long I took them for walks, the children were entirely in my hands. I began to notice that they were picking up the way I spoke and expressed myself, and I was picking up their mother's English accent. I also picked up her English habit of drinking tea. Whereas I picked up from her husband that his shirts should always be ironed, neat, and hung, ready for wear. Every little rule in the house was now fixed in my head. But fixed happiness and rewards are not meant to stay forever. There is always something trying to interfere or ruin a state of harmony.

The planes and ships were coming and going during this beautiful summer. One afternoon, there was a knock at the front door, and I went to answer it. Who should be at the door but the instigator. I was glad to see her and was excited by this surprise visit. I had not seen her for almost five years. I invited her in and gave her a cup of tea. We sat and discussed many things, the many people that we knew and our relatives. She asked me about my job, my pay, about the couple, and what I planned to do later. I told her everything, as I felt that she was concerned about me. It seemed she had changed and had grown up. I convinced myself of this, because even I had changed in small ways. Suddenly, after I had told her everything, her manner, which had been understanding a few minutes before, became impish, and that old instigating nature was in her eyes. Though I did not show it, I felt apprehensive inside me while she went on: "Mini, you don't have to be here, these people don't own you, you don't have to be a maid, you don't have to earn measly pay. You are Weetaltuk's granddaughter—you can do better than this. Why don't you come with me back to Hamilton and finish nursing? Why don't you get another job with better pay? You don't have to look after someone else's brats, you don't have to do without nice clothes, and you don't have to stay here at Moose!"

My hands were behind my neck, my long hair over my arms and my elbows leaning against the table. I was looking at her while she spoke, my head nodding in agreement to more or less make peace so that I wouldn't arouse her temper. I knew she was right in many ways, but I couldn't help but think that she had not really changed. She was still her old self: she thought of no one but herself, she was still a spoiled brat, she did things for her own gain. All she had on her mind was me, me, me, me and mine, mine, mine. She still didn't know how to consider other people's feelings. I agreed with my people that some people stayed makkutuk all their lives, while others take longer to get out of that teenage stage. She was one of them. She became quiet, because I was not responding very well. She knew me too—that I was a long-time thinker, that I took things as they came, and that I respected and was a great deal influenced by my parents' advice. She realized that I had known her for many years. Suddenly, she remembered that she had a date with one of the pilots who had flown in that morning. She was proud to tell me that, because she knew I was not as open and forward as she was—nor able to get a date as fast as she could. She knew that I had been there almost two years, and still I had no dates. I did not care. Who the heck was the pilot? I didn't know him—he didn't have any importance to me. He was nameless to me, though he would have a face when at some point he would fly me home. He had come to my land to find himself a job and would disappear when the winter came.

She left as unexpectedly as she came. Though I was glad to see her, as she was one of my Inuit group, I soon forgot her again. She did not forget me, though. No, she did not. Probably she wondered about me long after she left. A few days later, a letter was found by the woman, written to her husband, saying that I was madly in love with him, and supposedly signed by me. I could not even begin to write on this page all the other things that it said. I tried to deny the whole thing to both of them, but everything got worse. She took it very seriously, while he laughed at the whole thing. The more she got suspicious, the more he teased me in front of her, acting out gestures and saying, "Yes, darling; yes, dear; anything, dear; oh sweetheart" with that Native humour he had inherited from his mother. I could see that he was a true Native of his people. If someone is accused of doing such a serious thing when it is not true, the only thing to do is to make a joke of it.

He knew that he was not guilty, but did his wife know? She was very doubtful. I could not believe that she did not know her own husband after all those years. I could not understand why she did not believe me. "But you signed the letter," she kept reminding me. But I did not write it, was all I could say. I could see that she did not believe me. She could not even understand the simple fact that I was the one who was supposed to be in love, not her husband. And he just made it worse. I could see that the more suspicious she was, the more he got a kick out of the whole thing. It was as though he was enjoying her jealousy.

For a while, we all forgot the whole thing, and our daily lives went on. But every now and then, I felt her doubts. I could see that he had forgotten completely because he did not tease me anymore. I felt glad that at least one of them believed that I did not write the letter.

The dismal fall weather seemed to arrive so quickly. The grey skies, rain, and sleet made me feel dismal, too. I became very aware of the kind of weather we were having because I was going out more often to visit friends to get away from the suspicions of the woman. She was tearing apart my relationship to every one of them, including the children. Though she did not bring up the subject anymore, I could see that she did not trust me. She watched every move I made, and I was dying inside. She was killing my natural innocent behaviour. Sometimes at nights, long after we had gone to bed, I would hear her questioning her husband. He would be so gentle with his voice and give her all the expressions of love that he had for her, even if he had not spoken them so loudly in the past. I would fall asleep while she still questioned him.

I would wake up the next morning, hoping that she had gone back to normal. Though their waking, eating, and work habits were the same, her suspicions lingered on. She did not have to speak them, but I felt them anyway. When I felt them, I became unnatural. I did not have that happy willingness to serve her anymore. I did not want to greet her husband when he came home, afraid that she might read something into it.

One late afternoon, he came home early. The door opened: I turned, and there he was, moving slow and limping. His massive red curly hair stood out against his fair, pale face. He limped over to the nearest chair and ordered me to get him a bowl of water. I did not ask what happened— I just followed his orders. The children asked him, but as usual, he just acted like a child, coming down to their level. "Daddy hurt," he said, "Kiss my foot and make it better." They wouldn't kiss his foot—instead, they laughed and enjoyed their father's humour. I could see that they did not believe that their daddy could get hurt as easily as them. As far as they were concerned, their daddy never gets hurt or gives hurt. The three of them conversed while I started to get supper ready. I could see that he was anxious for his wife to come home from work, because he kept asking what time it was. No doubt he meant to express his pain more and get more meaningful sympathy when she got home. I could see his foot in the clear water of the bowl, swelling and blue up to his ankle.

I had the supper ready when his wife came in. She was shocked to see her husband sitting there. She never even greeted any of us, but started firing questions at her husband. "Well, how long have you been here? Why did you come home? Did you come home to Mini sooner than I so that you could enjoy her more?" She never once noticed his foot in the bowl. There was silence while she stomped into the kitchen. "Well, at least the supper is ready. I am surprised you had time to make it," she went on, glaring at me. My mind said, "Oh no! Not again!"

She went on at me, and suddenly the man spoke. He was mad, so mad, that the colour came back to his face. I have never seen him so mad—I thought that violence was going to start. I could see that many things had been bottled up in him ever since the episode of the letter. The house was echoing with his voice. "Christ!" He was blurting out all kinds of words that I had not heard him use in the past: "I came back home because of this," he pointed to his foot. "A crate full of Coke bottles fell on it. Christ! Of course you weren't here to look after me—I had to get Mini to bring me this bowl." He was moving now, and water was splashing all over the floor. "If you can't have any trust in anybody in this ------- house, I am going to fire Mini and you can stay home and look after us for a change." Silence fell.

She went to him and started apologizing with all her heart, while the children and I kept silent, grouped together at the doorway of the kitchen. I could see that they felt secure with me. I felt secure with them too. She began to tend to him—she got a towel from the closet and dried his foot. In the meantime, supper was getting overdone on the stove. She began to think a little more normally and ordered me to start serving. We ate, and the two tried to make the meal as normal as they could. The children broke the coldness of the air around them. As for me? I had no more desire to be there. I had no wish to live amidst ugly feelings. I decided that I would talk to both of them about leaving when they had calmed down. I knew the happy relations that I had built so patiently and quietly were no more. I learned that jealousy and suspicion created for no reason are very destructive to human relations, and that harmony is not forever.

DID THE DRINK DRIVE ME CRAZY?

Winter was soon half over, and Christmas was in the air. I ordered a set of dishes from Eaton's to give to the couple. Though I had always known Christmas to be a happy occasion, I felt heavy in the heart. The relationship between the woman and me seemed artificial. I kept waiting for the right moment to tell them that I wanted to leave, but I had a lot of things to think about first, before I could tell them. I had no place to go. I had no other job. I did not want to move in with any of my friends. I could not go home as there were no planes or ships running. There was only the train, but that went the other way. I felt utterly stuck. I had to think a bit more. I put the whole thing at the back of my mind and tried to run the household as best I could. At least the children helped cheer me up, and they brightened my grey days.

As the days went by, I began to think about one of the things that the man had said during his raging madness when he had his foot in the bowl of water. He said that he would fire me if there was no more trust in this ------- house. I tried to think of a way for him to fire me, or at least to get his wife to fire me. I was sitting on the cold steps at the back door with my heavy coat on, watching the two children trying to make a snowman. For a while, I could not even see them as I was drowned in evil thoughts: maybe I would arouse her husband, just enough to get her raging, and then she would fire me. She had given me enough ideas with her accusations. Maybe I would turn my services into evil, loving services to him—that would give her some ideas. The deeper I was evilly plotting, the more I thought that was a good idea. But I did not know how to go about it. The very thought of arousing that towering, red, massive curly-haired man made me feel scared.

Suddenly, two voices were coming into my head: "You are the woman, the foundation of a home. You are the woman, who is capable of thinking, of planning, and even of plotting. It is women who lure the men into trouble." It was my father's voice, and I began to understand that he was very right. The other voice I was hearing was one of the children. The boy was calling for my help to put one of the big snowballs on top of another, which was to be the middle of the snowman.

I came to reality and shivered as I got out of my thoughts. I got up and went over to them. The snowball was not even round, but practically oval-shaped. I sort of shaped it and put it on top of the other one, which had no shape at all. It was mostly a clump, a mound with no base. I fixed it a little better for them, trying to live up to their excitement as they saw the man shaping up. They were delighted, bubbling, and hoping that it was going to be the biggest surprise for their daddy. They made me realize that evil thoughts did not go with innocent children. How could I ever put them through pain—or even their father, who had never given me pain? Was I beginning to think of just me, me, me, and mine, mine, mine? Was I going to force something to happen when the very idea was against my culture? Grandmother had always said that nothing ever stays the same, good or bad. I was getting greedy for my own freedom, when I should be learning lessons from my unhappiness. I put the whole plot out of my head and completely forgot about it. I am Inuk—I do not shape my future for my own gain. I let others shape it for me and learn to take whatever comes, good or bad.

The children and I went into the house, and the three of us had hot chocolate. It was two days before Christmas Eve. Everybody seemed to be in a happy state of mind. I, most of all, tried to keep them that way. The couple would sit in the living room, planning the Christmas dinner and who to give which presents to. I was glad that Christmas was here again, because it meant that the summer was coming too, and I would go home for sure. The couple gave me a day off before Christmas so that I could babysit when they went out Christmas Eve. I did not mind that. I was used to it and expected nothing else. I had no special friends with whom to celebrate the occasion.

The couple went out as planned. The children and I were alone. We were sitting in the living room, playing games while I was preparing their little minds to know that it would soon be bedtime. At the same time, I was trying not to cut off their fun-loving state of mind. We kept on playing, and I could see that I was over-playing with them. The more I played, the more out of hand they were getting. They got silly, and instead of trying to control their silliness, I joined them. I came right down to their level and acted like them—even my speech became baby talk. I had not had a release of fun like this for a long time, and I was enjoying the whole thing.

Though their bedtime was overdue, I did not bother to put them to bed. The little boy, who was always sillier, ran over to a small bookcase.

On the top of the bookcase was a carafe of liquor. It was always there, always full, and the husband and wife dipped into it every now and then. But they had never offered me any, nor was I anxious that they should. It was just one of those things that sat in the house, just like the other knick-knacks. I never paid any attention to the carafe, even though I had handled it many times while dusting. I was never tempted to try it; as far as I was concerned—it belonged to the man and his wife.

But the boy made me think. As he was being silly, he began to pour the liquor into one of the glasses that sat by the carafe. I ran over to him and told him not to touch it. As I was taking it out of his little hands, the vapours of the liquor hit my nose. I put my nose closer to the glass while the little boy was urging, "Here, Mini, drink it. It stinks!" I took a sip very carefully, as I was a little scared of it. Somewhere at the back of my mind, I heard that this kind of drink made you crazy. I took another sip, and each time my throat would burn and sting. Will I really go crazy? Maybe not. I had not seen the couple go crazy. I took another sip, but still I did not feel crazy. The little boy had filled the glass. I sipped until it was empty. My body began to feel warm. I felt light and became sillier with the children. The liquor was beginning to work on me.

I was starting to enjoy my feeling. I kept pouring some more into the glass. I got sillier with the children. They were having a ball with my playful nature, which was coming out like it never had before. The three of us began to run around playing tag, hide-and-go-seek, asking each other to jump around the corners and say boo! The more we ran around, the more I was sipping liquor. The carafe was getting empty. I was tickling and hugging the children more than I ever had. They were loving and enjoying the whole situation. They would poke at me, lure me to run more after them. I forgot all about the time, and the children did not know any better. As far as they were concerned, they were loose, and I was loose.

Suddenly, the front door opened, and the couple walked in. It seemed that one of them said, "What is all this?" I guess they were astounded to come home and find everything not the way it was when they left. I hugged them both and wished them a merry Christmas. The wife started screaming, giving me hell and telling me that I was fired. I could hear her husband trying to calm her down in the middle of her screams, telling her get me out of my silliness and to put the children to bed. She kept accusing me of harming the children. Then he would speak, "Christ! Make some coffee and get it into her. She doesn't know or understand a ------- thing you are saying. Can't you see her condition? Christ! Calm down, will you?" She went to make coffee, but I refused it. I told her loud and clear that I did not want any of the coffee. I suddenly found myself enjoying her coldness and madness. I kept going to her husband who was putting the children to bed. I would try and help him and give him more hugs, which he was neither enjoying nor pushing away. He gently kept telling me to go to bed, that he would talk to me tomorrow. He would yell for his wife to get me away and order her to get me into bed. Every time she came near me, I walked away from her. She could see that I was not going to listen to her. She would try and give up. She tried to get me to drink coffee, and I would not even pick up the cup.

Her husband came out of the children's bedroom and came straight to me. He was calm, towering, and he did not wear a mad face like his wife did. His head came down to my face as if he was trying to reach the sensible part of my mind. He said, "Christ! Mini, you don't want the children to know you like this, do you?" He knew what to say, knew what I cared about. I said, "Of course not," more loudly and more clear than I ever spoke to him before, without feeling shy or awkward. He went on: "You know where your bedroom is? Go there, and go to bed. My wife and I will speak to you tomorrow." I did not have to listen to him either, but I got up and went to bed, mainly because I wanted to show his wife that there were other ways to get through to me, other than screaming. I did not do anything else, just went to bed, clothes and all.

I must have been in a stupor, as I could not remember anything until the next morning. I slowly began to wake and moved around a bit on my bed. My body was stiff and still attired in clothes. I tried to think a little better. Then I began to remember. I thought about the children and tried to get up. Oh! My head was thumping and aching. I felt sick in my stomach. I lay down again. I wondered what the couple would do to me. I became more awake and began to think more deeply: they will be so mad, they will give me hell, fire me, maybe. They won't even give me a chance to look for a place. Where will I go? I can't face them, ever. I will have to stay in my room until they leave for work every day. No, that will be impossible because I have to get up and make their breakfast. Out of fear, I began to hope for them to fire me.

I could see through my window that it was high noon, cold and sunny. I wanted to make a move, to go out to the kitchen and tell them how I was feeling. I could hear both of them once in a while, talking to the children. The children were asking where Mini was. The mother urged them not to come to my room. I figured they were waiting for me to come out and would give me hell before I could say anything. So I just lay there and waited.

A couple more hours went by, and finally the wife opened my door. Her first words were, "I see you have been awake for some time. You are not ashamed, are you?" That was all I needed to hear. I turned away from the door and decided that she could fire me. I could always go to one of my friends and get a job at the new school. She closed the door and I could hear her footsteps going into the kitchen. A few minutes later, my door opened wide, and there the husband stood. "Did you have fun last night?" were his first words. That was not what I wanted to hear either. I tried to turn away, and he wouldn't have it. He became stern. "Christ! Get up before I get the children in here." I did not want the children to see me either, at least, not until I looked a little better. "Get up and come into the kitchen and have some breakfast. Or lunch, whatever you fancy."

He left and left the door wide open. I tried to get up and oh, my head ached. I washed and went into the kitchen. Not one dish was clean, and the counter had no space left to put anything on. I looked around a little further. The living room was a mess—there were toys, books, and bits of food everywhere. I looked at the carafe; it was completely empty. I wondered if I drunk it all last night. The children came over and the little boy said, "We had lots of fun before we went to bed, didn't we, Mini?" I did not want to hear that either. Everybody was saying something I did not want to hear. I only wanted to hear, "You are fired!"

Instead, the couple began to talk to me. "Mini, we don't like what you did here last night. We are hoping that you won't do it again. On that basis, we have decided to keep you." Since they were being so understanding, I wanted to apologize very much. I wanted to tell them that I had not planned it that way—that I just meant it to be fun with the children.

I wanted to tell them that I became curious about the drink, to see if it would drive me crazy, but I could not. They reminded me that I could have easily harmed the children. That was the end of that. It was forgotten, though I was very disappointed that they did not fire me.

GRANDMOTHER WAS ALWAYS RIGHT

Christmas went by, and the new year arrived. Chores in the house went back to normal. My home kept coming to my mind. I decided that I would tell the couple to start looking for someone long before I left— that way, they wouldn't have any reason to hold me back. I kept waiting for the right moment, but it never seemed to come. Some days, I just did not think about it. The month of February was approaching. It was the coldest month of the year. The weather was bitter, so cold that anyone who made a track in the snow could pick it up, mount it anywhere, and show it off. Every time any door was opened, a smog of cold clouds would sneak in, making anyone feel like getting into a nice warm bed and staying there until the warm sun came back.

One night, the woman and I were alone in the house, and the children were asleep. Her husband had gone to Moosonee to arrange some orders for the confectionery. I thought it was going to be one of those evenings when we might sit and converse about anything, but it was not so. She asked me bluntly if I loved her husband. What could I say? In my culture, I had been taught that I could love in many ways. I was young and did not know how to answer her silly question. I did not want to say no, because I did love the man in the way I would love anyone who had been a good guardian to me. And I did not want to say yes, either, because she would not understand what kind of love I meant. I could not answer her and just kept looking at her. I wondered if she would understand me, and I wondered if she knew her husband at all. He seemed to be so good to her.

Of course, she did not wait for an answer but went on: "You could make him happier, since you understand his Native ways. His parents would probably accept you better." I was utterly aghast. I could not believe my ears. It was like a nightmare while I was wide awake. She was still thinking about that crazy letter, written by someone who was as crazy as her. I sat there wanting to explain to her about the letter, how it came to exist. I wanted to tell her that I grew up with someone who had tried to ruin my growing years for a long time. I wanted to tell her about the instigator's personality. But would she understand what a complicated story that was? I doubt it, and I had no words to explain my past experience to her. I felt thankful that tomorrow was Saturday, my day off. I could spend it going over to the school to find a job.

Finally I spoke: "Tomorrow I am going to look for another job." That was all I said, and then I went to bed. She tried to speak to me, but I wouldn't hear her. Tears were running down my cheeks, which made it harder for me to face her, or even to listen to her. I undressed and put my whole body under the covers so that she wouldn't speak to me anymore. Her last words were, "Mini, you can't do this to me. I'm sure you will feel better tomorrow." My mind was determined that I would not give in, no matter what she or he said to me. I would turn my soft heart to stone and think of me, me, me and mine, mine, mine. Like my culture says, some people take longer to grow up than others. I fell asleep.

The next morning, I was woken by voices screaming at each other from the direction of the living room. "Christ, why can't you just leave her alone? How do you think I run the confectionary? You have to understand people if you want to keep them under you. When are you ever going to learn? If serves you ------- right! You can try and find someone else during the weekend, or stay home, like you should have a long ------- time ago! Christ! I'm not trying to keep her back again—I've done everything to keep her happy! You will have to work it out yourself! No! I'm not going to talk to her for you anymore! It's about time she left, like all the other girls have. Just you don't ever ------- forget that she had the gumption to stay this long. At least she told you that she is leaving—the others did not even used to show up after a week with you!"

Then the silence fell. I guess the children were outside. Wherever they were, they were not making a sound. Though I had never thought that I would leave this way, I began to dress and planned to head to the new school. I had to do it—there was nothing else for me to do. I stood for a second at my door and wondered how I should get out without arousing any flare-ups. I decided to head straight for the front door. I went past the living room, and both were sitting there, looking exhausted. Nobody said a word, and I went out the door. It was late Saturday morning and the air was bitter cold. When I got outside, my breath started to smoke. I walked toward the school, my mind determined to get a job.

I had never been in the new school. It was towering and scary. I rehearsed in my mind what I was going to say to whoever I met there. Near the door was a sign that read "Principal." There, inside the office, sat a very thin man behind a desk. I suddenly relived the scene I had experienced so long ago, of Grandfather signing the papers when I first went to the old school. We startled each other, but he greeted me politely. I felt shy, but I was determined to find a job. "What can I do for you?" he asked. "I am looking for a job," I replied. "What would you like to do?" I didn't know, but I was willing to do anything. "Who is your present employer?" I told him. "Why are you leaving?" I was not happy there. He sat back in his chair. "I don't know if I have anything that you could handle on your own. You see, Miss Aoodola, we don't have enough staff who could take the time to teach you quickly. We do have two openings, one in the laundry. The matron is going to have a baby and plans not to return to work. The other is supervising forty-four intermediate girls. I don't think you can handle forty-four children—some of them are bigger than you. No, you don't look tough enough. Would you like to try the laundry?" I said yes—in fact, I just about sang it out. "Fine," he said. "Do you have a place to stay?" No. "Then you can move to the staff rooms—that will be even better for everyone. Come on Monday, first thing in the morning. I will speak to the matron who will show you what has to be done." That was that! I felt too shy to thank him, so I just gave him an appreciative smile. I was leaving his office when he suddenly got up, hesitated, and spoke: "You can move in during the weekend or even today, if you like." Why didn't I think of that myself? I wondered. I was so relieved.

I went back out into the cold air. But I did not feel cold—I was too happy to feel anything else. I could have danced all over the snow. But I kept walking back towards the couple's house. I had to start thinking again. I decided to move right away, the sooner the better. I reached the house, and as I opened the door, the couple was still sitting there, like they had never moved or were in a state of shock. I said nothing and headed straight to my room to pack. There was a knock at my door, which was opened right away by the woman. She wanted to know if I had had anything to eat, and I said no. She wanted me to come to the kitchen and said that she would fix me something. I said that I was not hungry. She tried to give me a smile, which I did not want to return.

Then she began: "Mini, I can't do without you. Look at the house, look at my kitchen sink, the children will miss you." Like my culture says, some people take longer to grow up than others. I did not answer. I felt that if I answered, I would begin to feel sorry for her again and would probably stay on, unhappy, until next summer. That summer was so long away. I did not answer. She kept on: "Mini, we have made up in the past—let's make up now and forget everything." I did not answer and kept on packing. Finally, she closed the door, and I could hear her talking to her husband, probably trying to urge him to talk to me, but he never came to my door. I was glad—I knew that he would have used the children to make me stay on. I probably would have melted for the children and stayed on. But he knew when he'd had enough nonsense, too. I was glad that he had a Native nature and that he understood how people felt, how much people can take, that people can be pushed only so far.

I finished packing. I wanted to hug the children and tell them where I was going, that I would never come back. But I could not. I headed straight for the front door and closed it behind me. I felt neither happy nor remorseful. As I was walking on that cold snow with two suitcases in my hands, I had all kinds of mixed feelings. I had never thought that I would leave that way, from the home that I had tried to feel at home in. I had always imagined that when the time came for me to leave, these people, who had taken me in, who had come to care about my well-being, would see me off to the ship as friends forever. But, like Grandmother always said, some things don't stay the same forever, and you can't plan to stay the same forever. Grandmother was always right when it came to human nature.

MACHINES ARE COLD

I moved into the school just as lunch was being served. I had not eaten the whole morning, but I was not hungry. I was shown to my room, which was on the third floor. The whole third floor was a staff area, and at the other end was a little dispensary for minor accidents and sicknesses. The nurse had her own room beside it—she was a motherly elderly woman. The second floor was where all the children and their group supervisors slept, and the chapel was on the same floor. The first floor contained two play-rooms for boys and girls, two dining areas for the staff and the children, a kitchen with all the modern conveniences, a sewing room where all fabrics were mended, and the laundry room. All were run by different people.

During lunch-time, I was introduced to the rest of the staff. Though the principal did not live at the school, he, too, came to the dining room to welcome me. I felt very shy, as usual, and could not express myself. I just smiled an ordinary smile and thought to myself that here was another life for me to get used to. I went to bed early, as I did not really know any of the staff well, even though a couple of them were my old Indian schoolmates. They had changed and so had I, so we had to get to know each other again.

The children were many. Though I didn't have anything to do with them, I still had to handle their many clothes. There were six senior boys, twenty-six juniors, twenty-four senior girls, forty-four intermediates, and forty-two juniors. There were six supervisors, two workers in the kitchen, one nurse, one engineer and his wife who managed choir singing, one jani-tor, whose wife was pregnant and had to give up the laundry, one sewing-room matron, and four teachers. Neither the minister and his wife, nor the principal and his wife lived in the school. There were two outside helpers who came in every day, one for the sewing room and one for the laundry.

In my room, I prepared my mind to my new job. I planned to do it well. My father's voice came to my mind, as it always did when I was confronted with a new situation: "Work with patience and learn all you can." Though I had not worked in a big laundry, I knew a lot about wash-ing clothes by now. I had gotten to know about different fabrics and had learned which kinds shrink and which ones run their colours. My day started at nine o'clock every morning and ended at five in the afternoon. My pay was seventy-five dollars a month.

The principal had said that there would be new outside help com-ing soon to the laundry. I hoped very much that person was someone I already knew or had seen in the community. I hoped that whoever it was was going to be a good working companion, and that I would be as well. I spent the weekend just having meals and going back to my room. I organized my room and prepared my daily clothing. I wanted my room to be in order so that I would always feel refreshed when I came into it. I could see that I was going to be in it a lot, since I was too shy to mingle with the other staff so soon. Though I love people like animal-lovers love animals, I would rather be among people I know well. I have always been very slow to open up to them. I was going to be slow to get to know them, but after all, I thought, I will have to live under the same roof with them, maybe for a long time. Maybe until I went home. I discovered that I still had not forgotten my home, and I probably never would. I decided to put home at the back of my mind for a while, at least until I got used to things in my new home.

Monday morning arrived. I was up at seven. I looked out the window as I got out of bed—the weather still looked cold. I washed and dressed. As I was a live-in employee, I had to conform to the school rules. After breakfast, everyone had to go to the chapel for prayer service. From there, the staff went to their jobs and the children went over to the classrooms, which were right next door. When I found my way to the laundry room, the former matron was already there. I did not know her, but I had seen her around the community. She was very pregnant and looked uncomfortable when she walked, but she was pleasant and showed me around the laundry. There were three big steel washing machines, two big dryers, one big bed sheet presser, two big sinks, and lots of little boards and hand irons. There was a closet full of laundry supplies. The former matron showed me how she usually started, but said that it did not really matter how I ran the laundry, as long as I finished by five o'clock. She also showed me where to put the clothing that needed mending and alterations. The sewing room was right outside of the room. I had to pass through it whether I was coming or going. She told me that each individual segment of the school had laundry days—Monday was the senior boys' day, and so on. She said that when the supervisors did not bring the laundry around, it was not my fault, as it was not my job to run around and look for the careless supervisor. "You will like it here," she said. "It's noisy, but you will enjoy it." She wished me luck and left. I sighed deeply as she closed the door behind her.

I began to divide the different colours. I looked inside the big machines and made an eye judgment to see how much I should put in each machine. I had wondered earlier how I could finish all this laundry in eight hours.

Now I could see that it was possible. The machines just seemed to devour the clothing. I put in the soap, closed the lid and switched on the switch. The noise scared me. I kept wondering if the machines were going to go off like a shot gun, but nothing happened. Around 10:00 a.m., the sewing-room matron came in and asked if I would like to have a break for coffee. I was not a coffee drinker at the time, and I did not want any, but I did not refuse her, as she was an elderly woman. She, too, like the nurse, had a motherly look and was practically bald. She introduced herself as we were walking towards the dining room—her name was the same as the principal's. He was her son. He had come to Canada from England, and she had followed four years ago. "Yes, I left my old home, all my friends, so I am a stranger here," she said. "My husband is dead, and when he died, I had a terrible shock and lost all my hair. At least you are at home," she commented. I told her that I was not really home either. I tried to tell her where my home was, but she had no idea. I kept trying to open doors for her and to serve her the way I was taught to treat my elders, but she wouldn't have it because I was a stranger to the school. I did not argue. She had her coffee, and I had a glass of juice, and then we went back to work.

By noon, I had the whole laundry done. All that remained was the drying, ironing and folding. The afternoon went very fast. As the day drew to a close, I thought about the couple's home and especially about the wife. I felt glad to have left. I opened the laundry-room door and looked back in to make sure everything was in order. The machines were cold, but at least they would not hurt my feelings, ever!

THEY WERE STRANGERS MORE THAN I

The next day, my new helper arrived. Although I did not know him very well, he was no stranger to me. I recognized him right away when he came in by the back laundry door. We both smiled at each other with recognition. His grandparents, who adopted him, knew my parents well, as the grandfather had been the Anglican minister at Old Factory. Now, he had been transferred here to Moose Factory. I was happy to see this grandson, knowing that he knew all about my people. He was known at Old Factory as a very good guitar player. He had befriended my father and taught him how to play guitar. Although I did not know his style of working or his ability to cope with this task, or even how he would take my orders, I was glad to see him. We were both young and very shy. We spoke to each other in Cree, as that was the language we used back home at Old Factory.

My helper handled the heavy machines for me and we helped each other lift the baskets of laundry. We came to know each other's ways of working. We never spoke about anything other than our work and what had to be done. Every day, we just worked on finishing what had to be done for that day. We eventually got to know how the laundry room was supposed to work, and we conformed to its rules. I didn't have to tell him anymore what needed to be done. We both got automated by the machines we had to work with. We never had any problems, and we never made any problems among ourselves. We worked together in harmony. He seemed happy, too, and he was always so polite and gentle in his manners. I responded to him the same way. Eventually, our work in the laundry became routine and automatic.

Although I was happy at the laundry and willing to do my job well, my mind yearned for more challenge. I was beginning to find that I could turn my mind on and off just like the machines. My reflexes became automatic, and I knew in my heart that it was not for me. I was meant to use my head, and I would never satisfy my curiosity among these automated machines. I craved for people who could make me use my thinking and challenge my mind. Even though I did my job automatically, without losing interest, I became bored with it. I knew that I needed something new to get rid of my energies.

One day, as I was taking my break with the other staff, my ears perked up when I heard one of the supervisors complaining about her job. She did not like all those children who were giving her a lot of trouble. She was about to go and see the principal about quitting. She sounded hopeless and sick of her job. It gave me an idea. That same evening I went down to her bedroom, which was between two dorms of intermediate girls. I had gotten to know her, so she asked me to come in.

Wow! Her room was a mess! I couldn't tell which were her own things and which were the clothes of the girls she supervised. There were piles and piles of clothes in almost every corner of her room—stockings, aprons, underwear and tunics. No wonder she was not happy. Grandmother had always said, "if you want to be happy within yourself, keep your living area in order."

I greeted her, and she asked me to sit on her bed, which was not made. She apologized for the mess, and I made no comment. I sat down and wondered if she would consider switching jobs. She asked me how I liked my job. I did not answer her, but said, "That's what I came to see you about. How would you like to change jobs with me?" She almost jumped at the idea. Then she asked me if my job was hard, and I said no—it was noisy, but not hard. She thought a little more, then spoke again: "Do you think you can handle the smirks, disobedience and smart-alecky behaviour of forty-four brats?" I said that I was willing to change if she was. We made an agreement that we could always change back if it did not work out. We decided to go and see the principal the next morning during our coffee breaks.

Together we went to the principal's office and came right out with what we wanted. The principal wouldn't see us together—instead, he talked to us individually behind closed doors. I don't know what he said to her, but to me, he said, "Mini, you are so small, smaller than some of those intermediate girls. They are hard to handle. You are so young and look too gentle. They will run all over you! Besides, I have not heard one complaint from the staff about shrunken sweaters since you came to the laundry. We haven't had to order new ones and pass on the shrunken ones to the juniors." I was not saying anything and felt shy that I had ever come to see him. It looked like he would not go for the idea. I felt very disappointed and did not bother to hide it. He became silent. Finally, he said that he had to keep his staff happy and agreed that I could try. If the children were too much for me, I could always change back to the laundry. I felt elated and got up to leave his office. I opened the door and the supervisor was still out there, waiting. The principal wished us both lots of luck.

It was Friday, and we decided to change jobs during the weekend. During Sunday supper, the principal came and got me out of the dining room. He said that he was going to introduce me to all the children during their supper, when everybody was together. The children, both boys and girls, were all eating. The dining room supervisor came over to us as we entered. The noise of spoons and dishes and little whispers completely stopped. There was silence for a second, and those little heads were turned towards us. The principal asked for attention and spoke: "You children all know Miss Aoodola. She has been your laundry matron, but now she is going to supervise the intermediate girls." "OOOOooooh," was the response! He went on: "You intermediates will have to listen to her, obey her orders and rules, tell her when you have problems, tell her when you feel sick. As you can see, she is small. If you give her any troubles, she will come to me." I could see that he was still very doubtful, and he put doubts on the faces of those children. But I was determined.

We left, and I went up to the second floor, to my new room, which was now half empty. All the children's clothing was still there, though it looked as though someone had tried to put it in a neat pile. There was a knock at my door—it was the former supervisor. She wanted to know if I would take the children to the Sunday church service that evening in the village. I said yes, and she left, looking relieved. I had to think and think fast. I had one hour to ready myself, but it was not just me that I had to think about—I had forty-four others to consider. My girls were all downstairs in the playroom. I made myself neat and went down. I opened the playroom door, and the noise of many mixed languages came to my ears. Some were speaking their own Indian language and some, English. They noticed me, and all stopped. There was silence. I told the intermediates to line up, to go up to their dorm room, and to change into their Sunday service clothing. They all obeyed right away. I wondered if it would always be as easy as this, but I knew it was only temporary obedience. They were feeling strange to me, as I was to them. On the stairs, the line broke up, and they all started talking. They knew this was not the rule—already they were testing me. I did not say anything. I wanted to wait for a better time to remind them about the school rules.

I went to my own room, more or less to test if they knew how to prepare themselves for church. It was not so: some of them came to my door, wanting to know what to wear, to show me their torn stockings or unstitched dresses. I felt pressured and knew that the principal insisted on the children being on time for church. We had quite a way to walk. I told them to wear what they had, and that I would see to them in the coming week. At least they were satisfied. I got into my own coat and lined them up in the dorm hall. My heart sank as I began to notice their coats: some were torn, some unstitched, some had buttons missing, and some did not fit anymore. But we had to get moving. I lined them up facing the outside door. I told the biggest girl to go ahead, and I walked behind them, next to the smallest one. As we walked towards the church,

I felt ashamed to see these children in their tattered clothes. I knew that for many years, the residential schools were always talked about by the villagers—how the schoolchildren ate poorly, wore rags, and that the school did not really look after them well. I decided right there that I would not be a part of it. By next Sunday, the children's clothes would be in better condition.

The service ended. The Anglican ministers always stood at the church doors to shake hands with the congregation. I saw the former Old Factory minister for the first time since he arrived at Moose. We greeted each other with recognition. The children and I walked back to the school, still in line. We entered, and I went up to take my coat off after I told them to hang up theirs. I knew that the principal's rule was to have all the children in bed by eight o'clock during the week and by eight-thirty on Sundays. Once my coat was off, I realized that there was not much time for me to talk to the children about all the things I planned to do with them. There were only fifteen minutes left for them to play around before bedtime. I took my time in my room before I went down to get them back up to their dorms. I went down and lined them up. While they lined up and became quiet, I took advantage of the chance to speak to them.

I reminded them that there was silence on the stairs, that there was no pushing each other, and if that happened again, I would punish not just the culprit, but all of them. At this point, I did not know what I was going to use for punishment, but I took a chance. It was for me to think about. As we went up, not one got out of line, and no one dared speak. Their line was so neat that I instantly fell in love with them. From then on, I knew that if I were willing to make my rules stick, the children would eventually conform to them without hate. They washed and brushed their teeth, and all went to their beds. As I checked the individual bedsides, I found that some had odours that stunk. Something else I had to think about. I said goodnight, and the chorus came back, "Good night, Miss Aodla," and I turned the lights off.

I went into my bedroom. As soon as I had disappeared into my room, whispers began in the darkness of the dorms. I stood for a while and thought. Should I ignore it or do something about it? I decided to do something. I went to one of the dorms and switched on the light. All was silence. I could see that they were sneaky and probably growing hypocrites.

I asked who was whispering, but no one dared to answer. I was not satisfied, so I said, "Okay, you will all have to supervise yourselves tomorrow while I sleep all day!" All heads were raised and eyes turned to one girl. I went to her. I asked for her name and made her stand in the centre of the floor. I made her look around the room and said, "See all these girls? You are keeping them awake. They want to sleep so they can have a good rest." I knew that she had no sense of responsibility for the needs of the others, but I also knew that she did not like to stand out in front of all those eyes. She felt small, and I told her to return to her bed and to go to sleep.

I went back to my room. I heard no more whispers, and in time, all I could hear were sleep sounds. Some of them talked in their sleep and some slept like they never had before. Though I had to share the toilet with the children, I had my own sink in my room. I washed and went to bed. I lay there and thought, plotted, and planned how to get all this mess organized. First of all, I had to get my room tidied up, and I kept remembering the smell in the dorms. I planned to do two things tomorrow: get my room cleaned, and also the dorms. I went to sleep after I set my clock for seven in the morning.

The next morning, I got up and dressed. When I went into the dorms, some of the girls were already awake, lying there, enjoying their beds without a sound. I had a little bell that I used to wake them. I shook the little bell, and everybody slowly got up, some yawning and some very quickly. I could see which of them were going to cause problems in the mornings in terms of speed, with such little time to dress, to get to the dining room, to the chapel, back to the dorms, put on winter clothes and finally to have them ready for the teachers to walk over to the classrooms. I went back and forth between the two dorms, encouraging them to hurry a little. I got them lined up for the dining room, and then I went to have my own breakfast. Every staff member had something to say as I entered. "How is it going, Mini? How are you going to manage all those girls? Did you sleep well? You are so small—some of them are bigger than you." I made no comment, just smiled and ate. But I was determined to get rid of their doubts, to demonstrate that my smallness had nothing to do with my capabilities.

That very day, when classes and supper were over, I asked the girls to come up to their dorms. I had every one of them take their beds apart and told them to turn over their mattresses and clean their bedside tables. I told them to put everything that they did not need or personally own in the centre of the floor. Everything went flying as the mattresses were turned over—paper, old rags, soiled underwear, socks without mates, crayons and chalk. It was no wonder that the dorms stank! I wondered, too, if some of these girls were menstruating or had any knowledge of what it was, or even what to wear for it. Oh, what a mess! All of them knew how to make the beds, though some of them tried to just sit there. I started cleaning my room to give them more encouragement. We did not stop until everything was spic and span. In the end, I brought out all the clothing that had been in my room and put it in the centre of the floor. I asked the girls to form a circle and help me to find all the matches to the socks, fold the underwear which was clean and make another pile with soiled underwear. I asked them to put all the things they wanted to throw away in one corner. Soon, that became a huge pile too. I tried to make the whole clean-up a happy event, and they soon caught on. They started asking, "What about this? That? What? Where? And how?" We finished the messy job in one hour.

Out of the pile, I picked up a bloody pair of underpants, lifted it up in the air, and said, "Anyone who has to wear something like this, please come to my room, because I want to talk to you about it." I did not want to come right out and talk about this to everyone, just in case some of the older girls were shy in front of the little ones. I said, "The rest of you go down, dress and go outside and play." They were all delighted and looked at each other with pleased smiles. Eight girls came to my room. I sat them on the floor, and I sat on my bed facing them. I wanted to tell them all about menstruation, truthfully, not the way I was told by my grandmother or the nuns. When I had finished, they were full of questions, which I tried to answer as truthfully as I could. None of them had ever been told about menstruation. They didn't even know what it was, and they didn't know they should wear Kotex. Poor, poor souls, is all I could say to myself. I told them that they should come and see me whenever they needed Kotex and to never, never leave the soiled ones under their mattresses. "They will smell," I said, and they all laughed. I wanted them to leave my room with the feeling that it was not scary. If I built trust, they too would trust me. Then I sent them outside to join the others. They deserved it, after all the dust that went flying everywhere during clean-up. Bed time arrived and two more girls came to see me about Kotex—I guessed that they had been informed about this by the others.

As time went by, I soon had everyone organized. I never stood around to order them. Whenever there was something to be done, I involved myself with them. I got to know each of their individual ways: some tried to be smart, some were even-tempered, some tried to tattletale, and some tried to avoid their work. I didn't ignore a thing and always got to the bottom of whatever they tried. I never screamed or scolded. When I had to punish them, I did it right in front of all the others. They hated that and felt shy and ashamed. I never made any promises to them that I could not keep. I used all the ways of making the rules stick that I had learned from my grandmother. I made sure that they conformed to my rules along with the school rules. They were never late for meals, church, or classes. I fell in love with all of them. I hugged them when I felt it was the right moment. I gave them compliments to encourage their efforts. Father had always advised me, "If you are good to people, they will be good to you."

When I got together with the other staff, all wondered how I could manage those girls without ever looking tired or ever complaining. All said that it was the first time they had seen the intermediates looking neat, always on time, and most of all not turning their heads during chapel service. I just thanked them. They didn't realize that I had some advantages over them. I spoke four languages, two of which all the children understood. I also knew some of the girls' parents, and some of their sisters and brothers had gone to this same school with me. I said nothing, and I had no time to explain long stories. They had no time to listen, either. They never realized that they were strangers more than I. Some were from England, from Scotland, from Toronto, from Woodstock, Ontario, and even one from the United States.

THE AGENT WAS STILL AFTER ME

Spring was in the air again, but I had not been thinking about home, as I was too busy. The children were talking about their homes, though—that they would be so glad when school was over, that they were missing their own food. It sounded so familiar to hear them talk about their homes, just as I used to think about home when I was their age. I could not help but share their emotions in my private thoughts. They got me thinking about home. I began to plan. Yes, I would go home that summer when all the children had left. Most of the staff had already decided what they were going to do with their summer holidays. Yes, I would tell the principal at the end of the school year. I felt elated. I knew that the principal had no reason to hold me there. He had all summer to replace me. I felt even more elated and told one of the staff about my plans.

The school routine went on, and spring was here. It was almost the end of April, 1957. I began to take the girls for long walks when we had nothing else to do. Sometimes, on my days off, I went down to the river. It was on one of those walks to the river that I ran into the Indian agent. He stopped me. He wanted me to come with him to his office. He was serious, more stern than usual, and he did not melt with the humour I attempted. I walked with him without any words between the two of us. We reached his office, and he told me to sit on a chair. He wasted no time and began: "The people in Ottawa still want you. They need a translator right away. If I were you, I would go. Not many girls in your situation get an opportunity like this. I am telling you, you should go. I will lend you the money for the fare and accommodation. I'll make all the arrangements. I'll even go and see the principal myself and tell him about it. Okay?" I began to say "But...." He would not hear me and told me to go, that he would let me know when everything was arranged. That was that!

I walked back to the school, thinking. Surely I will get home before he has a chance to make any arrangements. Some of these qallunaat talk a lot without ever doing what they say they are going to do. Or so I thought! In a couple of days, the principal called me down to his office. He said that he had been very happy with my services, that not many could take my place, but.... He used the very words of the agent, and that was that. I had one week to get ready—this would give him some time to make arrangements for someone to take my place. In the end, he decided that other supervisors would take turns to tend the intermediates, since it was almost the end of the school year. As for me, I had to pack, think and plan all over again.

The day before I left, the staff gave me a going away party. They gave me a trunk tied with a great big red ribbon, and there was a little note on top that read, "May you always be your cheery self. With love, the staff and the intermediate girls." My heart was touched! I wanted to cry. Instead, I barely said thank you.

It was now the second of May, and the ice on the river was long gone. The two elderly women, the nurse and the sewing-room matron, came with two other supervisors to take me to the other side, to Moosonee, where I would catch my train. I was very glad that we did not have to stand and wait around, as my throat was in pain, needing to cry. I boarded, and my friends were no more. It was a long ride to North Bay, where I had to stay overnight. The hotel knew who I was, and a bellboy showed me my room. I was glad that he left quickly after he opened my door for me. I wanted to be alone to think. I could not believe that I could get myself this far away from home. What was I doing? I felt tired and went straight to bed. I had an early train to catch the next day. Suddenly, the phone next to my bed rang. It startled me so much. I picked it up and a man asked what time I would like to be woken up in the morning. I said seven o'clock in the morning. My next train was leaving at nine and I wanted to eat before I left, as I had not even had supper.

The phone wakened me. Yes? "It is seven o'clock," the voice said and hung up. I dressed and looked out the window. All I could see was cement and many cars parked. The weather looked warm and the sky so blue. I went into the dining room and sat down and waited to be served. I waited and waited. I sat there for almost half an hour before I was served. The waitress finally came, and I ordered an enormous breakfast: two fried eggs with bacon, two pieces of toast, a glass of milk, and juice. I paid at the counter and went back up to get my suitcase. I paid my hotel bill and got a taxi to get to the train station. I paid the driver and got my ticket checked.

The train did not take long to come, and soon, I was on my way again, heading to Ottawa. I sat and looked out the window. I saw many strange things and wondered if all these strange things and people would eventually push into my Inuit land. I shivered as I saw a polluted river, tall buildings at a distance, and many, many cars.

Everything looked cemented and cold as steel. Hours went by until I arrived at Ottawa. Everything was scary, noisy, smelly and so very strange. I knew that I was strange, too, because everybody was staring at me while I stood there waiting for the man who was supposed to pick me up. This was how I arrived in southern Canada to start learning all over again about fear, sadness, gladness, disappointment, excitement, lovingness, and rewards—to wonder, to gain, to care, to humour, to lose and meet many people, to have an adventure among these strange qallunaat, while I seemed to be invisible.

HOW DO I LIKE THE WEATHER?

Twenty-one years have passed since that strange day. I am used to many things by now. I am immune to the weather by now. I have found ways to cool myself during heat waves. Sometimes, I'm even cold during winter. I look at myself when I am cold. Upinnarani! It is no wonder! I am dressed like a qallunaat lady: just a coat, no head wear, and flimsy little stockings. Tall buildings do not give me a chance to see what the weather is going to be like. I have learned that I don't have to depend on the weather like I used to when I was a nomad. I don't have to take my furnishings along every time I want to travel. For that, the weather is just fine. I have learned to take its unpredictable ways. I have decided, though, that there is no spring weather for the stranger in the South. Spring, to me, is when the snow begins to melt slowly, when I suddenly can see and hear streams running into one another, when the mass of ice begins to have big cracks, when I hear Canada geese flying over my head, when I begin to run outside without a heavy parka, when I see hunters dressed in white, stalking basking seals in the sun, when I suddenly see wild, tiny flowers blooming. That is the kind of weather I dearly miss, and I miss my dear people who are becoming stranger, covering their familiar ways with a strange culture.

AFTERWORD

LIFE AFTER
LIFE AMONG
THE QALLUNAAT

By Julie Rak, Keavy Martin, and Norma Dunning

Our afterword has several aims: to outline briefly the publication and
reception history of *Life Among the Qallunaat*; to locate the book in the
context of other Indigenous autobiographical writing; to summarize the
Inuit history of James Bay (with an emphasis on the tumultuous changes
of the mid-twentieth century); and to explain how we became involved
in bringing this book back into the hands of readers. In the 1970s, it was
usual practice for editors to hide the evidence of their own work. At the
time, editors were supposed to remain behind the curtain, making the
"magic" of the text possible. But this arrangement sometimes had the
effect of taking decision making out of the hands of Indigenous authors.
Now, after decades of important work by writers, editors, translators, and
interviewers who recommend that editorial work should be as transparent as possible, it is happily much more common to be open about the
editorial process itself and to look to the author for guidance in decision
making. We therefore explain our own editorial process so that readers

can understand how we made decisions and what Aodla Freeman's own role in the process has been. All texts are the product of negotiation, and this one is no exception. In this new edition, however, Mini Aodla Freeman was consulted throughout the editing process, and her preferences were always honoured. We are honoured to have had the chance to work with her, and we are very grateful for the kindness, generosity, and patience that she showed us as we worked to bring *Life Among the Qallunaat*, with restored material from the original typescript, to a new generation of readers.

How We Got Here: Stories of Publishing, Editing, and Writing

So, how did we end up sitting in Mini Aodla Freeman's living room, talking with her about reissuing *Life Among the Qallunaat,* a book that had been out of print for more than thirty years? The answer partly has to do with changes to the image and use of memoir as a genre and partly to do with the rise of Indigenous literature and orality as recognized areas of study. Mini Aodla Freeman wrote about her own experiences in the 1970s, in the wake of a burgeoning awareness amongst southern reading communities that the stories of Indigenous people in Canada are important. While some early scholars of Indigenous life writing emphasized what they saw as the alien nature of the autobiographical mode, with its emphasis on an individual's experience, a split between public and private identities, and a belief in the inner life of the protagonist, scholars like Deanna Reder (Cree/Métis) and Robert Allen Warrior (Osage) have since pointed out the ways in which personal and/or life narrative have always been central to Indigenous rhetoric.[1] This principle holds true in Inuit contexts, where the protocol to speak from one's own life experience (and the refusal to speak about things outside of this) is emphasized consistently, particularly by elders of Aodla Freeman's generation.[2] Aodla

1. Reder outlines the positions of early Indigenous autobiography scholars like Arnold Krupat and Penny Petrone; as the latter wrote in 1990, "[Autobiography] was a new form, alien to an oral heritage where the communal and collective were celebrated" (qtd. in Reder 155).

2. As Saullu Nakashuk says in Vol. 1 of Nunavut Arctic College's *Interviewing Inuit Elders* series, "I can be asked what I know. I state only what I know" (Angmaalik et al. 1).

Freeman's use of the memoir form therefore allowed her to adhere to Inuit ways of doing things by telling stories about her own experiences. But, as she suggests in the interview that prefaces this edition, the form also helped her to realize that she was a writer. Building on her career as an interpreter for the Department of Indian Affairs and Northern Development, Aodla Freeman was able to make use of the memoir form as an instrument of translation, as her narrative weaves together inherited Inuit knowledge, a "reverse ethnographic" account of her time in Ottawa and Hamilton, and reflections on the history and activity of the people of James Bay during a period of intense political and social change.

Aodla Freeman accomplished all this at a time when Indigenous writers, including Maria Campbell (Métis), Alice French (Inuvialuit), Anthony Apakark Thrasher (Inuvialuit), and Jane Willis (Cree), were writing memoirs about their experiences and publishing them with major Canadian presses. There was an audience for this work partly because a decade of civil rights unrest in North America, along with the advent of the Red Power movement and the activity of AIM (American Indian Movement) in the United States, created a public awareness of the political situation for Indigenous people all over North America (Josephy et al., 1999; Chaat-Smith and Warrior 1997). This meant that the readership of life stories by Indigenous people began to grow as well, and more non-fictional books by Indigenous authors began to be published. In the Inuit context, many of the first generation to have been sent to residential schools were surprising southern policy-makers by using their Eurowestern educations both to pursue land claims and also to record their experiences in print. Again, this built upon a pre-existing tradition of telling stories from life experience, and as a result, the appearance of *Life Among the Qallunaat* followed a number of other Inuit life narratives: Nuligak's (Bob Cockney's) *I, Nuligak* (1966), Peter Pitseolak's *People From Our Side* (1975, with Dorothy Eber), Anthony Apakark Thrasher's *Skid Row Eskimo* (1976), and Alice French's *My Name is Masak* (1977).

Memoirs like these were published by smaller presses such as Fifth House, medium-sized presses like Hurtig Publishers Inc., or Douglas and McIntyre, or large presses like McClelland and Stewart. Books found publishers and reading audiences partly because of a growing awareness among English-speaking Canadians of what was later called "cultural nationalism," the idea that Canadians should read stories and other literature by writers in Canada, about Canada, and not let their ways of thinking be determined by others in the English-speaking world, especially Americans (Edwardson 2002). The books produced at this time have aspects of "testimony," a type of non-fictional writing that is sometimes (but not always) a combination of Western and non-Western traditions of witnessing and storytelling. Testimony uses personal experiences as a way to create awareness of an injustice in the public sphere (Franklin and Lyons 2004). In the Canadian context, testimony often provides information about a group that was previously not part of the national Canadian story. Memoir, therefore, can be a conduit which links personal experience to wider political realities. Although the writing of memoir by "non-professional" writers often has been characterized as the work of narcissistic hacks or amateurs—particularly by writers who want to preserve the category of the "literary" for fictional productions—since the 1980s, a recognition of memoir's worth as testimony has been on the rise in Canada, along with a growing recognition that nonfictional forms such as memoir and biography can be as good as, or better than, their fictional counterparts (Rak 2013).

As we are writing this in 2014, Indigenous literatures in Canada are no longer "up-and-coming." Joseph Boyden's *Through Black Spruce* won the Giller Prize in 2008, while his novel *The Orenda* took first place on the CBC radio program Canada Reads in 2014 (a position narrowly missed by Richard Wagamese's *Indian Horse* the year before). Meanwhile, the works of numerous other prominent Indigenous authors are taught in every university in the country. In the midst of this success, a number of scholars of Indigenous literatures—led by Warren Cariou at the University of Manitoba—formed the First Voices, First Texts editing collective (and ultimately publication series) to explore the complexities and the possibilities of bringing the many out-of-print "classics" of Indigenous literature in Canada back into circulation—and back into our classrooms. High on the list of priorities for several members was Aodla Freeman's *Life Among the Qallunaat,* a book that had received fairly significant critical attention but—for reasons that we will discuss shortly—had hardly been available even when it was in print. Keavy Martin, a member of the collective, was encouraged to pursue this project by a conversation with her colleague, Julie Rak, who had studied the text during her doctoral program at McMaster University and had hoped for years to bring it back into print. When Martin got in touch with Aodla Freeman—also living in Edmonton—the author confirmed that she had long been interested in seeing her work widely available in paperback. Aodla Freeman not only agreed to a reissuing of the text but also provided the editorial team—which by this point had been joined by the Inuk writer and graduate student Norma Dunning—with a copy of her original typescript.[3]

As we began this project in 2013, the timing seemed right for a reissue of *Life Among the Qallunaat*. Inuit writing and storytelling—long underrepresented in Indigenous literary studies—was also starting to gain recognition in the South, thanks to activities of Inuit filmmakers like Igloolik Isuma Productions, to the republication of classic literary works like Mitiarjuk Nappaaluk's *Sanaaq*, and to the innovations of contemporary Inuit writers and publishers. Public awareness of the impacts of the Indian Residential School system in Canada was mounting as the Truth and Reconciliation Commission continued its work at high-profile events across the country. Contemporary Indigenous political concerns—such as the causes championed by the political movement Idle No More—were making issues facing Indigenous peoples in Canada front-page news in Canada and around the world. As scholars, we understand these events to be closely connected to the world of Indigenous literature. The pursuit of restitution—whether in the courts or in the streets—has been and continues to be bolstered by the work of Indigenous authors; their inroads into the publishing industry, after all, have galvanized Indigenous communities across the country—and have helped to awaken Canadians to the urgent and ongoing injustices stemming from their colonial history. For this reason, readers across the country were turning not only to contemporary Indigenous writing but also to the "classics" of Indigenous publishing, as represented in part by the other books in this series by the University of Manitoba Press. Clearly, it was time to reissue one of the pathbreaking works by a talented Inuit writer for a new generation of readers in the North and around the world.

---

3. See p. xviii of this volume for an image of the first page of the original typescript.

While the 1978 edition of *Life Among the Qallunaat* has received enthusiastic critical attention, we anticipate that scholars will find this new edition to be even more fertile, particularly with the restoration of its original structure, of the author's idiomatic use of English, and of her detailed explanations of Inuktitut terms.[4] There is much to be said about *Life Among the Qallunaat* as a work of autobiography, as a memoir of residential school, as a subtle critique of Canadian society, as a representation of a woman's experiences during a time of major cultural change, or as an extension of Inuit narrative tradition—whether the autobiographical mode of the inuusirminik unikkaat (stories from life experience) or of the unikkaaqtuat (stories that go on for a long time, or myths).[5] It is our hope that there will be many other scholars in diverse fields who will now help to give this text the critical attention that it deserves.

A History of Change: the James Bay Inuit in the Twentieth Century

"Life Among the Qallunaat" was not the original title of this book. As Aodla Freeman mentions in the interview that acts as the preface to this new edition, Mel Hurtig chose the title in order to frame the book as a response to the extensive history of qallunaat (southern) writing about Inuit and the North. In particular, it spoke back to the writings of the German ornithologist Bernhard Adolph Hantzsch (1875–1911), whose memoir, *My Life Among the Eskimos* (1977), had just been published by the University of Saskatchewan. While Hurtig's title—with its promise of "reverse ethnography," made doubly effective through the use of the

---

4. For critical discussion of the 1978 edition, see Robin McGrath's *Canadian Inuit Literature: The Development of a Tradition* and "Circumventing the Taboos: Inuit Women's Autobiographies," Margaret Harry's "Literature in English by Native Canadians (Indians and Inuit)," Heather Henderson's "North and South: Autobiography and the Problems of Translation," Peter Kulchyski's "Primitive Subversions: Totalization and Resistance in Native Canadian Politics," Dale Blake's "Inuit Autobiography: Challenging the Stereotypes," Sherrill Grace's *Canada and the Idea of North*, Bina Toledo Freiwald's "Covering Their Familiar Ways with Another Culture: Mini Aodla Freeman's *Life Among the Qallunaat* and the Ethics of Subjectivity," and Keavy Martin's *Stories in a New Skin*.

5. As Robin McGrath suggested in 1997, Inuit writing may resonate with long oral narratives such as the story of the epic hero Kiviuq, a character who travelled widely and who also ended up in the South ("Circumventing" 226). For more on Inuit genre, see Keavy Martin's *Stories in a New Skin*, 107–113.

Inuktitut term for "southerners"—may entice qallunaat readers eager for a different perspective on themselves, it also to some extent misrepresents the focus of the book. When Aodla Freeman talks about her writing process, after all, she frames this work as being not so much about qallunaat (or even her life among them), but rather as about her own people—the Inuit of James Bay. This is the context out of which this story emerges and to which Aodla Freeman, as a writer, continually returns.

Aodla Freeman was born in 1936 on a small island called Nunaaluk, or Cape Hope Island, which was then home to the most southern Inuit community (and today forms the southernmost part of the Nunavut territory). The rich political history of this region features the complex relationship between Inuit and local Cree people and also the rising presence of missionaries and of fur traders, who had been active in the area since even before the founding of the Hudson's Bay Company (HBC) in 1670.[6] By the late nineteenth and early twentieth centuries, one of the key players in the area was the HBC pilot, community leader, boatbuilder, and artist Weetaltuk (also known as George Weetaltuk), Mini Aodla Freeman's maternal grandfather. In 1892, Weetaltuk—then working as an HBC ship's pilot—moved south from the Belcher Islands to Charlton Island, which was at the time the northern terminal for the HBC James Bay trade (Milton Freeman 1983).[7] After the 1933 completion of the railroad to Moosonee shifted economic activity away from Charlton Island, Weetaltuk moved his people to Cape Hope Island, where Aodla

6. While the post at Rupert House (now Waskaganish, Quebec) was established in 1668, before the HBC was formed by the granting of a fur trade monopoly, the Company's first official trading post was founded in 1672 at Moose Factory, and by the mid-1800s the Inuit who spent winters on the coast—termed "mainlanders" by the Company men—were acting as trade intermediaries to the "islanders" living in the Belcher Islands (Francis and Morantz 141).

7. During his time on Charlton Island, Weetaltuk met and ultimately collaborated with the visiting filmmaker Robert J. Flaherty, the eventual creator of the 1922 documentary *Nanook of the North*.

8. Another one of Weetaltuk's grandchildren, Freeman's first cousin, Eddy Weetaltuk, is the author of a memoir entitled *From the Tundra to the Trenches* (first published in French translation under the title *E9-422: Un Inuit, de la toundra à la guerre de Corée*, edited by Thibault Martin), which will soon be published in English by the University of Manitoba Press.

Freeman's earliest experiences take place.[8] The community remained there until 1960, when government policies bent on Inuit relocation required its removal to Great Whale River (Kuujjuarapik), in northern Quebec.

As is suggested by the life of her famous grandfather, Aodla Freeman was born into a time of tremendous change and upheaval for Inuit communities across the North. The influence of the Hudson's Bay Company had gradually shifted Inuit traditional economies so that the trapping of white fox—and subsequent visits to the trading posts—became a central component of Inuit life. As the reliance on the trading posts grew, however, the HBC became less willing to provide assistance to its fur suppliers in times of famine or disease and began instead to shift these responsibilities toward the federal government. This led to a dispute between the federal government and the province of Quebec over who should be responsible for Inuit welfare, and in 1939, the Supreme Court case *Re: Eskimos* ruled that the term "Indians" as used in section 91 of the 1867 British North America Act (which outlined Canada's legal jurisdiction) did include people known as "Eskimos"—and therefore that Inuit welfare was a federal responsibility.[9] The period following the Second World War therefore saw a major change in federal Arctic policy, as the state began to intervene drastically in the lives of Inuit, relocating families living at seasonal camps on the land to larger and more permanent settlements, where they would allegedly have

9. The beginning of the Second World War, however, shifted the government's attention, and the *Re: Eskimo* decision was never fully implemented; as a result, Inuit were never subject to the Indian Act.

10. Or, in some cases, Inuit were sent to establish new communities in the High Arctic, where their presence was intended to bolster Canadian sovereignty in the region. See Kulchyski and Tester 103.

11. A 1958 report by Northern Service Officer D.W. Grant speaks to the bureaucracy's belief in the emancipating possibilities offered to Inuit by the transition from traditional subsistence economies and fur trapping to wage labour: "Above all, our aim is to develop these men to a stage where they can make their own decision as to the type of life they wish to lead. When they have progressed to a point that they fully understand the responsibilities of wage employment in the mining field and also understand the possibilities of other alternatives offered in the new community, they will make their own choice" (qtd. in Kulchyski and Tester 294). Susan Lofthouse also points out that in the case of the Cape Hope Island community, government officials were keen on having the Weetaltuk family's boatbuilding expertise available for the economy at Great Whale/Kuujjuarapik (46).

greater access to services.[10] They could also be recruited as wage-earning labour in the growing resource extraction industries.[11]

The upheavals of this period were made even worse by the growth of the residential school system. While the federal government did not assume full responsibility for educating Inuit children until 1955 (significantly later than in the rest of.the country), church-run residential schools had long been operating in the James Bay region.[12] A 1920 amendment to the Indian Act (Bill 14) had made attendance at residential school compulsory in Canada; this legislation may not have been applied to Inuit families in James Bay during Aodla Freeman's childhood, but the influence of church officials in encouraging Inuit parents to allow their children to be taken to school seems to have been comparably strong. As Aodla Freeman writes of the moment when her paternal grandfather Symma agreed to send her to school: "He always preached that refusing people in authority can lead to a bad mark on the refuser" (Aodla Freeman, *Life* 2015, 102). In the end, generations of young Inuit were subjected to the profoundly disruptive and assimilative impacts of the residential schools. Both of the institutions that Aodla Freeman attended—the Anglican school in Moose Factory, Ontario, and the Catholic school in Fort George, Quebec—were included under the 2006 Indian Residential Schools Settlement Agreement, which arranged various forms of compensation for tens of thousands of survivors.[13] While Aodla Freeman's interview references the restraint that she exercised in describing her own residential school experience in this book, she has since worked actively to address the impacts of the system by serving as an elder both at Bowden Institution (a prison located at Innisfail, Alberta)

12. The Anglican school in Moose Factory that Aodla Freeman attended for two years as a young child was founded by Bishop Horden in 1855, and the Catholic residential school that she subsequently attended in Fort George, Quebec (St. Joseph's Mission) opened in 1936 (though an Oblate-run day school had already been in operation for almost a decade).

13. The 2006 Indian Residential Schools Settlement Agreement (the largest class action settlement in Canadian history) required the federal government and churches to fund both the Truth and Reconciliation Commission and other measures to support healing and commemoration—and also to provide residential school survivors with individual monetary compensations.

and at the 2014 Truth and Reconciliation Commission National Event in Edmonton, Alberta.

Another major factor in mid-twentieth-century Inuit life—and in the events of *Life Among the Qallunaat*—was the epidemic of infectious pulmonary tuberculosis (commonly called TB). While TB had been rampant in Inuit communities for decades, following the Second World War, the federal government began to address this issue by removing tuberculosis patients to southern sanatoriums. By 1957, a staggering 10 percent of eastern Arctic Inuit had been sent to the completely alien environments of southern medical facilities (Kulchyski and Tester 53). As Pat Sandiford Grygier writes, "in 1956 the largest year-round Inuit community in Canada was situated in the Mountain Sanatorium in Hamilton, Ontario," where 332 of the 1,578 Inuit patients being treated for TB in southern hospitals were staying (xxi). Aodla Freeman experienced this epidemic from many sides, having apprenticed as a nurse at the Mission hospital at Fort George before contracting TB and being sent to Hamilton herself. Later, during her employment as a translator for Indian Affairs and Northern Development, she visited Inuit patients in southern hospitals across the country, where she noted the substandard conditions of some facilities and the difficulties experienced by the patients, who had minimal contact—sometimes for years—with their families in the North.[14]

Life Among the Qallunaat thus sheds light on the real-life impacts of Canada's heavy-handed and paternalistic mid-century northern policies, exposing not only the innocent misunderstandings between northern and southern culture but also the deliberate ways in which qallunaat have both misrepresented and disrupted Inuit life. While the critiques presented are subtle, couched always in the protagonist's own personal feelings and experiences, Aodla Freeman's narrative also functions as a powerful antidote to the actions of the traders, missionaries, and administrators as it reasserts Inuit histories and perspectives. As it did in 1978, her story will not only educate qallunaat but will also empower generations of younger Inuit, who continue to grapple with the impacts of the twentieth century.

14. The experience of Inuit tuberculosis patients in southern medical facilities is also represented in Benoît Pilon's 2008 film *Ce qu'il faut pour vivre* [*The Necessities of Life*].

Note on the Text: Restoring the Structure of Life Among the Qallunaat

In our initial conversations, Aodla Freeman did not express overt concern about the editorial process that her work had been through in the 1970s. Yet as we compared her original typescript to the published version of *Life Among the Qallunaat*, it was apparent that—as the author had warned us—substantial portions of the original text (particularly near the end of the manuscript) had been cut out or significantly altered. Aodla Freeman's original manuscript was divided by its initial editors into three parts, which, we feel, emphasized the importance of the qallunaat sections more than the section about the people of James Bay.[15] In some cases, phrases had been added that were not written by Aodla Freeman at all.[16] This left us, the new generation of editors, in a challenging situation: while in many respects, Aodla Freeman was content with Hurtig's editing of her work, her repeated emphasis on the amount of material that had been cut, along with our own observations of the ways in which the author's vivid writing style had been altered in the name of "correctness," meant that we needed to find a middle ground.

As we detail below, we therefore decided to reinsert the omitted sections of Aodla Freeman's original typescript, restoring as much as possible her original phrasing, while editing some passages for grammatical consistency in terms of subject-verb agreement and verb tense. In all cases, we tried to balance the need for clarity with the originality of Aodla Freeman's writing style, expecting that phrases that were not completely clear to us may be perfectly transparent to other readers. In some passages

15. The three subheadings added to the Hurtig edition of the text were titled as follows: I. *Ottawamillunga*: In Ottawa, II. *Inullivunga*: Born to Inuk Ways, and III. *Qallunanillunga*: Among the Qallunaat. While the first two subtitles represent quite faithfully the content of the early sections of the manuscript, the third seems to be an attempt to create continuity with the 'reverse ethnographic' thrust of the first section, thereby shaping the text to fit Hurtig's title and rendering the second section a mere colourful interlude. While the final third of the book does include several episodes where the protagonist is "among the qallunaat," the setting of most of its events (with the exception of the trip to the TB sanatorium in Hamilton) is James Bay. By removing these subheadings, then, we hope to allow Aodla Freeman's intended focus on the Inuit of James Bay to come through.

16. For instance, to signal the end of the second section, the editor took Aodla Freeman's sentence "My grandparents seemed to have made the boat for me" and added the phrase "and that it was meant to take me to another world" (*Life* 1978, 100).

of this new edition, then, Hurtig's edits are preserved, while others have been restored to a version identical (or very close) to the original. We then decided to remove some of the trappings of the original edition: we determined, in consultation with Aodla Freeman, that the original preface to the book by the government administrator Alex Stevenson was of its time and would not make a fitting introduction to a contemporary version of *Life Among the Qallunaat*. We also removed the original editor's three section headings, instead listing Aodla Freeman's own subheadings so that readers can see more easily how the author organizes her narrative. And while the spelling of Aodla Freeman's first name has been corrected according to her wishes—the name "Mini," while easily anglicized, is actually an Inuktitut word meaning a "gentle rain"—the author opted to retain Hurtig's clever title.

Life Among the Qallunaat is an extraordinary text in many ways. In an early meeting with us, Aodla Freeman said that she typed the entire manuscript straight onto the page; there was almost no editing within it, and yet it is very tightly constructed, featuring cleverly interwoven sections that often comment on and refer to each other. This is a very unusual composition method: few writers can put their thoughts directly onto a page in such a finished manner. Aodla Freeman's method of composition shows that she is able to depend on her memory about places, events, and people in detail, even when she is writing about events that happened decades earlier. As she says in *Life Among the Qallunaat*, she "had been taught by my people how to memorize—the practice that has been used by my people from generation to generation, either for remembering stories, events, objects or travel routes" (*Life* 2015, 197). Her ability to both to memorize and to construct complex narratives in a singular rhetorical performance is strongly apparent in the writing of this book.

Aodla Freeman uses short sections, each with a header, to show that she has a specific story to tell. The stories relate to each other in a number of ways. For instance, the story "Second Look," a meditation about the way that qallunaat perceive (and often mistake) her ethnicity, ends with "whoever heard of Inuk in the South anyway?" (*Life* 2015, 62). This phrase links this story to the next one, which is a long discussion of the differential treatment of qallunaat and Inuit by the Department of Indian Affairs and Northern Development. This, in turn, leads to the story "The Situation Was Familiar," the story of a photo taken of Aodla Freeman that was used without her permission to sell government bonds. Within this story, Aodla Freeman tells another one—a recounting of political struggles within the James Bay group—which leads her to the conclusion that "qallunaat too had politics. That, of course, I had been raised with ever since I was born, and I knew well to keep away from it when I looked at my picture" (*Life* 2015, 66). In other words, Aodla Freeman demonstrates the ways in which the history of her own people can be employed to glean insights about life in the South—particularly about the pervasive and interlocking misunderstandings of qallunaat about Inuit. A careful consideration of Aodla Freeman's arrangement of anecdotes reveals strong connections between them; rather than being haphazardly ordered and therefore unaffected by edits for length or "coherence," the narrative is purposefully and carefully structured. One story creates the conditions for another to be told, and the stories can be used to explicate each other.

The original editorial work on *Life Among the Qallunaat* often obscured these kinds of connections, which happen frequently in the book. Whole sections, such as the inset story in "The Situation Was Familiar," were left out, presumably because the editor thought that the story of Aodla Freeman's own group was not related directly to the story of her mistreatment in the South. Stories were sometimes edited out entirely or given a different order. When we edited *Life Among the Qallunaat*, we decided to restore the order of Aodla Freeman's original and to reinsert sections of material that were omitted in the 1978 publication. We also restored lines and original wording wherever we could so that Aodla Freeman's own voice and way of telling a story are as strong as they are in her typescript. We did, however, make some changes to the orthographic and grammatical conventions such as verb and subject agreement; sometimes, we altered wording in a restored section in order to try to make the author's meaning clearer to all readers. For instance, in her original typescript, Aodla Freeman writes the following: "Getting into a car was, I think the moment I was ever to be quiet in full five minutes" (*Life* ms. 2). The original editor changed this to the following: "My first ride in a car left me speechless" (*Life* 1978, 17). We much preferred Aodla Freeman's witty phrasing, but we also thought that we could not restore the original text exactly. We finally decided to render the sentence like this: "Getting into a car was, I think, the first moment I was ever to be quiet for a full five minutes" (*Life* 2015, 3).

Generally, we aimed for balance between clarity and Aodla Freeman's own way of telling her readers what she wants them to know. Most of the time, these goals are in harmony with each other, with minor adjustments. When they were not, we opted to let the author's way of writing things stand, particularly when the earlier edit seemed too aggressive. For instance, the story "Novelty Creates Smells" was retitled by the original editor as "Still an Innocent," with this phrase inserted by the editor at the end. The original story is about an attempt a nun makes to find out whether the young Aodla Freeman had been sexually assaulted or sexually active. Another section of the same story explains how, at school, Aodla Freeman and other girls were told how to wash cloths after they menstruated. This is the source of Aodla Freeman's realization that using cloths (which she had not used before) would create a smell and she would have to take care of this "novelty" at school, unlike the way she took care of her bleeding at home. The story is not in fact about being "innocent." It is about learning something new and the consequences of using a new technology and way of doing things. And so, we opted to restore Aodla Freeman's original subheading, as well as the other part of the story, and we took out the editorial phrase "still an innocent."

Out of the Basement

As Aodla Freeman explains in our interview, something very strange happened to *Life Among the Qallunaat* after its publication: half of the print run was somehow acquired by the Department of Indian and Northern Affairs and kept in storage for up to eight months. The author suspects that the Department, then dealing with rising concerns about its many violations of Indigenous rights, was worried about what *Life Among the Qallunaat* might reveal to the public. As any author knows, this kind of control of distribution—whether accidental or intentional—will have an adverse effect on the sales and distribution of a book. Before this action by the Department took place, *Life Among the Qallunaat* appeared to be headed for best-seller status, or at least excellent sales as a respected book. Carole Corbeil, in a 1978 review for the *Globe and Mail*, called the writing in *Life Among the Qallunaat* "episodic, extremely simple, honest" (35), while the *Toronto Star*, in September 1978, devoted a multi-page spread to an excerpt from the book (H16–H18). Peter Buitenhuis, one of the committee members for the 1978 Governor General's Award for Non-fiction, argued in deliberations that *Life Among the Qallunaat* deserved to be among the finalists. When it was not chosen, he was so convinced of the merit of the book that he discussed it at length in a 1979 *Globe and Mail* article about reading three hundred books for the Governor General's Award shortlist (6). It looked like Aodla Freeman was poised to become a major writer on the Canadian scene, the author of a critically acclaimed work that might become as well-known as Maria Campbell's *Halfbreed*, published five years earlier.

But this is not what happened. Instead, Mini Aodla Freeman's book was tucked away. Over half of the 6,254 published copies were stored in an Indian and Northern Affairs Canada (INAC) basement, until—it seems—someone at the Department actually read the book and realized that it could be distributed, as it did not reflect badly on the Department's northern administrative practices (such as the residential school system and forced relocations). The result was that there were very few, if any, copies of *Life Among the Qallunaat* available to the reading public. No one in the northern communities Aodla Freeman wrote about even saw the book for a number of years, as the author says in her interview. The book was never reprinted, and a paperback edition was never published. And so, direct government intervention in the book market contributed to making the story of *Life Among the Qallunaat* relatively unknown to readers.

Digging around in old Hurtig Publishers papers, Norma Dunning found the only evidence that alludes to inventory movement, the shuffling of numbers on a page that represent where Aodla Freeman's book was stored—in places called "sheds" and in small numbers in local Edmonton bookstores. What was never accounted for on the Hurtig inventory lists were over 4,200 copies of *Life Among the Qallunaat*. Dunning hunted hard for that one waybill that would show a large shipment to Ottawa, but she couldn't find it. She looked in every file hoping that something had been misplaced, some error, anything, but came up empty-handed.

Sometimes, books are locked away in basements, gathering dust, hiding from public view; and sometimes, books make it out of the basement, changing the way that we think about things. As Aodla Freeman says in her interview, she suspects that her book was locked away, awaiting review in case she talked about "it"—"it" being residential school. It was as if she had become a threat of sorts, simply by being an Inuk author who talked about what it was like to move amongst the qallunaat while memories of James Bay wove through her life. The re-releasing of this book therefore becomes very important—perhaps more important because of the way it was first handled. As the author says in her interview, she's "ready to take it again," but this time, her work will not be hidden away out of fear of the power that it contains. Aodla Freeman's words will fall into the ears of a new generation, and her voice will continue to sing and to strengthen us all.

We are grateful to Mini Aodla Freeman for her patience and her trust; it has been an honour and a pleasure to work with her. We also owe thanks to Louise Abbott and Niels Jensen, creators of the film *Nunaaluk: A Forgotten Story*, who generously provided us with beautiful archival and contemporary photographs of Aodla Freeman and her family; to Cascy Germain for his photo-editing skills; and to Elsa Cencig and Susan Lofthouse of Avataq Cultural Institute, who gave us access to their resources dealing with James Bay Inuit territories. We would also like to thank Warren Cariou and the members of the First Voices, First Texts editorial collective for their guidance on the complex practice of bringing these classic Indigenous texts back into circulation.

WORKS CITED

Angmaalik, Pauloosie, Saullu Nakasuk, Elisapee Ootoova, and Hervé Paniaq. *Introduction*. Edited by Frédéric Laugrand and Jarich Oosten. Vol. 1 of Interviewing Inuit Elders. Iqaluit: Nunavut Arctic College, 1999.

Aodla Freeman, Mini. *Life Among the Qallunaat*. Edmonton: Hurtig, 1978.

———. Excerpt from *Life Among the Qallunaat*. *Toronto Star*, 30 September 1978, H16.

Blake, Dale. "Inuit Autobiography: Challenging the Stereotypes." PhD diss., University of Alberta, 2000.

Bonesteel, Sarah. *Canada's Relationship with Inuit: A History of Policy and Program Development*. Ottawa: Indian and Northern Affairs Canada, 2006.

Buitenhuis, Peter. "Choosing a Winner Among 300 Books." *Globe and Mail*, 14 April 1979, 6.

Ce qu'il faut pour vivre [The Necessities of Life]. Directed by Benoît Pilon. Performed by Natar Ungalaaq. Montreal, ACPAV, 2008.

Chaat Smith, Paul, and Robert Allen Warrior. *Like a Hurricane: The Indian Movement from Alcatraz to Wounded Knee*. New York: The New Press, 1997.

Corbeil, Carole. Review of *Life Among the Qallunaat*. *Globe and Mail*, 23 December 1978, 35.

Edwardson, Ryan. "'Kicking Uncle Sam out of the Peaceable Kingdom': English-Canadian 'New Nationalism' and Americanization." *Journal of Canadian Studies* 37, 4 (2003): 131–151.

Francis, Daniel, and Toby Morantz. *Partners in Furs: A History of the Fur Trade in Eastern James Bay*. Montreal and Kingston: McGill-Queen's University Press, 1983.

Franklin, Cynthia, and Laura Lyons, eds. "Personal Effects: the Testimonial Uses of Life Writing." *Biography* 27, 1 (2004).